HOW THE GLOBAL FINANCIAL MARKETS REALLY WORK

Praise for *How the Global Financial Markets Really Work*

"An essential handbook for anyone hoping to understand the financial world of the 21st century."
William Kay, The Sunday Times 'Money' columnist, London

"This book provides an easy-to-read and up–to-date overview of the players and products of the capital markets, explaining how and why things went so spectacularly wrong in the credit crunch."
Janette Rutterford, Professor of Financial Management, Open University Business School

"An excellent introduction to financial markets. Wide-ranging, easy to read, and with a wealth of information for investors."
John Calverley, Head of Research, North America, Standard Chartered Bank, and author of When Bubbles Burst: Surviving the financial fallout

"Alexander Davidson has provided a very useful overview of the structure and operation of the broad range of financial markets. This provides a framework in which the challenges and implications of the credit crunch can be explained."
Duncan McKenzie, Director of Economics, International Financial Services, London

"A concise and readable commentary, particularly focused on making sense of recent events. Its scope is remarkably wide and the descriptions are well complemented by the glossary and other appendix materials."
Professor Stewart Hodges, Faculty of Finance, Cass Business School, London

"Never has it been more important for all of us to understand how financial services work and this superb general guide deserves to be widely read. Alexander Davidson has done an excellent job in explaining how it all fits together and how the 'City' impacts the rest of society, and the world."
Lord Mayor of London, Alderman Ian Luder

"The author provides a thorough analysis of the global financial markets and sets out in clear terms the interdependence of markets in the modern era. The book is a valuable aid for policymakers, campaigners with an interest in global financial markets, and students alike."
Mick McAteer, Director, The Financial Inclusion Centre, London

THE TIMES

HOW THE GLOBAL FINANCIAL MARKETS REALLY WORK

The definitive guide to understanding international investment and money flows

Alexander Davidson

KOGAN PAGE

London and Philadelphia

Publisher's note

Every possible effort has been made to ensure that the information contained in this book is accurate at the time of going to press, and the publishers and author cannot accept responsibility for any errors or omissions, however caused. No responsibility for loss or damage occasioned to any person acting, or refraining from action, as a result of the material in this publication can be accepted by the editor, the publisher or the author.

First published in Great Britain and the United States in 2009 by Kogan Page Limited

120 Pentonville Road
London N1 9JN
United Kingdom
www.koganpage.com

525 South 4th Street, #241
Philadelphia PA 19147
USA

ISBN 978 0 7494 5393 0

The views expressed in this book are those of the author, and are not necessarily the same as those of Times Newspapers Ltd.

British Library Cataloguing-in-Publication Data

A CIP record for this book is available from the British Library.

Library of Congress Cataloging-in-Publication Data

Davidson, Alexander.
    How the global financial markets really work : the definitive guide to understanding international investment and money flows / Alexander Davidson.
        p. cm.
    Includes index.
    ISBN 978-0-7494-5393-0
    1. International finance. 2. Investments, Foreign. 3. Money market. 4. Capital market. I. Title.
    HG3881.D3287 2009
    332′.042—dc22
                                                                2009014889

Typeset by Saxon Graphics Ltd, Derby
Printed and bound in Great Britain by Thanet Press Ltd, Margate

LONDON   PARIS   BERLIN   MADRID   TURIN
FIVE CAMPUSES - ONE ROUTE TO YOUR SUCCESS

At ESCP Europe we understand how competitive the job market has become and how it's never been more important to lead the race

With our finely-tuned programmes taught across five European campuses, we offer a metropolitan and truly international education.

Our London-based programmes:

Master in European Business
Master in Management (ranked 1st in the UK and 2nd worldwide*)
Master in Marketing**
Specialised Master in Finance
Executive Education (EMBA ranked 19th worldwide*)

A hands-on approach combining the latest thinking in management education, internships, and consultancies has made us one of the leading business schools in Europe.

Lead the way with ESCP Europe

For more information and upcoming Open Days, please call **+44 (0) 207 443 8800**, visit **www.escp-eap.eu** or email us at **ukadmission@escp-eap.net**

ESCP Europe ranked 6th best in Europe, FT 2008
To be launched in 2010

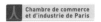

PARIS LONDON BERLIN MADRID TORINO

The Times' Guide to the City

Anthony J. Evans
anthonyjevans@gmail.com

ESCP Europe is the oldest business school in the world, founded in Paris in 1819 by Jean Baptiste Say. The original vision was to unite the intellectual rigour of political economy with the practical relevance demanded by businessmen, and the balance between rigour and relevance still drives the research agenda of the school today.

Say was one of the first great economists, and his understanding of how individuals coordinate their planning through the institution of market exchange helped to define the discipline. This "Classical School" of economics and accompanying model of laissez-faire has since lost favour amongst some commentators and intellectuals, but is little understood. However, if you talk to the entrepreneurs and investors that anticipated the current financial crisis and are critical of the government intervention that has followed, you will find three important lessons about free markets.

Firstly, *markets reveal new information*. It was the short sellers trading on their concerns about banks that were proven right, and the regulators who failed. A holistic approach to financial regulation would realise that no public agency can ever accumulate and act upon the local and tacit knowledge across an entire economy, and would appreciate the role that markets can play in bringing this information to light. We could very quickly discover the extent of a bank's toxic assets by allowing anyone with relevant information to trade on it. This would give potential whistleblowers a voice that would actually be heard. Companies such as Koch Industries and Google have pioneered the use of internal prediction markets to allow executives to utilise the combined wisdom of their employees. One of the key lessons is that the people with private information are the ones who improve market efficiency.

Secondly, *value comes through exchange*. The reason that socialism has led to economic chaos wherever it has been tried is because the market-clearing price of a good is not merely a technical problem that can be solved through statistical modelling. Prices can only be established when subjective valuations combine and two parties actually trade. The quantitative analysts on Wall Street failed to realise this, since their models used current market prices as estimates of the value of an asset. However, we only find out the real value when that asset is sold, and if there is a systemic event that compels many banks to sell at the same time, this model will have been hopelessly optimistic.

Thirdly, *central banks are not market institutions*. In the UK, our monetary system is centrally planned by a nationalised bank which holds a monopoly over the issuance of currency. Each month, a committee meets to set the Bank rate of interest; if they cannot set it any lower, they resort to directly expanding the supply through quantitative easing. If this were any other industry, it would be viewed as the Soviet-style planning board that it is, and we would be duly sceptical about its ability to intervene without creating wide scale misallocations of capital. Interest rates are not an arbitrary price of money - they are the devices that coordinate savings and investment. Manipulation of interest rates obscures the signal between consumers and producers, and when they are set too low people borrow too much. Many economists warned that central banks were creating too much credit, and that this would lead to an unsustainable boom, an inevitable credit crunch, and a subsequent recession. Many businessmen foresaw the crisis, and this is largely due to age-old economic truths about how markets operate.

We are currently seeing policymakers blame the failures of laissez-faire to justify unprecedented amounts of intervention and indebtedness. The message of Jean Baptiste Say and the vision of what an economy would actually look like if markets were allowed to operate freely are more relevant than ever. Markets are not perfect, but they create more prosperity than any rival system. On this academics and businessmen can agree.

Anthony J. Evans is Assistant Professor of Economics at ESCP Europe and Course Director of the Master in European Business (MEB) Programme in London. He is co-author of "The Neoliberal Revolution in Eastern Europe: Economic Ideas in the Transition from Communism" and has published research in a range of academic journals, trade publications and policy reports. His email address is anthonyjevans@gmail.com.

dbFX.com

Invest your Money in Money

Foreign exchange (FX) trading presents an opportunity to diversify an investment portfolio and make money from money – particularly when times in the equity or bond markets get tough. FX is proven to have low correlation with returns in these markets and market volatility actually increases trading volumes in this asset class contributing to the massive liquidity of the FX market.

It is now almost as simple to invest your money in money as it is in shares. Until 10 years ago, FX was the domain of large institutions or the very wealthy. Over the past ten years, this has changed largely due to the revolutionary growth of the Internet, which has led to the development of sophisticated online trading systems such as dbfx.com from Deutsche Bank, the first platform set up by an investment bank that caters exclusively for retail investors – giving ordinary investors the opportunity to apply for an online account with an initial investment of just £2,500. Clients are given access to real-time executable prices, charts from which they can trade and research to help make educated and sound investment decisions in the fast moving 24 hour a day world of FX. Margin requirements can be as low as 1% of the value of the trade, clients can go long or short individual currencies and funds are deposited directly with Deutsche Bank AG London.

There are three crucial strategies which are often used when trading FX; the carry, momentum and value trade. Momentum tracks the direction of currency markets; carry sees investors selling low interest rate currencies and buying those with high rates; and valuation takes a position based on the investor's view of a currency's value. Deutsche Bank research follows a range of indices that track the performance of these strategies.

Getting started with dbFX is simple: visit dbfx.com/TT for complete information on the service. Start by testing your trading skills with a $50,000 virtual trading account. dbFX sales staff are available to give you a personalised demo of the full functionality and power of dbFX. When ready, apply for an account with the self service application for individuals and corporations.

Deutsche Bank

Contents

Acknowledgements

The opinions and perspectives in this book are mine alone, along with any errors. But I would like to acknowledge great help from many on Wall Street and the City of London, including contacts arising from my work generally as a financial journalist and writer.

The London Stock Exchange, Chi-X in the United States, Lloyd's, the Alternative Investment Management Association, the Investor Relations Society and the Association of Investment Companies are among those who provided background information and answered questions specifically for this book.

Link Up Markets, the Depository Trust & Clearing Corporation, Chi-X and Ascot Underwriting provided useful perspectives. iMoneyNet kindly provided data on US money funds, and Financial Research Corporation provided data on exchange-traded funds. Denis Peters, director of corporate communications at Euroclear, gave this book a full reading, and made many helpful comments and suggestions.

At Kogan Page, I am grateful to Ian Hallsworth, publisher, for running with this title so enthusiastically. On a personal note, I thank Gulia and Acelia for making life so comfortable for me at home. I thank Starbucks outside Bank station where I did so much of the writing.

Wealth warning

This book is a general guide to how the global financial markets work. It has a broad educational purpose and the author aims to communicate in easy-to-understand language that does not have the status of legal definitions. The author has made every effort to ensure that the text is up to date, accurate and objective, but global financial markets change daily. This book is not primarily about investment and under no circumstances is it a substitute for professional investment advice.

Online information

It is worth mentioning that the online services of *The Times* are constantly evolving and therefore some of the information quoted in this book may have changed by the time you read it.

Abbreviations

When I use the name of an organisation for the first time, I spell it out in full, with its abbreviation in brackets. Subsequently, I use only the abbreviation. For example, you will find the Financial Services Authority (FSA) referred to subsequently as the FSA, and the London Stock Exchange (LSE) as the LSE.

Introduction

Global financial markets are chameleon-like. They advance, reinvent themselves and retreat, eventually repeating the process. The mechanics often take a new twist but the underlying principles remain constant. On this basis, the days of highly leveraged trading in structural products are over but they will be back.

The 2007–09 credit crisis and global economic recession, with the collapse of stocks and commodities, has left a plethora of investments that are cheap on fundamentals. Some say it is a once-in-a-lifetime opportunity to invest. Others say markets have not reached rock bottom and it is better to wait.

This book is only partly about the recent credit crunch. We are taking the longer view. Even so, we cannot ignore the present. London's status as a leading financial centre and, in the longer term, the status of the United States as the world's most powerful nation, have come under threat. So much growth has been built on credit that can no longer be supported under current market conditions. The clever structured products that made so many bankers rich have collapsed.

There is a case that China will eventually become a major power, challenging the United States or perhaps even nudging it from its perch. We are far from there. The banks of the United States and the rest of the Western world have so far survived the crisis, courtesy of our governments. Central banks in the most powerful nations are pumping liquidity into financial markets. Insurers continue to provide cover and asset managers still look after investment portfolios.

The message for bankers is to go back to basics: focus on vanilla products and reduce leveraging. Risk management and compliance will become increasingly important as regulation is likely to become heavier. With the run on Northern Rock, the collapse of Lehman Brothers and government rescues of companies across the world, we have lost the trust that we had implicitly placed in big financial names. It may take a long time to rebuild it.

In *How the Global Financial Markets Really Work*, I will give you a guided tour. I focus on the United States and parts of Western Europe and a few emerging markets. There is much of the world I have left alone. This is not just because encyclopedic coverage of even small economies is beyond the scope of this book, but also because the story repeats itself. One central bank is much like another. Many emerging economies face similar issues.

We will focus first on the global village that world financial markets make up, and then progress to banking, central banks, and then specific areas such as derivatives, stocks and bonds, and insurance. We will examine regulation and compliance developments and the role of the media.

The more you look, the more you will discover that financial markets and the real world are interconnected. The cliché of a 'small world' resonates. A family defaults on its mortgage in Florida and its house is repossessed, and this contributes to the write-downs of a bank in Europe. The US Federal Reserve cuts interest rates and sends out a message to central banks around the world.

This book attempts to bring the pieces together. You can read it in sequence or dip into it, ideally in conjunction with *The Times* or *Times Online* (www.timesonline.co.uk). This way, within days, you will start gaining knowledge of how global financial markets work. For greater depth of understanding, read some of the recommended books and visit websites listed in the appendices.

All this will stand you in good stead in whatever career you pursue or to which you aspire, or, in particular, if you are studying business, economics or journalism. If this book kick-starts an interest in global financial markets, it will have achieved its purpose.

A global village

Introduction

In this chapter we will take a look at how financial markets are linked across the world. We will focus on the credit crunch of 2007–09, its impact on global markets and how regulators are working together to combat the problems. This opening chapter provides the framework for the rest of the book.

The credit crunch

The global credit crunch that started in August 2007 has demonstrated that London can no longer be seen in isolation from financial markets in New York, continental Europe or elsewhere. Some economies were not hit immediately by the US sub-prime mortgage problems, the freezing of the money markets and the subsequent confirmed recession. By the end of 2008, however, the impact was far more widespread than a year earlier. Switzerland, Japan and some emerging markets such as India were among those who took a later hit.

The collapse of the US housing market was the initial cause. Lending criteria had slackened for borrowers and many mortgages sold were sub-prime, which means they were granted to borrowers with a bad credit history.

Back in 2005, US property prices showed signs of faltering growth and, the following year, the market crashed. In the foreclosures that inevitably followed, it was usual for lenders to obtain much less than the original mortgage value when the time and expense of the resale process had been taken into account. The originators of the loans had sold them on and the loan servicers had no incentive to restructure them.

By 2007, even borrowers with a solid credit rating were a risk, given that the properties they bought had in many cases slipped into negative equity, a proven catalyst for repossession.

Financial markets exposed to sub-prime mortgages felt the impact and this eventually froze the lending market. Banks were exposed to complex structured derivatives, known as collateralised debt obligations, which were backed by packaged slices of exposure to levels of risk on US sub-prime mortgages. The collateralised debt obligations are sold on, including across borders. It was a game of pass the parcel. When there were defaults on the mortgages that backed the collateralised debt obligations, the investors and banks that were left holding the baby took the hit – and some couldn't cope with the losses. Some had covered positions with credit default swaps, a form of derivative that also led to defaults.

The credit crunch exposed the huge risks that financial institutions had taken, typically off balance sheet and using heavy leverage. In good times it seemed clever and made many of them a fortune. Let me borrow from the heavily publicised words of Chuck Prince, the former CEO of Citigroup, in July 2007, in saying that so long as the music went on, everybody danced. As was inevitable, the music stopped.

The United States played the biggest part in triggering the global credit crisis but, given the state of some Western economies, and the reckless state of their banks, it was an accident waiting to happen. Banks in the United Kingdom and Europe particularly had been exposed to sub-prime mortgages. In times of crisis, central banks play a crucial role in restoring financial stability. There are some observers, such as investment guru Jim Rogers, who think that the central banks should not interfere with the workings of the market and should let failed companies go under.

In the 2007–09 credit crisis, central banks have intervened with unprecedented speed, innovation and coordination. They will have to face a lot more yet.

The Federal Reserve and the European central banks have led the way. In general, the approach has been to pump extra money into financial markets and, increasingly, into the real economy. So far, this has prevented more major financial institutions from collapsing. It has not yet restored public confidence.

Lessons from history

Governments have learned from history. After the Wall Street crash of 1929 and the subsequent Great Depression, Frank Roosevelt, on becoming US president in 1933, increased public spending. His government recapitalised banks by buying them with preferred stock, which gave it a priority claim on profits over common stock.

Sweden was another case study for governments today. In the early 1990s, the Swedish banking system was insolvent. In December 1992, Sweden guaranteed savers and creditors of banks, but not shareholders, against losses. The terms were that banks had to write off expected losses immediately, sell off collateral and give shares to the government so that shareholders could not be rewarded. 'Bad' banks were established to manage the problem assets. Eventually the global economy improved, Sweden's bad assets attracted buyers, and the government later claimed to have recouped the US$11 billion (£7.4 billion) in aid it had doled out to banks. It was a success story – although the Swedish loans were a simpler product than today's securitised assets.

The same could not be said of Japan's own drawn-out liquidity programme. The country's speculative property and stock market bubbles collapsed in the 1990s and there was an economic crisis. Central banks cut interest rates but not fast enough and, by the time they acted, there was deflation. The government increased public spending and stabilised the stock market. Japan rescued its banks, injecting in them more than US$500 billion (£335 billion) in return for preferred stock. One of the mistakes was that the government allowed the banks to keep their non-performing loans, and these became bigger. The Japanese economy has still not fully recovered from the crisis.

By early 2009, the US Federal Reserve had resorted to electronic printing of money to boost financial institutions and the economy, just as Japan had, and the United Kingdom had paved the way for similar action. In both the United States and the United Kingdom, there is a clear feeling of a need to increase government spending following moves to recapitalise the banks. It is all ultimately at the taxpayers' expense, although some of the investment may be recouped.

The global nature of the crisis means that it is a shared crisis, in particular when a multinational institution asks for a bailout. In September 2008, Belgium, the Netherlands and Luxembourg put €11.2 billion (£10 billion) into Fortis, the Belgian–Dutch banking and insurance group.

Supervisors and central banks

Financial services supervisors are suspicious by nature and do not always find it easy to smash the cultural barriers that impede global cooperation. The bureaucratic concerns of some continental European regulators can clash with the principles-based regime of the Financial Services Authority (FSA) in the United Kingdom. Neither the European regulators nor the FSA are natural bedfellows with the rules-based approach of the US Securities & Exchange Commission. Understandably, financial services firms are seeking opportunities for regulatory arbitrage, gravitating to the jurisdiction with the weakest regulation. Ostensibly at least, regulators, central banks and politicians are working to narrow the gaps. The Financial Stability Forum seeks ways to deal with the crisis at global level.

The Group of 20 (G20) meeting of central bank governors and finance ministers on 15 November 2008 did include emerging economies, which was considered of at least symbolic significance, but it did not reach consensus on major issues such as how to measure liquidity or establish levels of capital that banks should hold, arguably because US agreement was missing. The meeting took place just after the US presidential election.

The financial crisis is global because economies and markets are interconnected. Emerging economies lend their money to the West and export goods into those countries. The United States is the world's biggest economy, and if its stock market takes a pounding, so typically will the Far East markets overnight and, the next day, the stock markets in the United Kingdom and continental Europe will open well down.

Stock exchanges and similar rival trading facilities are increasingly global. The London Stock Exchange has welcomed applications by suitable companies from the ex-Soviet Union, China, India and other countries to launch an IPO in London, although the global credit crisis has blocked much of the pipeline.

Among those who take advantage of the shrinking global stage are the money launderers and fraudsters. Surveys show that fraud has boomed in the credit crisis. There are some jurisdictions where fraudsters have flourished. Some African or Latin American countries are steeped in corruption, as is most of the former Soviet Union. Other jurisdictions will give the crooks a tougher time. The United States throws large sums at investigating white-collar fraud and imposes lengthy jail sentences on the few crooks it catches, with a plea-bargaining system that encourages crooks to give evidence against their colleagues. The United Kingdom is moving in the same direction.

We have then a global financial services village, linked to the real economy, with one country learning from and depending on another, but with differences between jurisdictions. As the World Economic Forum notes in its report, *Global Risks 2009*, risks are interconnected across asset classes and countries. Global coordination is essential, but it means walking the walk and not just talking the talk, said Daniel Hofmann, group chief economist at Zurich Financial Services Group, in presenting the report in January 2009. He noted that while the G20 leaders made an agreement to abstain from protectionism at their November 2008 meeting, it was broken within 72 hours. His conclusion was that only if governments follow talk with action will they gain trust.

The World Economic Forum has proposed that country risk officers could serve as the focal point of communication between countries and with international bodies for risks of a global nature, including national catastrophes, food safety pandemics and terrorism. So far, there have been some moves in this direction. Singapore has instituted a 'whole government integrated risk management' framework to evaluate and prioritise risks in a holistic market. In Japan, the Central Disaster Management Council is an inter-ministerial body established to formulate and promote a comprehensive national strategy for risks.

In the global village, the banking system is ubiquitous. That is the subject of the next chapter.

2

Commercial banks

Introduction

In this chapter we will look at the role of commercial banks, how they work and how they have been hit by the credit crisis of 2007–09. We will refer to capital adequacy requirements. Read this chapter in conjunction with Chapters 3 and 4.

A new image

The credit crisis of 2007–09 and the economic recession that partly resulted from it have exposed the deficiencies of our banks. Some of the best known banks have been crippled by their lending and investment decisions and by reckless trading, much of it off balance sheet, coupled with their dependence on the money markets.

As has become apparent from the credit crisis, regulators have turned a blind eye to wholesale markets, and credit rating agencies have overrated assets that turned out to be toxic. The public image of a bank as a safe and solid institution has been destroyed. It is unlikely to be restored in a hurry. Confidence has been shattered.

Banks have a long history. The earliest bankers operated in Florence from the 15th century and conducted business from benches in the open air. In the late 14th and early 15th centuries, some Italian merchants came to London and set up as money lenders in Lombard Street. British banking started in the 17th century with rich merchants storing their money in the vaults of goldsmiths because these premises were secure. By 1677, there were 44 goldsmith bankers in London.

By 1900, London had become the world's largest banking centre, with about 250 private and joint-stock banks. During the First World War, the banking business expanded and, during the Second World War, banks became subject to foreign exchange controls. In the 1950s, these were relaxed and banks expanded. In the 1970s, the government encouraged competition and banks moved towards a broad provision of financial services.

Commercial banking, with its conservative culture, was once separate from investment banking with its gung-ho risk-taking approach. This stemmed from when the US Congress passed the Banking Act of 1933, the Glass–Steagall Act, which separated the two types of banking. Some saw this legislation as unnecessary on the basis that securities trading need not harm commercial banking, but other research rebuffs this claim. In 1999, Congress passed the Financial Services Modernisation Act, which eliminated the separation between investment and clearing banks. There is nothing now to stop universal banks, as they are known, from operating investment banking and securities activity under the same broad roof as their deposit taking.

Alberto Giovannini, chairman of the Giovannini Group, a group of financial market experts, has rejected reintroducing the Glass–Steagall style of separating securities from banking. Speaking at the seventh annual European Financial Markets conference in Brussels in January 2009, he said that securities and the lending business are very complementary. He said that the idea of conflict was due to a failure to recognise that the securities business is a repeater game.

Deposit lending

Banks lend to consumers, which is retail banking, or, at a lower rate, to businesses and governments, which is wholesale banking. On the balance sheet, any sums that banks lend, both from deposits and from wholesale funds borrowed, are assets because they belong to the bank. Deposits are liabilities because the bank owes money to customers.

At any given time, banks do not have nearly enough cash in hand to pay all of their depositors. Fortunately, however, depositors do not normally rush to withdraw all their funds at the same time.

In the United States, banks with more than US$43.9 million (£29.4 million) in net transaction accounts must have reserves of at least 10 per cent of that amount. In the United Kingdom, in contrast, the Bank of England has a voluntary reserve ratio system. In 1998, the average cash reserve ratio in UK banks was 3.1 per cent. In other countries, there are required reserve ratios, which are statutorily enforced.

Meanwhile, the banks use the money markets to gain interest on the money deposited. The business model works except when there is a run on the bank, as happened with Northern Rock.

Such a scenario was perhaps not foremost in the mind of US poet Ogden Nash when, in his poem, 'Bankers Are Just Like Anybody Else, Except Richer', he penned the lines:

> *Most bankers dwell in marble halls,*
> *Which they get to dwell in because they encourage deposits*
> *and discourage withdrawals.*

Such bankers can stay complacent only as long as the public has sufficient confidence in the bank, long enough to continue to deposit money. The trust could conceivably be manipulated. In fact, the public can be tricked. In his book, *Manias, Panics and Crashes*, Charles Kindleberger, a global economist, described how the Bank of England stopped a run in 1720 by placing stooges in one queue to withdraw funds, which they were paid slowly in sixpences, and the same people then joined another queue to pay the money back in. The sight of a bank operating in its usual way was enough to prevent the run.

When public confidence has collapsed, something more than a trick is needed. During the credit crisis, governments worldwide needed to provide financial bailouts.

Bailouts

The September 2007 run on Northern Rock came after the bank got into financial problems because it could no longer depend on the money markets to fund its mortgages, something its business model required.

The Newcastle-based bank relied on the wholesale money markets to fund about 80 per cent of its mortgage lending. In the first half of 2007, Northern Rock provided one in every five new mortgages in England but, after the money markets seized up in August, it had to refinance up to £4 billion of its borrowings by the end of October, and needed access to new finance, without which it risked default. It could not obtain this finance because it had a poor-quality mortgage book, including mortgages that gave first-time buyers a loan of up to 125 per cent of the value of their home.

The government stepped in and nationalised Northern Rock with a £55 billion initial bailout, saying that the collapse of Britain's fifth largest mortgage lender would not cause systemic risk.

On 29 September 2008, press reports confirmed that the UK government was to nationalise mortgage lender Bradford & Bingley. It would take control of the bank's £50 billion mortgages and loans, while the bank's £20 billion savings unit and branches would be bought by Spanish bank Santander.

On 3 October 2008 the US government's US$700 billion (£469 billion) bailout was passed through Congress. Under the Troubled Asset Relief Program (TARP), the treasury department would buy toxic and illiquid assets from financial institutions. The TARP limited payments to parting executives of banks that accepted the deal, and had scope also to capitalise institutions, which it subsequently did. In late November 2008, the Federal Reserve said it would inject a further US$800 billion (£536 billion) into the credit markets to stimulate the dried-up markets in mortgages, car finance and student loans.

On 13 October 2008, the UK government announced a £25 billion (US$37 billion) bailout of major UK banks. It would provide capital support in return for a stake in them. The move was backed with taxpayers' money and the government pledged further support if this did not work out.

There were three main pillars to the UK government bailout. The first was a £200 billion short-term lending facility, which doubled the amount available through the Bank of England's special liquidity scheme, allowing institutions temporarily to exchange mortgage-backed securities for government bonds.

The second pillar was that seven major banks and the Nationwide Building Society had a right to apply for £25 billion in permanent capital to improve their tier-one ratio (permanent reserves divided by risk-adjusted assets), with a further £25 billion available on standby and for other institutions. On this basis, the institutions agreed to increase their aggregate capital by the end of 2008. In return, the government would take a stake in participating banks through preference shares, which have priority over ordinary shareholders. The Treasury was to be entitled to a fixed dividend.

The third pillar was that the government would guarantee up to £250 billion of bank bonds of a maturity of up to three years, enabling banks to borrow long term again. It would allow banks to refinance debt from the wholesale markets as it falls due, relieving their dependence on short-term lending.

The UK bailout had forced larger amounts of capital on firms than similar recapitalisations in other countries, and on less generous terms. It consisted of preference share capital, taken from the taxpayer and charged at 12 per cent interest, which is onerous in comparison with the 5 per cent coupon at which the US banks were taking share capital. Later in October, a recapitalisation programme announced for French banks did not involve any form of equity, but was in the form of subordinated loans payable after other debts are cleared.

The UK deal was semi-nationalisation, with the risk and reward associated with the bailout going ultimately to the taxpayer. It was to be funded by government borrowings, with the cost, and any upside if the banking sector should recover, funelled to the taxpayer.

On the same day as the deal was announced, the Bank of England, the US Federal Reserve, the European Central Bank (ECB) and some other central banks implemented a 0.5 per cent cut in interest rates. The Bank of England said in a statement that the cut 'could not be expected to resolve the current problems in financial markets'. This was seen, however, as a defensive move against a potentially worse recession than might otherwise emerge, as well as recognition that the credit crunch had started making itself felt in the wider economy. The stock market reacted adversely.

As a condition of the bailout, the FSA, the UK regulator, was to look at executive remuneration. There was some feeling that the compensation culture in UK banks encouraged risk taking, which had led to the credit crunch.

Some of the banks to which the UK government made its offer declined to take it up, with Barclays announcing a plan to raise £6.5 billion independently. The UK government now has a 70 per cent stake in Royal Bank of Scotland, a 43 per cent stake in the combined Lloyds TSB and HBOS, and controls Northern Rock and Bradford & Bingley.

By late 2008, some of the rescued banks were not lending to businesses as freely as the government had hoped, and it has not ruled out the prospect of full nationalisation. The banks were not passing on the full benefit of interest-rate cuts to homeowners who held mortgages with them.

On 19 January 2009, the UK government announced further state intervention in the banking sector. It would provide credit risk insurance to banks and building societies for toxic assets held. This was an alternative to either setting up a 'bad bank' to house all the toxic assets, or outright nationalisation. The government was to set up a new guarantee scheme for asset-backed securities, including corporate and consumer debt, as well as mortgages. The securities could have a credit rating equivalent to government bonds. The government was to extend its existing state credit guarantee scheme for commercial paper issued by banks.

In addition, there was to be a new Bank of England facility for buying assets. It was to have a new fund of £50 billion, financed by treasury bills, which would be used to buy high-quality private-sector assets, including commercial bonds and asset-backed securities in the secondary market. This would provide the Bank of England's Monetary Policy Committee with a tool for meeting inflation targets, given the limitation its interest-rate policy in circumstances where interest rates were getting close to zero, and would boost liquidity in relevant markets. The Bank could create money electronically to pay for the assets, leading it into quantitative easing, and it eventually committed itself to this. The supply of new money to the economy in this way could create inflation risk – but the immediate risk is more of deflation.

Because of the various government rescue measures, UK national public sector net debt, previously known as national debt, had reached 40 per cent of gross domestic product (GDP). Some opposition politicians expressed concerns that the United Kingdom could eventually have to request a loan from the International Monetary Fund (IMF), as it had for a £2.3 billion loan in 1976. The fears are extreme. So far, the UK treasury has never defaulted on its debt, and UK government securities have been in demand during the credit crisis as a safe investment.

Icelandic banks

Iceland, which is in the European Economic Area, had a banking crisis that had become too big for the government to bail out. By the end of 2007, the three largest banks in Iceland had €125 billion (£111.1 billion) in assets, many funded by lending in wholesale markets, in an economy of only €14.5 billion (£12.9 billion).

In the credit crunch, the Icelandic banks could not refinance their debts because of the frozen money markets. In late September 2008, the Icelandic government partly nationalised Glitnir, the third-largest bank, and the Icelandic krona fell to a record low against the euro. In early October, the government seized the two other large banks, Landsbanki and Kaupthing. By 10 October, British councils and other organisations had lost about £860 million in savings deposited in Icelandic banks.

The British government threatened legal action against the Icelandic government in a dispute over frozen UK deposits in the collapsed Icelandic banks. In turn, it froze the assets of Icelandic companies in the United Kingdom where it could and invoked the Anti-terrorism, Crime and Security Act to freeze assets held by Icesave, owned by Landsbanki, to prevent it from stripping funds.

Iceland's prime minister Geir Haarde described the British action as an assault against the interests of his nation, and out of proportion to the issues. He said Icelanders could not accept being cast as terrorists by the British government.

In mid November, Iceland agreed to honour its obligations to depositors at failed Icelandic banks abroad, including in the United Kingdom. It was believed that this agreement may have been necessary for the country to secure a US$2.1 billion (£1.4 billion) loan from the IMF. In practice, this meant that Iceland would pay the first €20,887 (£18,568) of individual depositors' losses, and the United Kingdom's Financial Services Compensation Scheme (FSCS) topped this up to the first £50,000.

Bank runs and compensation schemes

Bank runs have had a disastrous effect on public confidence, as demonstrated by the Argentine crisis of 1999–2002, when the government closed bank accounts and would not let deposit holders withdraw cash. There were street riots.

In the United States, deposit insurance has effectively ended bank runs, according to Marin Gruenberg, vice-chairman of the Federal Deposit Insurance Corporation (FDIC). In a November 2007 speech on the international role of deposit insurance, delivered at the Exchequer Club in Washington DC, he noted that the FDIC had trained officials from China in establishing and operating a deposit insurance scheme and had entered a memorandum of understanding with the People's Bank of China, which had taken the lead in establishing a local deposit insurance system.

When Northern Rock ran into problems in 2007, UK depositors were covered by the FSCS, the UK's statutory fund of last resort, but this was only up to £2,000 in full and then for 90 per cent of the next £33,000. There were concerns that insured deposits could take up to six months to be paid. The FSA amended the FSCS's rules so that, from 7 October 2008, 100 per cent of the first £50,000 would be paid. In the United States, Congress has temporarily increased the FDIC's deposit insurance from US$100,000 to US$250,000 per depositor.

Capital adequacy and regulation

Regulators across Europe have set capital adequacy requirements for banks, based on recommendations from the Basel Committee for Banking Supervision. Basel II, the latest version, was made law by the Capital Requirements Directive, which allows for national discretion in some areas of implementation. Firms subject to the directive had to have adopted the new regime by 1 January 2008.

Basel II is intended to reduce the possibility of consumer loss or market disruption as a result of prudential failure. It aims to align economic risk with the capital charge on the balance sheet. There is a standardised or advanced approach to calculating credit risk. The capital charge is based not on the type of issuer, as was the case under Basel I, but rather on the rating of the debt. This has thrust credit rating agencies to the heart of the bank capital system.

One of the problems with Basel II, which has led to calls for reform, is that in a downturn, more credit lines are downgraded than upgraded. Banks then have to put more capital aside against unexpected losses. This means that they must provide funding at the worst time of the economic cycle, which could make them more likely to fail in a crisis.

Basel I had not been pro-cyclical in this way. It was a cruder calculation, but the capital charge would not have changed in a downturn. When the dot-com stock market bubble burst in late 2000, regulatory capital of banks remained constant.

By late 2008, regulators were discussing a cap on leverage so that, even in good times, capital under Basel II would not go below a given level.

This is the approach to Basel II in the United States, where the federal agencies set the correct standards and leverage ratio requirement of US capital rules. Basel II has a three-year transition period in the United States, a year longer than required under the international accord. Cumulative capital reductions under Basel II cannot exceed 5 per cent in the first year of implementation, 10 per cent in the second and 15 per cent in the third year. Basel II is compulsory only for the core banks, which are the largest, but smaller banks may opt in to the advanced approach, which requires sophisticated risk-management and risk-modelling skills. There is no option of using the standardised approach under the international accord.

National interests come first

As has become apparent during the credit crisis, countries seek to protect their national interests first. In 2008, German government ministers went so far as to say they did not want German taxpayers' money to bail out other countries' banks. In early October 2008, the Berlin government, Germany's central bank and some financial institutions rescued lender Hypo Real Estate with a €50 billion (£44.5 billion) bailout package.

There is a competitive motive in such attitudes. In September 2008, Ireland angered other jurisdictions when it guaranteed all deposits in Irish banks, causing some British depositors to shift their savings into branches of Irish banks. Greece and Denmark followed suit.

By the end of 2008, governments were providing more than £9,000 billion in support of banks across the world, which is more than a quarter of world GDP, at the ultimate risk of the taxpayer.

As the crisis continues, the systemic risks are high, particularly for those countries that have large deficits in their current account and have funded these with foreign borrowings. In December 2008, the IMF approved a €1.52 billion rescue package for Latvia, which was one such country. The aim was to stabilise its economy against the impact of the global credit crisis.

3

Specialist banking services

Introduction

In this chapter we will take a look at the now crashed world of shadow banking, where the respectable banks traded complex securities off the balance sheet. This in itself was a major factor in the credit crunch of 2007–09. We will turn to the secretive world of offshore banking. Finally we will investigate Islamic banking, building societies, savings and loan associations and credit unions.

Shadow banking

Shadow banking is about non-bank financial institutions that operate like banks but, unlike them, are not ultimately protected by deposit insurance or the support of a central bank as lender of last resort. The shadow banking system includes structured investment vehicles (SIVs), as well as broker-dealers, private equity groups, non-bank mortgage lenders, hedge funds, monoline insurers (see Chapter 8), conduits and money market funds.

Banks often sponsor and control SIVs, without actually owning them. The SIVs issue short-term commercial paper in the money markets at a low interest rate close to London interbank offered rate (LIBOR), which is the rate banks charge each other for loans and is based on supply and demand. They take the money they receive from this issuance and lend it out, buying long-term securities at perhaps 0.25 per cent higher than the rate at which they had borrowed through the issuance. The SIVs make a profit from the difference in rates, and the banks that set them up may extract this profit as fees.

In this way, SIVs operate like deposit-taking banks. The market exposure is, however, more volatile. The SIV must pay out on the commercial paper before the long-term money is due, so will refinance the short-term debt at a sufficiently low rate but, if that proves impossible, it may have to sell the securities into a difficult market. If the commercial paper becomes worth more than the long-term securities, the SIV faces risk of insolvency. This happened in the credit crisis of 2007–09 after the market for commercial paper dried up.

The banks have used SIVs to put their risky investments off balance sheet and so avoid having to meet the capitalisation requirements that would have applied under Basel I. It was a perfectly legal accounting ruse. An industry in SIVs had been set up to meet the demand and regulators applauded themselves for making banks themselves safer by hiving off the risky securities onto these vehicles. The risk exposure had simply been transferred to shadow banking.

Northern Rock demonstrated how it could be done. In 2007, the UK treasury found that this mortgage bank, which it was rescuing from collapse, did not own half its mortgages. Some of them had been removed to Granite, a Jersey-based registered charity and a form of SIV that allowed the bank to trade risky securities without having to be backed by required banking capital. Northern Rock had hived off liability into the shadow banking system. Other banks were doing the same and Germany experienced its Northern Rock moment when, in early 2008, its government rescued IKB Deutsche Industriebank, which had invested in sub-prime mortgage-backed securities through the SIV Rhinebridge.

In the aftermath of some failures of shadow banking, regulators have become less self-congratulatory but maintain a defensive stance. They argue that Basel II, the latest version of the Basel Accord, would have reduced the impact of the credit crunch if it had been in place earlier. Basel II puts a capital charge on the liquidity guarantees that some banks give to off-balance-sheet vehicles, but reforms to this process are under discussion. Greater disclosure requirements under Basel II would have enabled investors to better assess the toxic asset exposure of conduits.

In practice, banks had sometimes voluntarily supported SIVs and shadow banking vehicles with liquidity lines. Some banks brought lending through SIVs back onto the balance sheet, even when this was not a legal requirement. Others did not.

The Federal Reserve and other central banks have bailed out the conventional banking system, but have not yet provided much support to shadow banking. If shadow banking is to continue to exist, more stringent regulation, including accounting standards, will be required for hedge funds and rating agencies.

After the Great Depression of the 1930s, regulators tightened regulations for banks and, after this present crisis, they will do so for shadow banking.

They have left this area alone partly because it seemed to be wholesale. This is not the full story. Money market funds, which have been exposed to commercial paper issued by SIVs, restricted withdrawals by their retail investors.

Shadow banking operations, with the exception of money market funds, are more leveraged than banks. Philipp Hildebrand, vice chairman of the governing board of the Swiss National Bank, said in a December 2008 lecture at the London School of Economics that to deal with the high leverage in the traditional banking system, a leverage ratio, setting a lower limit to the capital-to-assets ratio of banks, should be provided to complement the risk-weighted approach in the current Basel framework.

Banking secrecy

Like shadow banking, offshore banking is about opacity. The credit crunch has brought calls for more transparency in tax havens. In late 2008, fears rippled through some parts of the banking world after a Florida grand jury indicted a UBS executive with helping 17,000 Americans to avoid tax by putting their money in secret bank accounts. According to the indictment, UBS had some customers sign a form in which they said they would like to 'avoid disclosure of my identity' to the US Internal Revenue Service. The indictment further alleged that UBS had assured clients in letters that it had concealed the identity of account holders from the US authorities and, in a September 2006 staff training course, it had instructed staff on discreet business conduct, including using the mail without UBS logos and in the use of encrypted computers.

UBS said publicly that it was cooperating with the investigation of its US business. In a late-November extraordinary meeting where shareholders of UBS backed a SFr6 billion (£3.6 billion) capital-raising scheme for the bank from the Swiss government, UBS chairman Peter Kurer said that Swiss banking secrecy is not there to protect against tax fraud cases.

Banking secrecy had already come under scrutiny. The IMF has been examining offshore financial centres since 2000, with an aim of helping to strengthen financial supervision of the centres so that international rules and arrangements will apply, and to promote greater cooperation among supervisors.

The Organisation for Economic Co-operation and Development (OECD) aims to improve transparency in tax havens and to establish an effective exchange of information in tax matters, goals which a Group of 8 (G8) meeting in July 2008 approved. In 2000, the OECD had identified over 40 tax havens and asked them to commit to the OECD standards. Initially, seven tax havens refused to cooperate and were included on a blacklist. By 2008, only Liechtenstein, Andorra and Monaco remained on the list and they have stayed resistant to the OECD's requirements.

Liechtenstein, located between Austria and Switzerland, is under pressure. Heinrich Kieber, a Liechtenstein citizen and former employee of the principality's main bank, the Liechtenstein Global Trust, famously stole secret client data from his employer, copied it onto DVDs and sold his information to US authorities. He attempted to make a sale to UK authorities and succeeded in selling data for more than £4 million to Germany's foreign intelligence agency, the Bundesnachrichtendienst.

Germany said it suspected 1,000 wealthy Germans of stealing €4 billion (£3.6 billion) from the taxpayer. The German chancellor Angela Merkel has demanded that Liechtenstein open its foundations to tax authorities and, unless this happens, she has threatened to refuse to ratify Liechtenstein's accession to the Schengen passport-free zone.

Liechtenstein's Crown Prince Alois has criticised Germany's government for spying on his country and putting fiscal interests above the law. Self-evidently, Liechtenstein would lose commercially if it lost some of its banking secrecy. The principality has 15 banks and more than 300 trustees, mostly lawyers, who manage thousands of foundations. These are both anonymous and fiscally convenient for foreign customers of Liechtenstein banks who put money into them tax free.

As part of its work, the OECD launched a project to give tax authorities within its membership better access to banking information. A standard of access was agreed and has been widely implemented within the OECD and beyond. It has been endorsed by the G8 and the G20, although some countries have not yet reached the standard. Since 2000, around 27 tax-information-exchange agreements have been signed, and 40 more are under negotiation.

The UK government has announced an independent review of British offshore financial centres and, in December 2008, announced that Michael Foot, a former FSA managing director, would lead it. The review was to cover financial supervision and transparency, taxation in relation to financial stability, sustainability and future competitiveness, financial crisis management and resolution arrangements, and international cooperation. However, offshore centres would retain existing constitutional arrangements and fiscal independence, including the setting of tax rates.

If the review leads to greater transparency and this prevents parties from hiding income offshore and so evade tax, the offshore financial centres will lose business. Apart from putting money into tax havens, however, individuals have opportunities to relocate to and live in low-tax regimes. Here they can pay small tax bills in accordance with local legislative requirements, as in certain parts of Switzerland.

In the European Union (EU), the Savings Directive aims to counter cross-border tax evasion by promoting the exchange of information automatically between member states. Every state should be able to apply its own tax rules to interest received by its residents from paying agents in other member states.

Another piece of EU legislation, the Savings Taxation Directive, has been amended to close some tax loopholes, including through the use of innovative financial vehicles instead of traditional bank savings accounts.

In February 2009, the US$8 billion fraud by Sir Allen Stanford (see Chapter 11) put the spotlight on how offshore centres are used. There is some concern that Stanford had been beyond US scrutiny because his main operation, Stanford International Bank, was based in the Caribbean island of Antigua, which has been under investigation for money laundering. The International Financial Sector Regulatory Authority in Antigua has a six-member board including an executive from Stanford International Bank, as well as three executives from other offshore banks it is supposed to regulate.

Stanford had previously set up a bank, the Guardian International Bank, on the Caribbean island of Montserrat, and the Federal Bureau of Investigation (FBI) had suspected it of involvement in money laundering. Stanford voluntarily gave up his banking licence in Montserrat, and a joint FBI–Scotland Yard investigation of brass-plate banks at Montserrat ran out of steam. Stanford then set up Stanford International Bank in Antigua.

Islamic banking

If shadow banking and offshore financial centres smell of secrecy and possible tax evasion, Islamic banking is at the other end of the spectrum. It is seen as a squeaky clean alternative to conventional banking, although it is not yet widely used.

The concept of Islamic banking is underpinned by the virtuous-sounding principle that money cannot be used to make more money. On this basis, no interest is chargeable on loans. Lenders must share in the risks and profits of the enterprise and wealth creation should aim to improve society as a whole.

In this framework there is not much space for complex derivatives transactions that contributed so destructively to the 2007–09 credit crisis. Islamic products have ventured only in a small way into credit default swaps, exchange-traded funds and hedge funds. Takaful, which is Islamic insurance, is becoming more widespread. Participants pay into a fund invested in Sharia-compliant instruments and any surplus after claims is distributed to them.

So far, Islamic banking is only a small part of the global banking system, not least because the 56 Muslim countries cannot agree on a strategy for the sector. But the growth potential is significant. In the Middle East, Bahrain has by far the largest concentration of Islamic financial institutions, including 24 banks and 11 Takaful companies. Malaysia has promoted Islamic finance vigorously. Hong Kong has signed agreements with Dubai to establish two working groups to develop each other's Islamic financial sectors. Turkey has a pro-Islamic government, and its general banking law, introduced in 2007, covers 'local participation' banks (Islamic banks) as well as the conventional kind, making it easier to launch Islamic capital products.

In Europe, France's President Sarkozy has launched an initiative to make Paris an Islamic centre. The City of London has embraced Islamic banking under Britain's social and financial inclusion policy. Gordon Brown's government aims to make the United Kingdom the international focus of Islamic trade, investment and finance. London has five dedicated Islamic banks and more than 20 other banks offering Islamic products, and it has relevant legal expertise. In late 2008, the UK was consulting on whether to issue its first sovereign Islamic bond, known as Sukuk, into the wholesale sterling market in 2009.

Building societies

Building societies are lending and saving institutions, and they compete with banks. They are mutual institutions that are run by boards of directors, and whose investors, borrowers and account holders have a right to vote, receive information and attend and speak at meetings. Banks, in contrast, are companies owned by, and run for, their shareholders.

There are 59 building societies in the United Kingdom, with total assets of £360 billion. They also exist in Ireland, as well as in New Zealand and Australia. In Finland, the Mortgage Society of Finland is a permanent building society. According to the UK Building Societies Association, building societies often offer better-value products than banks, particularly in savings accounts and retail mortgages, because, unlike banks, they do not have to use more than a third of their profits to pay dividends. But some building societies limit the availability of their offer to people living within a certain area.

One of the defining features of a building society is that it is not allowed to raise more than 50 per cent of its funds from the wholesale markets. On average, it raises 30 per cent of its funds this way. This is one reason why building societies were less exposed to the credit crunch than banks.

Building societies have the sole task of meeting customer needs, but the banks must make a profit from their customers. Some building societies have been undercapitalised and have needed to grow fast. Between 1989 and 2000, 10 UK building societies decided to become banks. This was after the Building Societies Act 1986 introduced demutualisation, which means conversion into an investor-owned company. Managers and directors favoured the move because it would increase their own income, and opportunists, known as carpetbaggers, sought windfall profits by opening temporary savings accounts in those societies most likely to convert.

Not one of those ex-building societies remains an independent company. In 2000, Barclays bought Woolwich, and in 2001, Halifax merged with Bank of Scotland to form HBOS. In 2004, Abbey was bought by Banco Santander Central Hispano, a Spanish financial group. Others sold themselves directly to banks. Cheltenham & Gloucester is now owned by Lloyd's TSB, and National & Provincial by Santander. Bristol & West is owned by Bank of Ireland, and Birmingham Midshires by Halifax Bank of Scotland.

The credit crunch has taken its toll. In February 2008, Northern Rock was nationalised, and in September of the same year, Bradford & Bingley was also nationalised while, in October, Santander bought Alliance & Leicester. The case has been made that the fall of Northern Rock was linked to its 1997 demutualisation. Once it had become a bank, Northern Rock had felt it necessary to expand into a competitive sector where some smaller players had not survived. The way it decided to do this was to securitise its mortgage books, which, as it turned out, did not work once the money markets seized up.

A great deal of talk about consolidation is going on among remaining UK building societies. Under new rules from September 2009, building societies that merge will be able to maintain separate compensation limits. The FSA announced the move after customers expressed concern about this issue in relation to the planned merger between Nationwide with Cheshire and Derbyshire building societies, announced in September 2008.

Savings and loan associations

In the United States, savings and loan associations (S&Ls), also known as thrifts, are based on the building society concept. They are a sector with a history of problems. Let us go back more than two decades. The Depository Institutions Deregulation and Monetary Control Act of 1980 removed upper limits on interest rates, following which interest rates on deposits rose, and both banks and savings and loan associations took bigger risks. They made some bad real-estate loans based on the fact that they could borrow at a high rate, and in the knowledge that the government could rescue them if all else failed. In 1986–95, there was a crisis in the sector and many S&Ls went bust, mainly due to their unwise lending. The Federal Savings & Loan Insurance Corporation, which was responsible for deposit insurance, became insolvent in 1989, and its responsibility was transferred to the Federal Deposit Insurance Corporation.

In late 2008, some insurance groups looked to acquire a thrift. This way, they would qualify for the US Treasury's TARP facility, for which ownership of a bank or a thrift was a prerequisite.

In November 2008, Hartford Financial Services Group said it had applied to the Office of Thrift Supervision to become a thrift and applied to the US Treasury Department's TARP. The company had signed a merger agreement to buy the Florida-based parent of Federal Trust Bank for US$10 million (£6.7 million). In the same month, Lincoln Financial Group, Philadelphia, said that it had applied to become a thrift and agreed to buy Newton County Loan & Savings, Indiana. The company has applied to participate in the TARP. Genworth Financial had similarly applied to become a thrift with respect to its acquisition of Interbank in Minnesota; it too applied for the TARP.

Dutch insurer AEGON had secured €3 billion (£2.7 billion) in capital from its government in October 2008, which it saw as more than adequate, combined with its own measures, to ensure a strong capital buffer. It was also looking at the possibility of acquiring a thrift. It was unclear at the time, however, whether AEGON, as an insurer domiciled in the Netherlands, would be eligible for the US TARP.

Credit unions

Credit unions, which are widespread in the United States, are organisations of people, usually in the same town. They take deposits and provide loans, including home mortgages. They are like savings and loan associations, but are not open to everybody.

4

Central banks

Introduction

Central banks have come under the spotlight in the credit crisis of 2007–09 as they have bailed out financial institutions and attempted to prevent financial instability. In this chapter we will see how they work.

Description and overview

Central banks control monetary policy in their country and oversee the stability of the financial system. They are lenders of last resort to the banks, distribute currency and act as the government's banker. Ideally, central banks are independent from government, so that they may legitimately decline to lend it money if, for instance, they see this as a significant inflation risk. The Federal Reserve, the US central bank, has always had this independence but the Bank of England and the Bank of Japan did not achieve it until 1997.

In conducting monetary policy, central banks change interest rates to make loans cheaper or more expensive, and they manipulate the money supply. One central bank may have a different strategy from another. For example, the Federal Reserve has a mandate balanced between minimising inflation and maintaining long-term growth, and is focused on cutting interest rates, including in the credit crisis of 2007–09, to stimulate the economy. The European Central Bank, in contrast, has a mandate to keep prices stable and so is less keen to cut rates.

Banking supervision is another variable. Only some central banks, as in the United States, Italy, the Netherlands, Portugal and New Zealand, are supervisors of banks. In the United Kingdom, Australia and Japan, banking supervision is done by an independent authority. This separation avoids conflicts of interest, but means that the central bank does not have a supervisor's expertise to draw on in its assessments of banking sector conditions, which is a drawback in addressing issues of financial stability.

The central banks have their own bank, the Bank for International Settlements (BIS), based in Basel, Switzerland. The BIS, which holds meetings of governors and senior officials of central banks every two months, is focused on regulatory supervision, including the Basel Accord, and fosters monetary policy cooperation. The BIS carries out traditional banking functions for central banks, including gold and foreign exchange transactions and agency or trustee functions, and conducts research. The BIS has provided emergency funding to the international monetary system.

In the current credit crisis, the banks that have got into the most trouble are those with large current-account deficits, meaning that imports are more than exports. To pay for this deficit, they need a capital account surplus, in the absence of which they will be raiding foreign exchange reserves. According to Michael Simms, director of political risk at Exclusive Analysis, in January 2009 Iceland, the Baltic countries, Greece, Spain and Portugal had the largest current account deficits. However, he said, countries such as France, Germany and Japan, with current-account surpluses, also experienced problems because they relied on external demand to drive their economies, which was difficult during the credit crisis. Let us now focus on some individual central banks.

US Federal Reserve System

The US Federal Reserve System, known informally as the Fed, was founded by Congress in 1913 as the central bank of the United States. The Fed performs the usual services of a central bank, including monetary policy, and acts as a supervisor and regulator of banking institutions.

The Fed is an independent, central government agency, and has its own source of funds, but is subject to oversight by the US Congress, which can pass laws affecting it. It is constructed in a non-centralised way, with 12 regional Federal Reserve Banks in 12 districts, representing the population spread in 1913, with more districts on the east coast of the United States than on the west, and two Federal Reserve Banks in the state of Missouri.

Each regional Fed bank has its own board of governors and issues stock to commercial banks, known as member banks, which must buy shares valued at 6 per cent of their capital. The banks cannot trade the shares, but receive dividends and participate in choosing directors and the president of the regional Federal Reserve Bank. They keep deposits at this Federal Reserve Bank and can borrow from it.

The Fed has a board of governors in Washington DC and a Federal Open Market Committee (FOMC). The FOMC, whose members include all the governors, the New York Fed's president and four regional Fed banks in rotation, oversees open market operations. These are the purchase or sale of securities, mainly US government bonds, in the open market, to influence overall monetary conditions.

Monetary policy

When money and credit grow too fast against the supply of goods and services, we have inflation. The Fed sees its task as keeping this growth neither too fast nor too slow. If money flows fast into the economy, banks are given more to lend and interest rates decline. Conversely, if less money flows, banks have less to lend, which means that consumers borrow less and spend less, leading to price declines.

The Fed, like other central banks, can control the money supply by increasing or decreasing reserves in the banking system through the buying and selling of securities in open market operations. If the Fed wants to increase the money supply, it buys government securities. In practice, the domestic trading desk at the New York Federal Reserve Bank, one of its regional Federal Reserve banks, buys on behalf of the Federal Reserve System from a group of securities dealers. The Fed creates the funds by crediting the account that the dealers' banks have at the New York Federal Reserve Bank. The transactions mean that the banking system has extra reserves.

Banks in the United States need to comply with a specified reserve ratio, which is a percentage of reserves that must be held in cash. Except for smaller banks, this is a tenth of the money lent out. In this way, US$1,000 of new reserves, based on a required reserve ratio of 0.10, will turn into new deposits in various banks, in amounts that dwindle down the chain, to an overall total of US$10,000. This is fractional reserve banking.

In the meantime, the Fed collects interest on the government securities it has bought and uses this to pay its expenses, passing anything left to the US treasury. As a reverse transaction, the Fed decreases the money supply by selling government securities and taking the cash.

The Fed does not issue the securities in which it deals. They are backed by the US Treasury, an entirely separate entity. As a department of the federal government, the Treasury collects taxes, makes payments on the government's behalf and issues government securities to cover the budget deficit, paying interest on them and redeeming them at face value.

On a day-to-day basis, the Fed typically engages in outright repurchase agreements, known as repos, which change the money supply only briefly. These are government security purchases or sales that are quickly reversed (more on them in Chapter 6). In the credit crisis of 2007–09, the Fed has bought toxic mortgage-backed securities from banks, which has increased the money supply.

In addition, the Fed sets the discount rate, at which it lends cash to depository institutions. As a way to control the money supply, this is its second most important monetary policy instrument after open market operations. If the Fed changes the discount rate, it is signalling its intentions to the market. The Fed has sometimes set a target for the federal funds rate, by which banks lend to banks, and which it can influence indirectly.

In practice, banks need not hold more than the minimum reserves required by the Fed. Should they need to top them up, they can go to the Fed's discount window and borrow what they need at the discount rate. They do not do this much or it would suggest that they were problem banks. The banks can otherwise borrow at the federal funds rate from other banks. If they have excessive reserves, they can *lend* to other banks.

As a third policy instrument, one that it rarely uses, the Fed can change reserve requirements, which are the proportion of deposits a bank must hold in its reserves as it lends the rest out.

The Fed's methods have attracted critics, including, at the extreme, conspiracy theorists. Some think that the Fed's power to create money should be held in check with a return to the gold standard, by which the dollar represented an amount of gold that never changed. The United States dropped the gold standard in 1933, two years after the United Kingdom had dropped it. Soon other countries followed suit. Under the gold standard, the Fed had been forced to keep interest rates high so that people would put funds on deposit rather than change them into gold, and this had damaged the economy.

The widely held view is that government intervention works better than the gold standard. There are limitations. Printing money to stimulate the economy can lead to rampant inflation in the long run, as in Weimar, Germany in the 1920s and in Zimbabwe today. In the credit crisis of 2007–09, some feared that the Fed, with its rescue programmes, was moving in that direction.

In a lecture on 13 January 2009 at the London School of Economics, Ben Bernanke, chairman of the Fed, said that the Fed's lending had resulted in a large increase in excess reserves held by banks, but they left most of this money idle, on deposit with the Fed. This, coupled with weak global economic activity and low commodity prices, meant that the Fed saw little inflation risk in the short term.

Measures in the credit crisis of 2007–09

In his lecture, Bernanke explained how the Fed had cut the discount rate in August 2007 as a first response to the credit crisis, followed by a reduction in the federal funds rate target. This policy action led to cheaper interest rates, although there were market concerns that it would stoke inflation.

In addition, the Fed took measures to support the credit markets and the economy. It provided short-term liquidity to sound financial institutions, including auctioning credit and making primary dealers (broker-dealers trading in US government securities with the Bank of New York Mellon and J P Morgan Chase), eligible to borrow at the Fed's discount window. The Fed entered bilateral currency-swap agreements with 14 central banks, enabling them to acquire dollars from the Fed to lend to local banks, easing global dollar-funding market conditions.

As a further measure, the Fed provided liquidity directly to borrowers and investors in key credit markets. The Fed has introduced, from February 2009, facilities to buy highly rated commercial paper at a term of three months, as lender of last resort, so reducing the risk that a borrower could not raise funds to repay maturing commercial paper. The Fed has thus provided backup liquidity for money market mutual funds.

The Fed is buying longer-term securities for its portfolio. This includes plans to buy up to US$500 billion (£335 billion) in mortgage-backed securities and US$100 billion (£67 billion) in debt. Mortgage rates dropped as a result of this programme, which should support the housing sector. The Fed is also considering buying longer-term treasury securities.

In his speech, Bernanke described the Fed's sometimes innovative approach to supporting the credit markets as credit easing. This involves expanding the central bank's balance sheet, with a focus on the quantity of bank reserves, which are liabilities for the central bank, but also considering the composition of loans and securities on the asset side of the central bank's balance sheet. The mix will affect credit conditions for households and businesses. Quantitative easing, in contrast, as practised earlier by the Bank of Japan, is focused on bank reserves only.

What both approaches have in common, which Bernanke did not describe in his speech, is the electronic creation of money to buy toxic assets, which the bank takes onto the asset side of its balance sheet. Later, it may or may not be able to sell these assets. This is an alternative to issuing bonds to raise money to buy the toxic assets.

European Central Bank

The Frankfurt-based European Central Bank (ECB) was founded in 1998, and took over some roles of the central banks in the euro-zone member countries of the EU. These still operate but no longer manage currency, which is centralised at the ECB.

The ECB, in keeping with its mandate to keep prices stable, as discussed early in this chapter, has focused more on controlling the money supply than the Fed or the Bank of England. In this way, it resembles the Bundesbank, the German central bank.

With Jean-Claude Trichet, former head of the Banque de France, as chairman, the ECB is a supra-national institution with its own legal personality. The ECB, together with the national central banks of all euro-zone EU member states, makes up the European System of Central Banks. With the national banks of all EU member states that have adopted the euro, the ECB makes up the Euro System.

The Euro System, which is functionally independent, carries out monetary policy, including decisions on the main ECB interest rates, conducts foreign exchange operations, holds and manages the official reserves of the euro-zone countries, and promotes the smooth operation of payment systems. The Euro System contributes to financial supervision, advises legislators and compiles financial statistics, and has the exclusive right to authorise the issue of euro bank notes.

The national central banks of the Euro System have a legal personality separate from the ECB, but operate in line with its guidelines and instruction. They carry out monetary policy and enable settlement of cashless domestic and cross-border payments. They manage foreign currency reserves, for both themselves and the ECB.

The governing council of the ECB meets twice a month, and has a main responsibility of formulating the monetary policy of the euro area, which is to decide the level of the main ECB interest rates. It steers short-term interest rates partly through Open Market Operations.

Euro-zone member countries cannot create money to repay euro-denominated debt, as the ECB controls this debt. They can, however, issue new bonds to rescue their banks. The cost of borrowing in euros varies: for example, the government in Greece must pay more than the government in Italy. EU member states do not have to rescue others that cannot service their debts.

Measures in the credit crisis of 2007–09

The ECB has temporarily taken an unusually flexible approach to providing liquidity during the credit crisis. On 15 January 2009 the ECB reduced the key interest rate from 2.5 to 2.0 per cent, the fourth interest-rate cut in just over three months. By late 2008, euro-zone governments had supported banks in their countries, partly by offering funds for recapitalisation and guarantees for loans, estimated at €2,000 billion (£1,778 billion), or 20 per cent of euro-zone GDP. In addition, some countries had announced or approved fiscal support.

In January 2008, Trichet said in the European Parliament that he was ready to take on responsibility for supervising European banks and that the EU's Maastricht Treaty allowed politicians to grant it this power. Some national regulators are sceptical about giving the ECB such sweeping powers. Banking supervision in the EU has, nonetheless, proved weak and uncoordinated, including across borders, which was a factor contributing to the problems of Fortis, the Belgian–Dutch financial services group, before it was rescued in September 2008.

Bank of England

The Bank of England, founded in 1694, is the central bank of the United Kingdom. It was once responsible for supervising banks, but this role came under scrutiny, initially after the July 1991 collapse of Bank of Credit and Commerce International (BCCI). In October 1992, a report by Lord Justice Bingham did not recommend that the Bank should be deprived of its banking supervisory role, but it found it had not pursued 'the truth about BCCI with the rigour which BCCI's market reputation justified'.

After Barings collapsed in 1995, as a result of its trader Nick Leeson losing over £800 million through unauthorised trades in derivatives, the Bank of England's authority to authorise banks and supervise the banking system was given to the FSA.

The Bank of England has responsibility for the stability of the banking system and other UK financial markets, and for maintaining price stability. Once, the chancellor of the exchequer would decide on whether to change interest rates, and the Bank of England only provided advice. Critics said that the government should not have such power because it had a conflicting political agenda. After Labour won the May 1997 general election, Gordon Brown, then Chancellor of the Exchequer, gave the Bank of England full responsibility for monetary policy.

The government has mandated the Bank of England to keep inflation at 2.0 per cent as measured by the Consumer Price Index, which equates to the European Harmonised Index of Consumer Prices. The bank seeks to achieve the target by changing the repo rate, the short-term rate at which it lends to banks. If inflation should rise or fall a full percentage point from the target, the governor of the Bank of England must write an open explanatory letter to the chancellor of the exchequer setting out what the bank will do to bring inflation back within the inflation-target parameters. The need for such letters arose in the credit crisis of 2007–09, when inflation rose from 2.1 per cent in December 2007 to 4.7 per cent in August 2008.

The bank, with the FSA and the treasury, is jointly responsible for tackling credit crises. This tripartite system of financial regulation came under scrutiny after the problems of Northern Rock.

In 2007, the Bank of England encouraged a rescue bid for Northern Rock by Lloyds TSB, but this came to nothing, and there was a crisis of confidence. Northern Rock asked the Bank of England for emergency funding, which caused panic among Northern Rock customers, many of whom rushed to get their money out of the bank. Following this run on the bank, the government issued a statement guaranteeing all deposits. The Bank of England lent Northern Rock an initial £2 billion, which had increased to £26 billion by the end of the year, shortly before the bank's nationalisation.

The tripartite system of financial regulation had not worked effectively. In the Northern Rock failure, it had been unclear who was in charge. The Bank of England lacked the powers to intervene. A Banking Bill, published in October 2008, replaced emergency legislation proposing a Special Resolution Regime giving powers to the tripartite authorities. Any of the tripartite authorities could apply for a failing bank to be placed in insolvency, and the Bank of England could apply for it to be placed in administration, which would mean that the bank was transferred to a bridge bank or private buyer.

Measures in the credit crunch of 2007–09

To address the credit crisis, the Bank of England introduced a Special Liquidity Scheme (SLS) whereby it lends treasury bills in return for security over assets. This was in addition to the government's provision of up to £50 billion to specified UK banks, in return for an equity share, and a government guarantee of certain debt instruments issued by eligible institutions.

To use the Bank of England special liquidity scheme, institutions had to be eligible to subscribe to Bank of England standing facilities, and the assets had to be backed by either residential mortgages or credit card debt. The participants retained the risk on 'swapped' assets. The scheme proved popular and was made available for longer, at a higher rate.

Working together

The central banks around the world have shown some willingness to cooperate in addressing the credit crisis of 2007–09. On 8 October 2008, the Fed, the ECB, the Bank of Canada, the Bank of England, the Swiss National Bank and the Swedish Riksbank cut interest rates simultaneously. It was an historic first attempt at globally integrated interest-rate action in response to a crisis.

The coordinated action made it less embarrassing for central banks to reverse rates, and eliminated the risk of cutting rates on an individual country basis, which had been a major concern for the Fed and the Bank of England. Since then, there have been further interest-rate cuts across the world in efforts to stimulate the global economy, including in Japan, which in October 2008 cut its benchmark overnight interbank lending rate for the first time in seven years. This was in line with earlier rate cuts by other central banks.

The efficient market fallacy

At the World Economic Forum in Davos in January 2009, there was a brainstorming session to assess which policy assumptions had contributed to the global financial crisis. The belief in efficient markets was the most widely held answer.

Within financial institutions, the efficient market theory is the underlying basis for the Value-at-Risk models with which banks and other financial institutions run their businesses, and these did not work in the credit crisis. Within the securities industry, the theory in its strongest form says that securities prices accurately reflect all known and knowable information, including inside information.

The efficient market theory, on a macroeconomic level, underlies how central banks have managed monetary policy, according to George Cooper, fund manager at Alignment Investors and the former London head of interest-rate research at J P Morgan. He says that what is missing in central banks is the understanding that global markets are inherently unstable, that there will always be crises, and that these are not anybody's fault.

In *The Origin of Financial Crises* (see further reading at the end of the book), Cooper observes that central banks do not worry about reining in excessive economic growth because it always moves toward an equilibrium; but in a modest downturn they stimulate the economy aggressively. Central banks have made it clear to financial institutions that they will bail out indebtedness, creating a risk of moral hazard, but, Cooper says, they would do better to practise 'tough love', allowing institutions sometimes to fail.

Cooper's view is that central banks have the wrong objective, namely to control consumer goods and services, which are efficient. Instead, he says, they should focus on asset-price inflation, targeting a reasonable rate of change.

Limitations

Central banks by themselves cannot guarantee financial stability in the long term and, in particular, cannot exclude that their intervention may create incentives for banks to be less cautious, said Philipp Hildebrand, vice-chairman of the governing board of the Swiss National Bank, at the Institut des Hautes Études Commerciales de Lausanne in September 2008.

In some cases, the mistakes of central banks can lead the country into crisis. This happened with Iceland, where wrong decisions by its central bank led to a commercial banking collapse in 2008.

For a long time, Iceland's inflation was over target, with market interest rates sometimes more than 15 per cent. Speculators brought foreign currency into the country, and the krona's exchange rate rose sharply. In 2008, they pulled out. The Central Bank of Iceland had failed to respond to pressure to increase its foreign currency reserves as Icelandic banks had foreign assets worth 10 times the country's gross domestic product. In the end, Iceland was rescued by a loan from the IMF.

International Monetary Fund

The IMF evolved from the Bretton Woods Conference, known formally as the United Nations Monetary and Financial Conference, in 1944. Representatives of 45 nations, including the United States and the United Kingdom, met at Bretton Woods, New Hampshire in the north-eastern United States and argued for a framework of international cooperation. They were aiming to avoid a repeat of the disastrous economic policies that had contributed to the great depression of the 1930s.

The United Kingdom's negotiating position was a proposition of John Maynard Keynes, the economist, who said that those nations with a large trade deficit and also, significantly, those with a large credit surplus, should be charged interest and otherwise penalised. The nations with a surplus would have a strong incentive to dispose of it, by which process they would dispose of other nations' deficits.

The United States, the world's biggest creditor at the time, refused the proposition. Instead, it proposed the International Stabilization Fund, which would put on those nations with the highest deficits the burden of maintaining the balance of trade. This was to become the IMF.

The IMF aims mainly to ensure the stability of the international monetary system. The fund advises its 184 member countries, makes finance available to help them address balance-of-payment problems and provides technical assistance and training. The IMF's resources come mainly from the quotas that countries deposit when they join the fund. The quota reflects the size of the member's economy, and is the basis for its voting power. The United States, the largest contributor, has the largest vote, at about 17 per cent of the total, giving it an effective veto.

Unlike its sister organisation, the World Bank, also arising from Bretton Woods, the IMF does not finance projects. Instead, its loans are intended to help members tackle balance-of-payments problems and restore sustainable growth. The lending programmes require countries to buy foreign exchange from the IMF's reserve assets, paying with their own currency. The borrower repays the loan by repurchasing currency from the IMF in exchange for reserve assets. Foreign exchange reserves must be held in US dollars, which help the US economy.

The IMF has been widely criticised for the strategy, sometimes called the Washington Consensus, that it has imposed on countries as a condition for financing. Borrowing countries must give priority to inflation control through high interest rates, and must create open markets and liberalise their banking systems. They must reduce government spending, except on repaying debt, and privatise assets. Such strategies have often made crises worse and have created new ones. To meet IMF loan conditions, governments have cut jobs and subsidies, and made credit unavailable. In the 1990s, the IMF strategy had a bad effect on Asia, where states paid back loans as quickly as possible.

The IMF has seen a revival since the credit crisis of 2007–09 because some nations have seen no other viable option but to borrow from it. By late 2008, the IMF had already agreed loans to some countries in crisis. The fund was to lend US$15.7 billion to Hungary, which it required to cut its budget deficit further, and US$16.5 billion to the Ukraine. It lent US$2.1 billion to Iceland and, as a condition of this, the Icelandic government has had to raise its interest rates by 6 per cent to 18 per cent in October 2008. In January 2009, the IMF said that, among other developments, it had made good progress toward an agreement with Turkey, and that it would be reviewing Ireland's economy in April 2008.

The G20 leaders in their meeting on 15 November 2008 had agreed that the Bretton Woods institutions had to be 'comprehensively reformed'. They suggested giving the IMF more money and poorer countries more representation. Such changes would not, however, reduce effective control by developed countries.

Gordon Brown, UK prime minister, and Nicolas Sarkozy, French president, have shown keenness to bring further funding into the IMF to raise the level beyond its US$250 billion available for lending, a level that has fallen in recent decades compared with world trade and income. In late 2008, Brown had asked China and Saudi Arabia for extra funding. If a non-Western country was to help this way, it would have more say in how the IMF was run. If it was to vastly increase its lending, the IMF would have to develop its infrastructure to cope with the defaults that would ensue. Some critics say that the IMF should increase only its monitoring role and that it is the central banks of developed countries that should be lending more money.

The world's capital market

Companies need capital to develop their businesses, to deliver products and services and to bring about progress from which we can all benefit. The London Stock Exchange provides the marketplace for companies and investors from across the world to participate in this process. The global financial markets need the world's most international stock exchange. The London Stock Exchange.

www.londonstockexchange.com

London
Stock Exchange

5

Stock markets

Introduction

In this chapter I will explain how stock markets work and the basics of investment analysis. Many readers will have an interest in investing, so this particular chapter is more about the concerns of private investors than of pension funds, insurance funds and other institutions.

Shares

If you buy a share, you are buying part of a company. You can have shares in companies that are not quoted anywhere, and these may be traded privately or over the counter, so making a market. The share price is set as a spread between a buying and a selling price. When a single price is quoted, it is often the mid price. Shares can rise or fall in value, which reflects supply and demand.

As an investor, you will typically hold your shares for several months, and perhaps some years, to make a profit. Traders do not buy and hold in this way, but come in and out of stocks quickly, within days or hours, hoping to profit from share price volatility.

If you own shares in a company, you may attend its annual general meeting, which offers you the chance to review the company's activities and to exercise your voting rights. Many companies pay a dividend, which in the United States is quarterly or in the United Kingdom is twice a year. This represents a payment from corporate profits to shareholders. It is the income from your share ownership. The price of a share falls by the amount paid out, which happens after the company goes ex-dividend. If you buy the shares after the ex-dividend date, you'll pay a lower price but will not receive the dividend.

Stock splits or, in UK terminology, scrip issues, are where a company's existing shares are divided into several. In a 2-for-1 split, each shareholder receives one extra share for each they hold. The stock split is an accounting exercise and does not affect financial ratios. It is sometimes done for psychological reasons. Retail investors sometimes believe, erroneously, that if the share price is low, it means better value. If, however, the company gives new shares to a director and does not increase investors' shares, this is a dilution, which is different from a stock split. There are also rights issues (see Chapter 7).

Broker-dealers and investment advisers

As an investor or trader, you will deal with a stockbroker, or you may have an investment adviser run a portfolio for you. You can invest globally through a broker in your home country, or you can often go directly to local brokers in the country where the shares are traded. If, for example, as a UK investor, you want to buy shares in a company listed in Russia, you can use a Moscow broker. Some shares listed on local exchanges are not accessible to foreigners, however, or not at the same price. Foreign stock markets can be fairly illiquid and subject to a lot of manipulation.

In the United States, there are around 5,000 broker-dealers, who have both a broker function, by which they conduct transactions in securities for others, and a dealer function, by which they buy and sell securities for themselves as principals. On a federal level, the broker-dealers are regulated by the Securities and Exchange Commission (SEC), with some regulatory authority delegated to the Financial Industry Regulatory Authority (FINRA), a self-regulatory organisation. In addition, some states regulate broker-dealers under separate state securities laws.

Broker-dealers are paid on commission. They sell mutual funds as well as equities, and do private placements of securities. They are to be distinguished from investment advisers, of which there are over 10,000 in number. They are regulated separately and have a fiduciary duty to clients that broker-dealers do not. They are paid by fees.

Only a small number of firms are dually registered as both broker-dealers and investment advisers, but there is, nonetheless, a substantial overlap. Some companies may have multiple business units or subsidiaries, each registered separately as an investment adviser or broker-dealer, according to research sponsored by the SEC (Investor and Industry Perspectives on Investment Advisers and Broker-dealers (1988) published by LRN-RAND Center for Corporate Ethics, Law, and Governance).

Why we should not lose faith in equities

The last 18 months has been a period of extremes for investors. Record declines in equity markets worldwide and shuddering moves in bond yields and currencies have undermined confidence, while a global financial crisis has taken hold, restricting the supply of credit and causing a global economic recession.

This turbulence on global stock markets has prompted many investors to examine why they should own equities. Although an understandable response given the destruction in equity values experienced over the last year, it's important to note how rare these extreme market events are. Over the long term, we still believe equities will continue to provide higher long-term returns than bonds or cash.

The historic case for equities

Historically, the main reason for owning equities has been to achieve attractive long-term returns driven by growth in corporate profitability and in the dividends that are paid to investors over time. Despite periods of inevitable volatility, ten-year real returns have been negative on only three occasions in the past century – in 1916, 1974 and towards the end of 2008.

Investment in equities means investing in actual companies. In simple terms, a company is a collection of physical assets and intellectual property, the combination of which caters to demand and produces profits. Equities in sum allow shareholders to participate in the underlying profits growth of companies over time.

In the past, participating in this earnings growth has generated attractive long-term returns. US equities, for example, have produced average returns of 6.2% per annum in real terms over the last 159 years according to Credit Suisse. Given this average level of return, the stock market weakness seen over the last 18 months appears anomalous.

Indeed, if we look back at the US stock market's annual returns since 1825, 2008's sharp 37% fall was very much a stand-out event. Actually, there have been only three years in the last 183 years that the US market has fallen by more than 30%, in 1931, 1937 and now in 2008. After last year's drop, the market has fallen below trend, given its long-term 6.2% annual average return. This suggests a likelihood of higher returns in the future.

Inflation and deflation?

One of the common themes behind some of the largest moves in equity returns in the past has been inflation. In the period from 1900, equities have on average benefited more from low inflation than from high economic growth (see table overleaf). Below trend inflation has brought double-digit returns on average, comfortably outperforming bonds. Even in periods of falling prices (commonly described as deflation) equity returns have been positive on average. In the 12 individual years since 1900 when US inflation has fallen below zero, equity returns averaged 8.3% pa, compared to 6.1% pa for bonds and 2.4% for cash.

Turning to Europe, real equity returns have trended around 7% pa, according to statistics that go back to 1926. With markets currently at the low end of the trend it would be reasonable to assume that equities will revert to their long-term trend, higher than today's position. A mathematician with no knowledge of, or interest in, financial markets, would probably go further and throw the onus on the pessimist to justify why future returns eventually would not revert back towards the trend.

Returns in different growth and inflation periods

Growth * rel to trend	Inflation * rel to trend	No. of years	Equity returns	Bond returns	Cash returns
Below	Below	31	11.4%	7.7%	3.4%
Below	Above	21	1.5%	-4.0%	-1.6%
Above	Below	25	14.8%	3.8%	2.3%
Above	Above	23	2.2%	-1.5%	-2.0%

Sources: Citigroup, Credit Suisse, UBS Securities, Global Financial Data, Sarasin & Partners, MacData, JPMAM   * relative to a 10-year trend

What drives real returns?

One of the reasons for holding equities is the exposure to future rates of growth in profits and the consequent dividends that are paid out. In general, profits are cyclical and although current earnings have fallen below trend, long-term profits growth remains strong.

Over the long term, however, the main driver of equity returns has been the dividend yield. From 1871 to 2008, the dividend yield in the US has averaged 4.5% pa. This yield, plus real growth in dividends, has generated total real returns of 6.1% pa. However, this long-term average has been dragged down by the past 25 years, during which the average market yield has fallen to 2.5% pa. Excluding the period of the worldwide equity bull market, which began in 1982, the dividend yield of the US market has averaged 5.0% pa.

What do statistics tell us about timing?

Equities give a positive return in 72% of years (based on 183 years of US returns data). Moreover, positive years often come after negative years. If we consider the eight worst years in this period when markets fell by more than 20% then a positive return was achieved in the following year three-quarters of the time. Half of the time, a rise of more than 20% was experienced in the following year.

So there are years that equity markets give very poor returns but investors have a strong incentive to remain invested because, after experiencing the pain, the markets have a high probability of recovery. As cataclysmic as things must have seemed when they fell dramatically, in the periods following the markets usually recovered. Even though history can only offer a guide to, but not a guarantee of future returns, precedent can offer encouragement.

Toughing it out

In equities, it is "time in the markets" that counts, not "timing the markets". Equities bounce before recessions end, with markets generally anticipating a recovery in business conditions some months before it happens. The same applies to the corporate earnings cycle. In general, the market troughs before earnings touch bottom.

In February 2001, commenting on why he was not investing, Warren Buffett wrote in his annual letter to Berkshire Hathaway shareholders, "Really juicy returns can be anticipated only when capital markets are severely constrained and the whole business world is pessimistic". In October 2008, Buffett wrote "A simple rule dictates my buying: Be fearful when others are greedy, and be greedy when others are fearful. And most certainly, fear is now widespread, gripping even seasoned investors". He was buying American stocks even though he acknowledged that he could not predict short-term market movements.

However, there's another more compelling reason for investing in equities at present, and it's based on the fact that equities are a financial investment that competes for your cash with other financial assets. This is especially pertinent now, because the past six months have seen a huge flight into cash and fixed income.

Indeed in Europe, holdings in cash funds exceed holdings in equity funds for the third time in 16 years – the previous occasions being the start of the bull market in 1992/93, and the start of the bull market in 2003. That on its own doesn't mean anything, but when we look at the rate of return on cash and fixed income it's difficult to forecast anything other than meagre pickings, whereas at least in equities you are compensated for your capital risk with a decent yield: 6.3% in the UK; just less than 6% in Europe ex-UK; and 3.5% in the US (as at 23 January 2009).

All of these dividend yields exceed the yield on local bonds. While it is true that many sectors will be under pressure to reduce dividends and the possibility that the relatively strong historical dividends we've 'seen recently may fall significantly, a lot of that expectation may be embedded in the price. Equity markets could move sideways this year in a volatile range, and still outperform cash and bonds because of the income they pay out.

However, as with all stock market investments, please remember that past performance is not a guide to the future.

Conclusions

Equities have provided higher long-term returns than cash or bonds in the past – this should continue in the future. History and forward-looking analysis suggests that the long-term trend of returns could remain intact. It is still reasonable to expect real returns in the 6%-7% pa range going forward – even after such carnage in the markets in 2008.

Markets are rocky at present and it is easy to lose all faith in equities. 2008 was a terrible year – one of the three worst years in the past century. But it would be wrong to assume that we will automatically see another year of negative returns. History shows that markets have a strong habit of rebounding after very poor years and investors with a longer investment horizon stretching over several years might be mistaken to bail out now.

It is "time in the markets" that counts, not "timing the markets". There is always a risk that a decision to enter equity markets could prove wrong on a one to two year horizon. However, a long-term investor should also consider the risk of being out of the market, as valuation, sentiment and timing signals all suggest that above average returns can be achieved if a long-term view is taken.

The main driver of long-term returns has been the dividend yield. Going forward, it is expected that dividend yields will play a more significant role in driving real total returns than over the past 25 years. With long-term growth expectations more open to question than before, it is clear that the case for equities lies once again as an income producing asset, with potential for future growth.

The report found that investors found it difficult to distinguish between broker-dealers and investment advisers, or to understand the difference in standards of care. In their responses, investors were mostly happy with their financial service provider, valuing personal service attributes such as trustworthiness and attentiveness.

In the United Kingdom, the equivalent to a broker-dealer is an intermediary; in Japan it is a securities company.

More about brokers

In the United States and United Kingdom alike, the broker fits into one of three categories: execution only, advisory, or discretionary. Execution-only stockbrokers simply execute deals and will not give advice. They typically advertise and operate through the internet. In the United Kingdom they account for around half of all retail-investor trading activity.

Advisory stockbrokers are more expensive but provide a fuller service. They will advise investors on which stocks to buy or sell and when, as well as executing the trade. Some specialise in, for example, small growth or high-income blue chips. The service is about getting the right balance between having the clients involved in decisions and protecting them from making mistakes. Levels of expertise vary widely, and success may depend partly on the relationship between the broker and client. In the United States, clients can be savvier about shares than in Europe.

Discretionary brokers take full charge of an investor's portfolio, and execute the trades. They make buying and selling decisions on the investor's behalf for a fee. Again, approaches and levels of expertise vary.

US brokers must pass the General Securities Representative Examination, known as Series 7, and UK brokers must pass the Securities and Investment Institute Certificate in Securities. These professional examinations test only basic knowledge. The broker's job is simply to trade shares.

Indices

The prices of publicly traded stocks help to make up market indices. Individual indices, specific to countries or sometimes multinational, cover stocks of a certain size or specification.

In the United States, the main stock market indices are the Standard & Poor's (S&P) 500 and (less followed nowadays) the Dow Jones Industrial Average. Also significant is NASDAQ (National Association of Securities Dealers Automated Quotation), the high-tech stock market index. These US benchmark indices have a ripple effect across the world.

If, for example, the S&P 500 index plummeted yesterday due to profit warnings from some companies or adverse trade figures just published, the Nikkei 225 index in Japan and the Hang Seng in Hong Kong are likely to have taken their cue and have put in a dismal overnight performance.

The combined effects of US and Far East markets will take their toll on European markets the following morning. Indices such as the United Kingdom's FTSE 100, consisting of the 100 largest companies by market capitalisation, and France's CAC 40 will probably start the trading day down.

Markets across Europe will move broadly in line for much of the day, influenced heavily by expectations for the lunchtime reopening of Wall Street, and the actual performance soon after. Institutional investors buy and sell shares on a pan-European basis, looking at sectors rather than countries within the euro zone. If, for example, telecom stocks in London fall, it is likely that they will fall in Italy and Germany too. Institutional investors will then focus on the telecoms sector component of their equities portfolios.

Company financial data

If you know the names of companies on which you want data, you will find a very useful tool on Times Online (www.timesonline.co.uk). Visit its business pages, find 'markets' and 'quote search', and you can look up details of individual UK, European or US quoted companies. You can find a share price chart over recent years and the latest share price, as well as the day's high and low prices. In addition, you will find the following financial data about the individual company:

- Market capitalisation. This is the current share price multiplied by the number of shares in issue. The bigger the 'market cap', the bigger the company's presence on the market.
- Shares in issue.
- Price earnings ratio (PER). This is the share price divided by earnings per share. It is also known as the PE ratio. The higher this figure, the higher the market rates the shares. Compare the PE ratio with the sector average. A comparatively high PE ratio indicates strong growth, which could mean that the market overrates the shares and they will decline in value; but in the meantime, the shares could keep rising in response to market demand. If the shares have a low PE ratio, this shows that the market underrates the shares, which could be for a good reason or, less likely, could indicate a bargain.
- Net gearing. This is the company's level of borrowing. Gearing helps the company to expand but can be risky. As a rule of thumb, if the figure is over 50 per cent, such a high level should be for a good reason or it spells trouble.

London
Stock Exchange

The London Stock Exchange is a global business and the world's most international capital market. Operating at the gateway to the world's largest single market, the European Union, the Exchange is the venue of choice for companies looking to raise finance and is also a highly liquid trading facility for a range of instruments including shares, bonds and derivatives.

The role of the Exchange has evolved over time from a simple club conducting business from coffee houses, to a complex and diversified global business. An important part of the Exchange's role is helping companies to raise capital by providing a range of well-regulated markets. The efficient trading of shares and other instruments, as well as the dissemination of data based on the trading activity represent further key strands to the business.

Financial markets around the world felt the strain in 2008 in the so called 'credit crunch'. A recession makes market conditions difficult for all, and yet businesses still need to develop, to grow, and to innovate to make progress. The link between what industries achieve and what happens in the City is often overlooked. A pharmaceutical company's research and development in healthcare may be made possible by financial investment although it has not yet produced a tangible, saleable product, let alone a profit. The investors are investing in the future and in their faith that the company will succeed. Transactions in the City enable and empower companies to develop, compete and evolve in various industries which may seem far removed from activities in the Square Mile.

As they develop, companies may need further funding. London's capital markets can help by providing the arena for further investment from existing or new stakeholders at a low cost of capital. There is a choice of markets for companies looking for debt or equity investment as a publicly traded entity, offering world class standards of regulation and corporate governance as well as flexibility, recognising that one size does not fit all. The Exchange's four routes to becoming publicly quoted are:

Main Market – home to many of the world's largest, most established businesses. A listing here gives access to the most international pool of investment funds and liquidity;

AIM – the world's most successful market for growth companies with a regulatory structure specifically designed to suit the needs of smaller companies;

Professional Securities Market – provides a London listing with additional flexibility, for example depositary receipts or debt instruments requiring the ability to report in local accounting standards; and

Specialist Fund Market – a market for London's highly sophisticated and international institutional investor base, for professional investors to provide capital to specialist investment funds, for example hedge funds and those with complex structures.

The Exchange's trading platform, TradElect, is world-class, with reliability, efficiency, and low latency being key characteristics. This has enabled the Exchange to diversify into ventures with other exchanges seeking these qualities. The Johannesburg Stock Exchange has for some years now used the London Stock Exchange's platform to host their own trading services, and in late 2008 the Oslo Børs announced an agreement to use the Exchange's trading system from 2009/10. Borsa Italiana also uses TradElect.

Expertise in running and regulating markets is demonstrated in the Exchange's joint ventures. Tokyo AIM, announced in early 2009, is the result of the Exchange's collaboration with the Tokyo Stock Exchange to build a market using the principles that have made AIM so successful and that could be adapted for the Japanese market. In October 2007 the London Stock Exchange announced its merger with Borsa Italiana, and the resulting London Stock Exchange Group recently created AIM Italia, again using the AIM framework for a flexible capital market in Italy for smaller, growing companies.

As a result of the merger with Borsa Italiana, the London Stock Exchange Group is now the leading diversified exchange group in Europe. The Group offers Europe's leading market for the electronic trading of ETFs and securitised derivatives; MTS, Europe's leading fixed-income market; the most efficient post-trade services through CC&G and Monte Titoli; and equity derivatives through EDX London and IDEM.

Beyond Western Europe, the Exchange has built on its ability historically to attract companies and investors from high growth markets overseas. Business development activity for listings has been devoted specifically to developing markets including Asia, Central and Eastern Europe, Latin America and the Middle East.

For the Exchange itself, this is a time when the effects of the European Market in Financial Instruments Directive (MiFID) are being felt in the form of increased competition and a proliferation of Multi-lateral Trading Facilities (MTFs) moving into the space of traditional exchanges as well as increased regulation. The Exchange continues to develop and diversify its business to ensure it meets the needs of companies and other market participants in a difficult financial environment. The London Stock Exchange is very much open for business and a key player within the global marketplace.

■ Percentage change in 12-month earnings per share (EPS) versus a year ago. This is any change in the EPS, which is profit after tax divided by the number of shares in issue. The City looks for a steadily rising EPS year on year.

■ Dividend for the year. Ideally, the dividend should rise every year in the same way as the EPS. If a company cuts its dividend, this sends out a warning message. Sometimes a company will dig into its reserves to maintain a dividend.

■ Return on capital employed (ROCE). This is profit before interest and tax divided by year-end capital employed. The ROCE is a measure of management efficiency. The City likes to see this figure both high and rising.

■ Country news and further data, including company results, revenue, pre-tax profit, EPS, dividends and rights, details of activities, indices on which the company is listed and its key executives.

Financial ratios from the accounts, as discussed above, are useful as a starting point for understanding what a company does, how it operates, and the scale and profitability of its business. To find out more, visit the company's website in the first instance. Company investor relations (IR) staff expend a great deal of effort ensuring the corporate website is an effective communication tool. This is not least because they do not have much time to speak to retail investors individually, who in the United Kingdom represent only 15 per cent of the money invested in quoted companies, although this is more like 40 per cent in the United States.

Meanwhile, bear in mind that accounting ratios are based at least partly on old data. The share price moves on how the City sees the company's underlying prospects, something that is uncertain. Analysts focus on prospective figures and, through their forecasts, may have significant influence on the share price. If an analyst for a high-profile bank changes a stock recommendation from *hold* to *buy*, this will affect the share price almost immediately. For more on how analysts work, see Chapter 20.

In forecasting share price performance, analysts use various methods but, in particular, discounted cash flow. Let us take a look at this.

Discounted cash flow

A company cannot manipulate cash. It either has it or it does not and, if it has, the cash is measurable. That is why analysts like to look at a company's cash flow. But they have to make forecasts about future cash flow and this involves an element of guesswork. Discounted cash flow analysis, the name of the procedure involved, translates future cash flows into present value.

To work this out, find the company's net operating cash flow (NOCF). You do this by taking the company's underlying earnings before interest and tax. Deduct corporation tax paid and capital expenditure. Add depreciation and amortisation, which do not represent a movement of cash. Add or subtract the change in working capital, including movements in stock, in debtors and creditors, and in cash or cash equivalents.

This is the current year's NOCF. You should calculate it also for future years, reduced in value to present-day terms by a discount rate broadly representing inflation in reverse. Also, cash flow will continue infinitely beyond the period over which the future cash flows are spread. This is the terminal value.

Present and future cash flows, together with the terminal value, make up the net present value, the accuracy of which depends partly on that of the future NOCF forecasts and the number of years used. The larger the discount rate used, the smaller the net present value of future cash flows.

The discount rate used by analysts is normally the company's weighted average cost of capital. This represents the cost of capital to the company weighted by debt and equity. This is split into its two parts. The cost of debt is the yield to maturity on the company's bonds. The cost of equity is typically measured by the capital asset pricing model (CAPM).

The CAPM is widely used, but controversial. It assumes that investors should be rewarded for acquiring investments which carry a larger amount of 'market' risk that cannot be diversified away. This risk is measured by beta, which is a historical figure, and therefore unreliable.

Given the uncertainties, analysts may plot discounted cash flow models using different discount rates to present alternative valuations. Although some abuse the method to paint an over-optimistic picture of a favoured company, discounted cash flow analysis is the most realistic method of valuation available.

Charts

Technical analysts focus on charts that show price movements of shares and indices and, sometimes, trading volume. They look at past performance and attempt to pinpoint trends. They scrutinise moving averages of the share price and other indicators. They aim to assess when to buy, sell or just hold shares. For more about how they work, see Chapter 20.

Investment strategies

Some retail investors dabble in the stock market and just buy a favourite share here and there, hoping to sell at a profit fairly quickly. This approach can work but, more often than not, it fails. It is particularly common in the stock markets of some growing economies such as China, which have been subject to speculative bubbles.

For serious investors, the conventional advice is to build a diversified portfolio, investing in a number of companies, each in a different sector, and ideally across asset classes, countries and continents. This way, the risk is spread. If one share falls in value, the others may outperform, balancing out overall performance. Should shares fall, bonds could hold solid. If one country falls into crisis, others may stay strong.

Among asset classes, bonds are less risky than equities, and cash deposits are the safest asset class of all. Risky commodities will broaden the spread, as will property. Geographically, Western Europe is more stable than emerging markets such as China and India, but it has less growth potential. For investors who do not have enough money to build a diversified share portfolio, the usual recommendation is to buy mutual funds, which enable significant diversification even on small funds invested (see Chapter 19).

Some successful investors argue that too much diversification is 'diworsification' – lessening the chances of benefiting from big gains as well as of suffering from big losses. The more skilled the stock picker, the less diversification makes sense. When it comes to picking individual stocks, the price paid is crucial. Value investors look to buy cheaply and sell expensively, and the credit crisis of 2007–09 threw up some opportunities. Others look for growth stocks, perhaps with a high PE ratio.

By early December 2008, the FTSE 100 had slipped 38 per cent, the S&P 500 was down 40 per cent, and the MSCI World Index had dropped 46 per cent in the year, all of which left some equities looking cheap. Price–earnings ratios on shares were often low and yields were high, based on a sustained dividend as a proportion of a sharply reduced share price. Yields on government bonds were low, indicating how investors had rushed into these safe-haven investments, sending up prices and so lowering the return as a percentage of the bond's value.

Legendary investor Warren Buffett focuses mainly on value but also on growth, and he made positive comments about stocks at 2008 price levels and put his own money into the market. Anthony Bolton, who achieved guru status as manager at Fidelity International's Special Situations fund until he retired at the end of 2007, was optimistic that the market had reached a bottom. Mark Mobius, director at Templeton Global Emerging Markets Equity Group, said in a *Times* podcast in October 2008 that bear markets last at most fourteen months and mostly six to seven months, and that he did not think this one would be long. He said that Templeton Emerging Markets was 'fully invested'. Pundits were reminding investors that stock market investment in the long term outperformed bonds or cash investment significantly.

However, many investors were holding back. Hedge funds were keeping cash available to meet redemptions. Sovereign wealth funds had withdrawn cash from emerging economies and were reinvesting it in the developed world's stock markets.

If there is a bear market, as in early 2009, a revival does not have to be in line with a revival in a weak economy. In 1933 the stock market boomed, but the economy did not. Brokers reassure investors that stock market investing makes money in the long term. True so far, but it can take years.

Where do we go from here?

Jeremy Batstone-Carr (Director of Private Client Research)

Bond markets, it is said, are dominated by pessimists, equity markets by optimists. Judging by the divergence of these two sentiments over the past two years there seems little doubt as to who takes the honours in the enduring relationship between fear and greed that dominates financial markets. Frankly, there is a lot to be negative about. Despite the best efforts of global leaders at the recent London G-20 summit to draw a line under the global economic and financial market crisis, precious little optimism suffuses investors at the current time. Little wonder. Both the International Monetary Fund (IMF) and the Organisation for Economic Cooperation and Development (OECD) have downgraded their forecasts for global economic activity and both confirm that the global economy will have a very poor year in 2009 before staging a partial revival in 2010. Corporate earnings estimates have been slashed and further downgrades seem certain as company analysts wake up to the realisation that, unlike previous post-WW2 recessions, the structural impediment to growth associated with aggressive deleveraging will have a severely negative impact on profitability.

Weak economic activity and falling inflationary pressure have enabled global central banks to cut short-term interest rates to multi-year and all-time low levels. The failure of conventional monetary policy to stimulate activity has resulted in a switch of emphasis towards quantitative easing, particularly so in the UK and USA, in an effort to expand bank reserves and encourage lending activity in the latest attempt to kick-start a return to economic growth. This policy action, in conjunction with attempts to ring-fence still significant 'toxic' assets on bank balance sheets, has fuelled the belief amongst many investors that the seeds have now been sown for eventual recovery. Only time will tell. Whilst share prices have responded favourably to what is being dubbed the "second derivative" associated with "less bad" forward-looking economic data contained within the blizzard of day to day releases, the fact remains that until the banking industry works through its debt and the residential property market stabilises (particularly in the United States), such rallies are likely to prove short-lived.

All that said, it is the view of Charles Stanley that aggressive policy measures will begin to gain traction and that on a quarter by quarter sequential basis conditions will gradually improve. This is not to say that the world will return to the go-go growth achieved during the past decade. A partial revival is all that can be expected and considerable uncertainty exists regarding medium-term prospects. A revival in activity, coupled with aggressive money supply expansion associated with unconventional monetary policy may call forth a period of inflation pressure, possibly hyper inflation pressure. In such circumstances we suspect that monetary authorities will be quick to alter course and this may serve to crimp the recovery and ensure a prolonged period of economic downsizing the world over.

Inevitably the low level of visibility associated with such an uncertain outlook severely hampers those investors with an investment time horizon of more than the next twelve months.

Whilst we know that the returns on cash or cash piles currently held by investing institutions on the sidelines are generating little by way of positive returns, few are prepared to commit funds aggressively at the current time either to bonds, despite rising actuarial pressure to do so, or equities. Index-linked bonds are proving popular with those who believe that revival will bring a period of inflation and corporate bonds have experienced heavy demand as a half-way house between conventional sovereign bonds which appear to some, if not all, to be in bubble conditions. Working on the assumption that a partial revival will take place as 2009 progresses, we expect to see enthusiasm for high grade corporate bonds morphing into demand for high yield bonds and thence, eventually, to equities.

The revival in global equity markets has been driven by a bear squeeze in cyclical and financial stocks. This looks premature, valuations are in no man's land, particularly so in the light of a downbeat operating backdrop and the strong likelihood of further earnings downgrades in the pipeline. Defensive equities have been sold off but may recover their appeal should the recovery not come through as expected. Investors continue to rate highly reliable top-line growth, robust balance sheets, dependable cash generation and the commitment to progressive dividend policies and, given the uncertain outlook, companies demonstrating these characteristics are likely to remain popular irrespective of relative over-valuation against more cyclical counterparts.

The lesson from history teaches us that prolonged bear markets are characterised by three distinct phases. The first is when share prices are aggressively sold off in anticipation of falling profitability. The second phase occurs when the trough in the earnings cycle can be viewed with greater certainty. Historically, this is the phase during which risk appetite revives strongly and stock markets can perform very well. If previous earnings recessions are anything to go by, this phase begins around six months before the anticipated trough in profitability occurs. During this phase caution is thrown to the four winds and cyclicals tend strongly to outperform defensive counters. The uncertainty presently plaguing the global equity market is synonymous with choppy activity ahead of the point at which phase one segues into phase two. Phase three occurs at the point at which the earnings trough is reached. At that point, and not before, it becomes safer to start buying financials in anticipation of a broader recovery in profitability thereafter. Until that point, bank shares and to a somewhat lesser extent, insurance company shares are likely to remain vulnerable to the vicissitudes associated with day to day news flow and should remain the domain of speculators only.

So how does the average private individual start investing in the markets?
Robert Gofton-Salmond (Head of Financial Planning)

Before deciding whether to invest in the stockmarket, you should assess your personal financial situation, taking into account any existing savings, pension arrangements, short and long-term savings schemes, life assurance and protection policies, as well as levels of indebtedness (such as mortgages). We recommend that you should be prepared to invest funds for at least five years.

Having decided that investment in the markets is the route to go, the important next steps are: to decide what your financial objectives are; establish the risks of investing in the different markets, sectors and instruments; determine the level of risk you are comfortable with; and only then to establish a strategy for managing the investment process to achieve your objective, within the risk parameter chosen.

Your objective may be growing your capital, securing a regular income, a balance between the two, or perhaps to improve tax efficiency. The level of risk you are prepared to take, together with your investment objectives, should determine which asset classes you intend to invest in and the weight that you allocate to each of them. Whilst risk is generally considered as the likelihood of a potential loss of capital, there are other risks to take into consideration, such as the risk that inflation will erode the real value of your assets over time.

Choosing investments with a low capital risk does not solve all problems, unless you are content to accept a lower return and an increase in the inflation risk. For example, many people, adverse to the risk of losing capital, put a high proportion of their savings into deposit investments, such as building society accounts. In doing so, they run the risk of the buying power of their wealth being reduced by inflation and, if dependent on the income generated from these savings, there is a risk that their lifestyle will be affected by the erosion of the real value of their capital.

Taking into account the considerations involved it is perhaps no wonder that well-established investment firms, such as Charles Stanley, are often seen as an attractive alternative to working your way through the above alone.

In addition to years of experience in interpreting the complexities of global markets, Charles Stanley's professional Investment Managers have a wealth of constantly updated technical information at their fingertips and can call on up-to-the minute stock prices, as well as research from their own award-winning research teams. They can also utilise in-house specialists in the fields of pensions, financial planning, inheritance tax mitigation, collective investments (unit and investment trusts), Exchange Traded Funds/Commodities, bonds and fixed interest stock, to name but a few specialist areas.

Whether you feel you would prefer to put your investments in the hands of specialists on either a Discretionary basis (you give us discretion to manage your investments according to agreed parameters), an Advisory basis (we provide advice on the investments and you make the decisions), or an Execution-only basis (you decide on the investments and make the decisions but you can use our experienced dealers to execute those trades), Charles Stanley will be pleased to talk to you about how our personal investment services can help you achieve your financial objectives.

6

Money markets
and bonds

Introduction

The money markets have featured prominently in the credit crisis of 2007–09. They are for short-term lending while bonds, also the subject of safety concerns, are for long-term lending. In this chapter we will see how both work.

Overview

When two Bear Stearns hedge funds in July 2007 explained the hit to their portfolios from sub-prime mortgages, the money markets stopped functioning properly and the central banks had to intervene. The seizure of money markets caused the subsequent problems at Northern Rock.

The September 2008 collapse of Lehman Brothers led to further problems in the money markets, on which it had sold its commercial paper. Concerns arose about the safety of corporate bonds issued by the banks, which are also long-term lending.

The money markets are wholesale cash markets, where governments, banks and other financial institutions, investors and companies can lend and borrow money for up to a year. In normal times, there is a high volume of lending on the money markets, and at low risk. Banks may lend to each other overnight or at call, meaning they may call the loan back at any time or at short notice. In London, the rate for borrowing overnight for the euro is the EURONIA, the euro overnight index average, and for sterling it is SONIA, the sterling overnight index average. EONIA is the euro overnight index average for the weighted average of all overnight unsecured lending transactions undertaken in the euro area interbank market.

As part of the money markets, banks may also lend to each other for slightly longer periods, from a few weeks to a year, on the interbank market. In this way banks with extra cash lend to others short of cash. Banks base their own wholesale lending rate on the interbank lending rate, which is what it costs them to borrow, and which in London is set at LIBOR, which as we saw in Chapter 3 is the London interbank offered rate. On the flip side, a bank's deposit rate is LIBID, the London interbank bid rate. LIBOR could be in a variety of currencies, and is the average of rates at which banks will lend, each being potentially different. For example, a bank could lend at LIBOR + 30 basis points, which is 0.3 of a point above the LIBOR rate. Countries in the euro zone use EURIBOR in the same way.

In September and October 2008, following the collapse of Lehman Brothers and the various government efforts to shore up financial institutions and money markets, the cost of borrowing on the money markets soared. This in turn made some corporate and consumer loans, including variable-rate mortgages, expensive. Let us look at this in numerical terms.

Usually LIBOR is a fraction of a percentage point above official rates. At times in the credit crisis of 2007–09, however, it was 1 per cent higher than official rates in the euro area, more than this in the United Kingdom, and over 2 per cent above the US federal funds target rate. The difference between the three-month dollar LIBOR and the treasury bill rate indexed on the so-called TED spread (the difference between the interest rates on interbank loans and short-term US government debt) was by late September 2008 more than 3 percentage points, compared with 20 basis points (0.2 per cent) in early 2007.

In addition to the lending of money, securities are traded on the money markets. Governments may borrow short-term money. Securities are issued at a discount to face value, and the face value is later paid. The difference between the discounted issue price and the face value is the interest equivalent. In the United Kingdom, the Debt Management Office, as an executive agency of H M Treasury, sells one- and three-month treasury bills on the government's behalf every Friday in a tender offer to banks, and six-month bills about once a month. The euro bill is like the treasury bill, but is issued in euros, and the Bank of England uses three- and six-month euro bills to help it fund euro liabilities. In the United States, treasury bills are sold in weekly auction to the primary dealers who buy bonds and federal notes. Variations on the distribution theme operate in other countries.

The treasury bill is traded less than it was because governments of developed countries such as the United Kingdom and the United States can issue bonds to borrow for longer periods. This is cheaper with current pessimism about the economic situation, based on the inverted-yield curve that reflects a decline in bond yields as maturity extends into the future.

Local authority bills are discounted short-term loans, used by local government bodies as a non-tradable investment with a maturity of up to six months. These and public sector bills have a much stronger market in the United States and continental Europe than in the United Kingdom.

A bank or building society may borrow money for a fixed period through a certificate of deposit (CD), a tradable instrument with a specified interest rate. The CD issue is typically for at least £50,000 with a five-year maturity. If the lender needs the cash back earlier, the certificate can be traded, in which case market conditions will influence its value and investors may receive more or less than the amount originally invested. CDs are actively traded in the United States and most foreign countries.

As an alternative to taking a bank loan, companies may borrow short-term money on the money markets by issuing commercial paper at a discount to face value. This is an unsecured short-term loan, and the borrower undertakes to repay the face value. In the United Kingdom, issuers must be publicly quoted, with a minimum £25 million balance-sheet value, and the minimum denomination for commercial paper is £100,000. These securities can also be issued by non-domestic companies.

An issuer of commercial paper will set up a programme. The bank, as dealer, will find investors among companies and financial institutions. The market is longest established in the United States, but has since spread globally, including to some emerging economies.

The credit crisis of 2007–09 has hit the market for commercial paper, decreasing lending volume. Short-term lending has risen and long-term lending has declined. Companies with weak financial status have had to pay higher rates.

A bill of exchange is a way in which companies can sell on their short-term debt. They will sell the bill, signed by the debtor company, to a third party that, on its own behalf, will collect the debt.

A central bank will help banks with any liquidity issues; this has become especially important since the credit crisis of 2007–09.

The commercial banks must keep reserves at central banks to maintain liquidity for paying deposits on demand. From May 2006, the Bank of England started paying interest on reserves held by banks, provided they maintain these reserves at an agreed level. This move, which was intended to stabilise market interest rates, gave the banks an incentive to put money in the reserves rather than square their book as much as possible daily on the open market.

In late September 2008, banks were depositing large amounts with some central banks, including the ECB. This was less risky than lending to other banks.

The central bank lends money to banks in the money markets, or borrows from them, through open market operations. The central bank's role is not to implement interest-rate policy but to satisfy the system's targeted level of reserves. In normal times, the central bank's lending is for a short period and against highly rated collateral, which means that the banks have to find a different way of funding weaker assets. The central bank may buy or sell such securities as the treasury bill. It may lend the banks money through the sale-and-repurchase agreement known as a repo. In implementing a repo, a central bank will buy securities, usually government bonds, from the banks for an agreed short period, perhaps 7, 14 or 28 days, after which it will sell them back at an agreed price that adds interest to the amount they had paid.

In its open market operations, the central bank determines as well as implements the repo rate. If it wants to reduce bank liquidity, it may issue a repo for a smaller amount than the previous one. This would reduce credit available to banks and send interest rates up.

In borrowing through a repo, the banks use low-yielding securities, mainly the government bonds they need to hold for reserves, as high-value collateral for the loans. These repos are part of the government open market operations. They are widely used across Europe, including between commercial banks. The collateral is typically 2 to 3 per cent more than the loan. For £100 loaned, the collateral may be £103, and the £3 difference is known as the haircut. There has not yet been a default on repos in the United Kingdom.

Government bonds used as collateral in the repo market have different risk profiles. Italian bonds have a lower credit rating than German bonds, implying a higher default risk, but the ECB has accepted both countries' bonds equally as collateral.

Interest-rate derivatives

Derivatives are financial contracts or instruments with values established from the value of something else (see Chapters 8 and 14). Interest-rate derivatives enable companies that have made large borrowings to hedge their positions and so protect themselves against adverse interest-rate movements. They are by far the largest component of the over-the-counter (OTC) derivatives market, which consists of those not traded on an exchange.

A common form of derivative is a swap, which is an exchange of payment streams, and the most common type is interest-rate swaps, where one party pays a fixed interest rate in return for receiving a floating rate. The overnight index swap, where fixed interest rates are swapped for floating rates, set according to SONIA or EURONIA is the most prominent trade after the repo in the money markets.

A forward is where one party is required to buy and another to sell a financial instrument at a specified future date. The forward rate agreement (FRA), which came to the market in the 1980s, is a forward contract between counterparties to pay or receive the difference between a floating reference rate and the fixed FRA rate agreed in advance. This is for a single forward period only, while the swap is an agreement for many forward periods. A number of FRAs are the equivalent to a swap.

Banks with a low credit rating find FRAs expensive and instead look to cover interest-rate exposures through futures, which are exchange traded, with the same institutional pricing available to all the banks (see Chapter 15).

The interest rate forward is when two counterparties agree to borrow or lend a fixed cash sum at an agreed rate for a specified period starting on a future date. In the past, it was used less than the FRA. It was based on real money, which means that it had to be recorded on the balance sheet.

In the past, swaps and FRAs, when used for hedging, were off the balance sheet, allowing a deferred profit or loss. Now, international financial reporting standards require that all derivatives are accounted for at fair value on the balance sheet and marked to market through the profit and loss account.

Domestic bonds

Overview

The bond is a medium- to long-term debt instrument. The issuer pays interest to the lender throughout the bond's term, which could be anything from 1 year to 30 years or more, and repays the principal sum borrowed on redemption. Undated bonds are not redeemed, however. In some markets, the short-term bond can be called a 'note'. The bond is popular among cautious investors because it offers a safe haven against equity risk, but it is also for traders who want to exploit price differentials.

Through bonds, investors receive a higher proportion of their return from income than through equities. Bond prices are less volatile than stock prices, particularly as the redemption date approaches. There is a price to pay. Over decades, bonds have underperformed equities, but have outperformed deposits in building societies.

How bonds work

The issuer of a bond may be a government or a company. The issue may be timed so that capital repayment will coincide with anticipated income from specified projects. Bonds are classified by the time remaining until maturity. If they are one to seven years, they are classed as short term. If the remaining time is 7 to 12 years, they are medium term. If it is more than 12 years, they are long term.

A bond will be issued and redeemed at nominal value, known as 'par', which for UK bonds is £100. At any time in the bond's lifetime, the market price may deviate from nominal value. When two redemption dates are shown, the bond must be redeemed after the first but before the second.

Bonds in the United Kingdom, as in Italy and the United States, pay interest twice a year. In some countries, including France and Germany, the payment is only once a year. In the period between interest payments, interest accrues. The pricing on bonds is normally *clean*, which excludes accrued interest.

A buyer of bonds pays not just for the financial instrument but also for any income accrued since the last interest payment. This is *cum* (with) *dividend*. If they buy it *ex-dividend*, it is the seller who has retained the right to the pending interest payment.

The coupon is the annual rate of interest on the bond, and is stated as a percentage of the nominal value. If, for example, a bond offers a 3 per cent coupon, it will pay £3 a year in interest for every £100 of nominal value. For UK bonds, the payment will be in two instalments. The coupon is decided by the level of interest rates in the market at the time of the bond issue.

The dividend yield that you receive from buying a bond on the secondary market can vary from the coupon because it is the return expressed as a percentage of the selling price of the bond, and the bond can sell at a different price from its nominal value.

The yield can also be expressed in different ways. The current yield is the annual interest of a bond divided by the current bond price. It is also known as the running yield, flat yield, simple yield or annual yield. The higher the bond price rises, the lower the current yield will be, and, conversely, the lower the price falls, the higher the yield.

The gross redemption yield, also known as yield to maturity, is widely used to compare the returns on bonds. It is the current yield plus any notional capital gain or loss at redemption.

The yield is a criterion for selecting bonds. So also is the duration, which shows how risky a bond is by measuring its price sensitivity to interest-rate changes. Investors also consider the spread between the yields for a given bond and the benchmark government bond, and any indication that the spread might narrow or expand.

The bond is priced precisely. In the case of a US corporate bond, the price is calculated to 1/8 of a dollar, and, for a US treasury bond, to 1/32. In continental Europe, decimals are used. The smallest price movement is known as the 'tick'. If a UK bond price moves by £1 per £100 nominal, it is one point. The press takes note of smaller movements, expressed as fractions of a point.

Pension funds are the largest traditional holders of bonds, because these instruments help to match their liabilities more precisely than equities or other types of investment. The factors affecting demand for bonds, whether government or corporate, are economic growth, inflation and interest-rate expectations.

For example, if interest rates fall, bond prices will rise. The underlying logic is that investors rush to buy bonds when their yields look attractive compared with the declining rates on bank deposit accounts. The bonds will then rise to a level that reflects the increased demand, and the yields will reduce accordingly until they no longer look attractive. A converse process also operates. If interest rates rise, bond prices will decline.

Bonds may be registered, as in the United Kingdom. Others have bearer status, which means that the physically held certificate is the proof of ownership. In the secondary market, bonds are sometimes traded on a stock exchange.

In most countries, the biggest investors in bonds are institutional investors, especially pension and insurance funds. Retail investors are much smaller investors in the United Kingdom, but significant in some other countries such as Italy.

Types of bond

Government bonds

Bonds issued by governments of developed countries are considered risk free, acknowledging that tax revenue could be used to honour commitments. Following the credit crisis of 2007–09, investors have sought refuge in government bonds as a safe haven for their money.

In the United Kingdom, government bonds are known as 'gilt-edged securities' or 'gilts', and they are issued by the Debt Management Office, an executive agency of H M Treasury, to raise cash so that the government can fund its annual spending requirements. In the United States, they are called treasury bonds.

Government bonds are much more liquid than corporate bonds (see below) and are more actively traded. Many bonds trade a lot just after they have been issued, typically in much larger sizes than shares, but less frequently. They subsequently trade very little. In the United Kingdom, institutional investors trade bonds with bond dealers, who trade with each other, often anonymously through inter-dealer brokers.

Corporate bonds

The corporate bond has slightly more risk of default than the government bond and so pays slightly higher interest. Corporate bonds are economically viable only for large company issues. More than half of all issuers are financial companies such as banks and insurers. Corporate fixed-interest bonds can be secured on specific assets, which is reassuring to investors in case of insolvency, or can be unsecured, with higher yields to compensate for the greater risks.

By late 2008, as a result of the credit crisis, corporate bonds had fallen substantially in value, which meant that their yields had risen accordingly. Corporate bonds of some banks such as Santander and Royal Bank of Scotland were looking cheap. Investors had lost money on corporate bonds including, in the case of private investors, through bond funds.

Generally, investors in corporate bonds face price risk, linked to interest rates, as well as credit risk, which is the likelihood that the bond issue will fail to pay interest or repay the principal. The credit rating agencies try to measure the credit risk, which depends on the underlying company's financial status. The higher the credit rating the bond issuer has, the less interest the issuer will have to pay. Highly rated bonds are unlikely to default, although the agencies do not always agree on their ratings.

'Junk bonds', also known as high-yield bonds, are those classified by the rating agencies as sub-investment grade, and, post-credit crunch, have fallen the furthest. Corporate bonds may fall to junk status due to the deterioration in the underlying company's financial performance, as happened with General Motors and Ford in May 2005. Junk bonds pay a high yield to compensate lenders for the credit risk of the issuer. In June 2008, the difference in interest rates on high-yield junk bonds from those on US treasury bonds with the same maturities was about 2.7 percentage points but, by early September, this had risen to 4.7 per cent.

Zero-coupon bonds do not pay interest in their life. Investors buy them at a deep discount from par value, which they receive in full when the bond reaches maturity. Equity convertibles are bonds with an embedded stock option. The holder may convert the bond into a given number of shares in the underlying company.

Covered bonds are issued by banks and collateralised by a cover pool of assets consisting of mortgage loans and/or public-sector debt. In case of default, bondholders have an initial claim against the issuer as well as a preferential claim on the cover pool of assets. The claim on the issuer is a main advantage that the covered bond has over the asset-backed security. No default on covered bonds has been recorded since they were first issued in the late 18th century, and the bonds offer a yield that is sometimes greater than on government bonds.

The Capital Requirements Directive requires a legal framework for covered bonds to be in place in the issuer's jurisdiction before a lower risk rating on covered bonds can be obtained, which would mean they would not attract high regulatory capital charges. The United Kingdom, like the United States, Italy and the Netherlands, does not yet have a national legal framework in place. Instead it has a *structured covered bonds* regime in which it uses contractual agreements to replicate issuance under a legal framework.

International debt securities

London has a large market in trading international debt securities, which include Eurobonds and foreign bonds. The Eurobond is a tradable bond with a maturity of at least two years, denominated in a currency neither of the issuer nor of the country where it was issued. It is listed on an exchange, which distinguishes it from a loan.

Large companies as well as banks, governments and financial agencies issue international bonds to borrow cheaply in a foreign market. Eurobond issuers need good credit ratings, because this type of bond is unsecured. The Eurobond is sold globally to high-net-worth individuals as well as institutions. Investment banking methods (see Chapter 7) are used to sell Eurobonds, rather than the commercial bank methods used to sell syndicated loans. A lead bank will run a syndicate of banks to underwrite the Eurobond issue. A group of selling banks that need not be underwriters will sell the bonds to investors.

Taking the advice of investment banks, Eurobond issuers will exchange the resulting money flows for those that they really want through the swaps market. Eurobonds pay interest gross, which gives time for the gross interest to be invested before tax is paid. They tend to be held in book-entry form by the international central securities depositories, Euroclear Bank and Clearstream Banking Luxembourg.

The Eurobond market can be subject to manipulation. In June 2005, Citigroup, the investment banking group, was fined £13.96 million by the FSA for a multi-billion euro Eurobond trade. The trading strategy, known as 'Dr Evil', had involved selling as many bonds in 18 seconds as would usually be traded in a day. A trading error forced Citigroup to buy back some of the bonds. The FSA found Citigroup had failed to conduct its business with due skill, care and diligence and failed to control its business effectively, but had not tried to distort the bond market. The deal is understood to have had adverse impacts on some of Citigroup's prospective mandates for issuing Eurobonds at the time.

You didn't get her

ABIT ABI Trust Ltd.

Tumultuous economic times may call for renewed scrutiny of your trusted advisor. We have been trusted advisors to high net worth clients, and providers of trust and corporate management services to professional intermediaries for the past nineteen (19) years. We are driven by four factors: efficiency, professionalism, customer satisfaction and integrity. We can withstand the scrutiny.

Our mission is to provide unparalleled wealth and corporate management services to a preferred clientele. Our goal is to become a major global provider of wealth and corporate management services with a reputation for efficiency and professionalism. Furthermore, one of our core values is to hold ourselves accountable to the highest ethical and regulatory standards.

We would like you to consider making ABI Trust Ltd your trusted advisor. Here are six (6) reasons to justify this:

1. **Integrity**
   We believe in maintaining the reputation of our institution and of our staff. We employ highly principled practices and persons, and are transparent in our dealings with clients and our regulators.
2. **Reliability**
   We do what we say we will do. Our word is our bond; we are serious about delivering on our promises.
3. **Industry Knowledge**
   Our staff members are highly qualified professionals that are able to respond to client queries accurately.
4. **Customer Service**
   We seek to be efficient and professional in all that we do. We uphold our core value of guaranteeing customer satisfaction through superior products and excellent service.
5. **Global Focus**
   Our company has a global focus; the nature of our business is global. We provide services to clients worldwide, and have representation in Latin America and the Middle East.
6. **Products and Services**
   We provide the full gamut of professional trust products and services across an array of jurisdictions.

We provide the following services:

Corporate Services
- Formation and management of various company types
- Company directors
- Shelf companies
- Safe custody
- Ship registration

Fiduciary Services
- Trustee and co-trustee
- Protectors
- Registration of trusts and foundations
- Family office services

We are a licensed trust company and a member of the ABI Financial Group, one of the largest indigenous financial conglomerates in the Eastern Caribbean. The ABI Financial Group provides services in banking, insurance, investment, brokerage, telecommunications, e-processing, property development and resort management. Visit our website today at http://www.abifinancial.com/ABIT/index.html or email us at abit@abifinancial.com.

7

Investment banking

Introduction

In this chapter we will see how investment banking works, and how it has changed. We will focus on mergers and acquisitions, and share issues, including IPOs and rights issues.

The business

Investment banking covers a range of activities, including raising money for clients in capital markets, mergers and acquisitions (M&A), securities trading and sales, treasury dealing and investment management. Banks have tended to specialise within these areas, branching also into proprietary trading, investing in private equity and becoming prime brokers for hedge funds.

This is a high-risk, high-reward business. Global investment banking revenues reached US$84.3 billion (£56.5 billion) in 2007, up by 21 per cent on the previous year, which was a rise for the fifth year running, according to 'Banking 2008', a report by International Financial Services London (IFSL). Europe, with the Middle East and Africa, accounted for 32 per cent of the whole and the United States accounted for 53 per cent.

The credit crisis since 2007 has forced a reshaping of investment banking. In March 2008, J P Morgan Chase agreed to buy Bear Stearns, one of the last few investment banks, in a rescue backed by the US Federal Reserve. The Fed provided a US$30 billion (£20.1 billion) guarantee, a move that was seen as preventing a systemic collapse. The Fed and the treasury were intervening only to protect Bear Stearns's counterparties, with which it had made many trades.

It was similarly to avoid a systemic problem that the US government on 7 September 2008 announced a cash injection package of up to US$110 billion (£73.7 billion) for Fannie Mae, the Federal National Mortgage Association, and Freddie Mac, the Federal Home Loan Mortgage Corporation. Between them Fannie Mae and Freddie Mac back three-quarters of all new US mortgages and own or guarantee US$4.8 trillion (£3.2 trillion) of US mortgages. They had combined losses of more than US$14 billion (£9.4 billion) over the year to September 2008 and combined debt of US$1.4 trillion (£0.9 trillion).

Lehman Brothers, an investment bank, was a different case. In mid September 2008, the investment bank was openly in crisis after it had incurred losses of billions of dollars on the US mortgage market through its entanglement in credit default swaps and collateralised debt obligations.

Until late in the night of Sunday, 14 September 2008, Lehman was locked in talks with potential buyers. Barclays pulled out of the talks after it could not win required government guarantees against future losses on Lehman's trading positions. On 14 September 2008, Lehman filed for bankruptcy protection after a weekend of negotiations failed to find a way of saving the company. At about the same time, Bank of America took over Merrill Lynch for US$50 billion (£33.5 billion), saving it from a similar fate.

The US authorities had allowed Lehman Brothers to collapse on the basis that this would not cause systemic risk. The decision, although logical, damaged market confidence and credit flows were frozen.

In later testimony in early October 2008 at a US hearing, Dick Fuld, head of the bankrupt Lehman, said he had done what he could to save his firm from collapse, but he was overwhelmed by a financial tsunami. He said he had been in close touch with regulators in the months leading up to the bankruptcy and, in summer 2008, had discussed with the Fed the possibility that Lehman could become a bank holding company, which would enable it to offer commercial banking facilities.

On 16 September 2008, shortly after the Lehman collapse, the US government seized control of American International Group (AIG), an insurance group. The group had been pushed to the brink of bankruptcy after its financial products unit had expanded into the market for credit default swaps, a product that protects investors in debt from the risk of a default, and this posed a systemic risk. The value of those credit default swaps sold by AIG collapsed because US$57.8 billion (£38.7 billion) worth was linked to the ravaged subprime mortgage market in the United States. AIG found it could not pay increased collateral demands on the credit default swaps it had written. The Fed agreed to lend up to US$85 billion (£56.9 billion) to AIG for two years in exchange for a 79.9 per cent equity stake.

A few days later, Goldman Sachs and Morgan Stanley converted to bank holding companies, as Lehman had hoped to do. In this way, they joined universal banks such as Citigroup, Deutsche Bank and Barclays, which offer investment banking services but only as part of their activities. In theory this was, as some journalists pronounced, the death of the bulge-bracket independent investment bank, but neither Goldman Sachs nor Morgan Stanley was expected in the short term to curtail any existing activities. In early December 2008, Professor Alan Taylor at the department of economics, University of California Davis Institute of Governmental Affairs, said on local TV that Goldman Sachs and Morgan Stanley had gone through the process of conversion to get under the federal authorities' umbrella of protection.

As bank holding companies, they have greater access to the lending facilities of the Federal Reserve than the temporary facility it gave to investment banks in 2008, and could borrow against the wider range of collateral allowed to commercial banks. However, the two firms have submitted to tougher regulations and supervision from several government agencies rather than, as before, only the SEC. They need more disclosure, and also more capital relative to borrowings.

By having complied with Basel II capital requirements, any former investment banks may have enough capital already to meet new US Federal Reserve requirements. However, lower leverage limits will reduce not just risk but also return on equity, and so put off investors. The firms may raise margins and fees to compensate, which could lead to fewer and more bespoke products.

The universal banks, among which Goldman Sachs and Morgan Stanley are now included, are able to diversify their businesses better than the old investment banks. They take customer deposits on the retail banking side and so are less dependent on money markets, which seized up since the onset of the credit crunch.

Both Goldman Sachs and Morgan Stanley have since made plans to expand their own modest retail deposit-taking businesses and would be allowed to buy commercial banks.

Meanwhile, some boutiques continue to offer investment banking services, although they do not commit their balance sheets in the way that the big banks had traditionally done.

Mergers and acquisitions

Mergers and acquisitions (M&A) is the area where investment banking has traditionally been compared and judged. Banks will advise a company planning a takeover or that is a likely bid target, and may help it to raise capital for the purpose.

The prospective buyer of quoted companies can be another company, from Europe, the United States or elsewhere. Alternatively, it can be a private equity firm, which is able to acquire a listed company and take it private. According to analysts, private equity has more resources to make acquisitions than quoted companies, and is not similarly encumbered with the need to make merger synergies.

Balance.

Global Bank of Commerce provides the perfect *balance* of world class banking services, security and convenience.

We have 25 years of experience managing your wealth across the globe, generation by generation.

Keeping in harmony with your lifestyle is important to us, today and tomorrow.

Global Bank of Commerce, Ltd.

Global Commerce Centre
Old Parham Road
P.O. Box W1803
St. John's, Antigua, West Indies

Tel: (268) 480-2240
Fax: (268) 462-1831
email: customer.service@gbc.ag
website: www.globalbank.ag

Private Banking

Wealth Management

Online Banking

Electronic Commerce Solutions

Global Remittance Services

Global Banking Solutions

GLOBAL BANK OF COMMERCE, LTD.

Cross Border Banking & Investments

As the world progresses towards becoming a global village, there are growing reasons for corporate and personal interests to seek banking services and investment opportunities across borders. Whilst the flow of funds have traditionally been towards the long established financial centres in North America and Europe, the recent financial crisis in those markets have highlighted the safety benefits of a global investment portfolio and management services.

Caribbean banks, for example, have clearly operated with more prudent lending practices, and their regulatory environment would not permit investments in the type of sub-prime and adjustable rate mortgages that have now been identified as part of the toxic debt held by some of the world's largest banks. Calls are being made for changes to the traditional economic paradigm and this heralds the growing opportunity for cross-border banking and investments which comply with global accounting and transparency rules together with international standards for the prevention of money laundering and financing of terrorism. Both the United Kingdom and the United States attract non-residents of these countries to bank with them and invest in instruments that do not attract tax. Similarly, Caribbean Financial Centres attract non-residents seeking international financial services. The concept of some funds being held "offshore" as opposed to "onshore" is less relevant as invariably the majority of non-resident deposits held in Caribbean banks are held in correspondent banks and investment firms operating in the major money centres of Europe and the United States. What is relevant is the need for strict regulation of all financial services operating in compliance with international banking standards. This includes the requirement of Tax Information Exchange Treaties and the use of Mutual Legal Assistance Treaties to provide a readily available legal process for regulatory authorities to exchange information.

Global interoperability of systems and secure online banking allows investors to make choices based on safety, convenience and service regardless of geography. The use of these services must be conducted in accordance with the requirement of some jurisdictions to have their citizens report all worldwide income, and investors are always encouraged to obtain sound professional advice to ensure that inheritance planning or the management of assets meets all lawful, moral and public policies. There are a growing number of wealth management and business reasons to seek cross border financial services. Caribbean jurisdictions can provide a legal environment and regulatory structure for international asset protection and wealth preservation. Caribbean banks are able to blend investment opportunities available in the region with strategic relations held with investment advisory services from the global financial markets.

Cross border services are also demanded by companies that require international ecommerce services and need to establish banking services with Caribbean banks experienced in conducting global services. The attributes sought after in cross border relationships included a democratic and politically stable jurisdiction, online merchant services, card processing facilities and a strong information technology infra-structure. International card payment systems also facilitate a borderless service for payrolls, employment benefits and remittances. Some Caribbean banks have invested in these technology-driven international services and offer the best of both worlds for cross border banking relationships.

By: Brian Stuart-Young CAMS, Chairman & CEO, Global Bank of Commerce, Ltd.
www.globalbankofcommerce.com

To finance an acquisition, a company may use the capital markets. The acquirer pays for a target company's shares with cash, its own shares, or a combination of the two. A company will make its own choice of a bank as M&A adviser, choosing the one with the best ideas. For smaller transactions particularly, there is a growing trend for companies to use in-house M&A advisers, perhaps ex-bankers, and avoid using the banks.

A bank's fee for M&A advice is up to 2 per cent of the deal's value, diminishing as the deal becomes bigger. The bank is paid only if the bid proceeds, which is a risk because the bidder may withdraw, perhaps after it has concluded a due diligence inspection or a rival bidder has muscled in. If a bank is advising a company making an acquisition, it may also raise capital for it, which is more lucrative.

Over the past 10 years, M&A has generated more than 40 per cent of investment banking revenue, according to the IFSL 'Banking 2008' report. It said that 2007 corporate M&A activity increased by a quarter to US$4.5 trillion (£3 trillion), the highest level since 2000, partly driven by emerging European markets such as Russia and Turkey.

In 2008, M&A activity dropped back sharply, impacted by the credit crisis. In the first two-thirds of the year it was down nearly a third globally according to data from Thomson Reuters. By late 2008, companies that had paid highly for acquisitions before the credit crunch expected in many cases to have to make one-off charges on their balance sheets because the acquired companies were no longer producing anticipated cash flow. Write-offs of this kind would affect accounting profits and net assets.

Initial public offering

Equity underwriting has generated between 30 and 38 per cent of investment banking fee revenue in the 10 years to 2007, according to 'Banking 2008'. If a company is going to issue its shares on the main market, it may launch an initial public offering (IPO). Ernst & Young has defined an IPO as 'a company's first offering of equity to the public'. London Stock Exchange (LSE) statistics refer to a company's first offer of shares on its market as an IPO, even when the company has issued shares on another market.

An IPO is used particularly by large issuers. In a bull market, IPOs are frequent and are often at an inflated offer price. When markets are bearish, the IPO market often dries up and, in any deals that get through, the company's shares may trade at below the offer price early on in the secondary market.

The IPO process starts with the *beauty parade*, in which banks compete for the role of book runner to the deal. In choosing between candidate banks, the issuer looks for a track record in floating similar companies. There are other criteria, including how well the bank understands the business, and its geographical distribution power. A bank cannot become book runner if there is an unresolved conflict of interest, which could arise if it is launching the IPO of a rival company. If two banks are selected as joint book runners, any historical conflicts will come under scrutiny in the selection process. In practice, many IPOs and secondary placings are handled by banks that have an existing corporate relationship with the issuing company.

The book runner takes lead responsibility for placing the newly floated shares with investors and, in a sizeable deal, may organise backup from a syndicate of other banks. The bank at the top of the syndicate may have the status of global coordinator and other banks within it may have key roles such as lead manager or manager.

In a pre-marketing phase, the book runner meets with potential investors and presents the investment case for the company it is bringing to market. It ascertains the indicative price of the company's shares upon issuance and sets parameters within which it believes the new issue should later be priced. The banks often make this indicative price range public.

The book build is based on investor interest that the banks have drummed up during the pre-marketing phase. A traditional book build lasts two to three weeks, but can be longer in difficult market conditions. Once the IPO date has been declared, the entire process becomes highly susceptible to market news and conditions.

The banks build an order book through a road show which, in the case of large issues, travels across continental Europe and the United States as well as the United Kingdom. Banks in the syndicate organise group presentations and, outside the visiting schedule, may use video conferencing. The company's chief executive, finance director and head of investor communications address potential investors alongside the book runner's investment banking executives and analysts. One-to-one presentations will be organised by the banks with *tier-one* clients, which are the biggest and most important.

From the start, clients are under pressure to subscribe to the IPO. Many hang back, watching market conditions and the progress of the deal, and will confirm orders only a couple of days before the book closes.

When a company is brought to the market, it is typically underwritten. An investment bank undertakes the role of underwriter by guaranteeing a price for a fixed number of securities to the issuer. The riskier the deal, the larger the underwriter's fee. 'The cost of capital: an international comparison', a study published in June 2006 by economics consultancy Oxera and jointly commissioned by the LSE and the City of London, found that underwriting fees on US transactions average between 6.5 and 7 per cent of the amount raised, compared with between 3 and 4 per cent on European exchanges.

The issuer and the book runner will have set the issue price at the maximum level acceptable to institutional investors. If the deal is oversubscribed, the price may have been too low, but some oversubscription is likely in a successful IPO because, to ensure adequate share allocation, investors tend to request more shares than they want. This in itself helps to create demand, including in early secondary market trading.

When pressed, major investment banks have admitted that the criterion for pricing the deal is not value but demand, which can partly be created. It is influenced not just by market conditions, but also by perceptions of interest that the issuer, the book runner and their public relations initiatives have been able to whip up.

With retail investors involved, a book runner may price a new issue higher. This is partly due to the extra take-up and the publicity it generates, but also because the price will usually then be more sustainable in early secondary market trading, helping to safeguard the reputation of the book runner. Retail investors often hold new issues long after they ought to have sold.

In good market conditions, a deal will typically reach a small premium, perhaps 10–15 per cent, over the issue price in early secondary market trading. This in itself creates demand for the shares. If the free float is small, meaning that the shares are tightly held by company directors and few are available to the public, demand may quickly exceed supply; then the share price may soar.

Institutional investors subscribing to the IPO often snatch a profit by selling the shares early in the profitable first days or weeks of secondary market trading. Such *flipping* is commonplace. The book runner may welcome this from favoured institutional investors because it needs liquidity to establish value in the shares and to meet buyer demand. After a few weeks the shares will lose their initial momentum and, at least for a period, may slip below the offer price.

Other share issues

As the credit crisis continued into early 2009, firms were launching rights issues and other forms of share issues to pay down debt. This was partly because alternative sources of financing had become scarce. Let us take a look at the main capital market solutions.

Rights issues

This method of capital raising, where shareholders have pre-emptive rights, is widely used in the United Kingdom and Europe. The company will issue new shares to existing shareholders pro rata to their existing holdings. For example, in a one-for-five rights issue, shareholders will have the right to buy one further new share for every five they hold. Through this process, shareholders may acquire new shares without paying their stockbroker a commission. They do not have to buy, however, and, if they are to do so, must be convinced that the company will use the cash properly.

The issuing company will usually appoint an underwriter, usually a major bank, to the deal, which guarantees full subscription. If the issue fails, the underwriter will take up the rights. Some rights issues are not fully underwritten, which can be a high-risk strategy for both the issuer and the underwriter.

On rights issues (and open offers: see below) there is a 14–21-day period in which the prospectus is posted to shareholders and they can reply. Some companies work on a timetable of a rights issue early, then freeze work until there is a need to proceed, and this gives them a head start.

Once the rights issue is under way, the company's share price can fluctuate, which may happen more in uncertain markets or if the issue is for a purpose that may not benefit shareholders, or if it is not underwritten.

The new shares in a rights issue will be priced lower than the market value of the existing shares. In difficult markets, the discount might be as high as 40–50 per cent, which is known as a deeply discounted rights issue. This encourages existing shareholders to buy, failing which their holding would be diluted. In early 2009, underwriting fees had risen from 2 per cent of the issue to 3 or 4 per cent, reflecting the bigger risk of deal failure in the adverse market conditions of the time. Underwriters were asking companies to put a bigger discount on the issue. In January 2009, office space provider Workspace confirmed a rights issue at a hefty 69 per cent discount.

Following a rights issue, the overall share price will find a balance based pro rata to the price of the old shares and of the cheaper new shares. In the example of the one-for-five rights issue, if the share price had been £1.00 and the rights price 40 pence, the ex-rights price will be £5.40 (which is the value of five shares plus one right), divided by six (which is the number of shares after the rights issue), which is 90 pence. This is the theoretical figure, although it will likely also be influenced by market and business conditions. For capital gains tax assessment, the UK tax authorities consider the new shares were acquired at the same time as the original ones.

Shareholders not interested in a rights issue may in most cases sell the rights to which they have not subscribed, known as *renounceable* rights, to other investors or the underwriter, after which they are called *nil-paid* rights. The rough value of the nil-paid rights will be the ex-rights price less the rights price, which in the example is 90 pence less 40 pence, which is 50 pence. Sellers of renounceable rights, after receiving the proceeds, and once the share price has adjusted down as a result of the rights issue, will theoretically be in a cash-neutral position. Shareholders offered rights also get the option to do nothing, which is not recommended, as it means their rights would expire and their shareholdings would become diluted.

During the rights issue offer period, there is trading in the shares and, separately, the rights to buy the shares are traded. The share price can go below the rights price, in which case there is no incentive to subscribe because the shares can be bought in the market more cheaply.

This happened in some deeply discounted rights issues in 2008, to which retail investors subscribed but institutions did not, leaving underwriters with those shares not taken up. Hedge funds have sometimes taken short positions during rights issues, which forces the share price down.

Among the low take-up rates on capital-raising initiatives in 2008, Bradford & Bingley in August had a 27.8 per cent take-up; for HBOS in March, it had been only 8.3 per cent. Some companies experienced changes in their financial position during capital raisings, which was a contributing factor to the low take-up.

In the case of HBOS, the regulators claimed there had been market abuse through the spread of rumours by short sellers, who had hoped to buy back HBOS shares at a lower price. The FSA launched an investigation, but five months later called it off, unable to find any culprits.

The Rights Review Group was established by UK chancellor Alistair Darling in summer 2008 to review the rights process. Represented on the group were the Bank of England, the treasury, the FSA and various financial institutions and other parties, including trade bodies and lawyers. They recommended in the medium term to simplify disclosure requirements under the Prospectus Directive and recommended a number of short-term measures that were implemented.

Acting on the group's recommendations, the Association of British Insurers (ABI) in early 2009 moved to increase the limit on the amount that may be raised in rights issues without obtaining approval at an annual general meeting from one-third to two-thirds of share capital. The FSA reduced the minimum subscription period for companies that undertake a rights issue from 21 calendar days to 10 business days. According to the FSA, the new minimum timetable and the extended amount that may be immediately raised together reduce the period of a rights issue from 39 to 16 days.

The new abbreviated timetable is, however, voluntary. Some rights issues have been big and complex; there was one rights issue that needed a 200-shareholder meeting. According to Mark Hynes, managing director of Transparency Matters Ltd, such issues need a 39-day timetable and cannot be done in 10 days. His view is that a reduction in the rights issue period will be helpful in reducing the risks of rumours and related short selling. However, the FSA points out that the timetable reduction was entirely as a result of the Rights Issue Review Group's suggestions, and was not motivated by any focus on short selling.

The rights issue structure is also under review, and the Rights Issue Review Group has examined the Australian approach known as RAPIDS (renounceable accelerated pro-rata issue with dual book-build structure). This is a two-tranche shareholder offer, first to institutions within one business day, and then to retail. However, there are logistical differences between the UK and the Australian markets. The RAPIDS is preceded by a trading halt to allow time to establish who owns the shares and see to whom to make the offer. In the United Kingdom, there is a dislike of a trading halt, and the complexity of nominee holdings makes it difficult to find out if shares are owned by retail or institutional investors.

In the United States, by contrast, there are no pre-emptive rights and so companies issue shares without offers to existing shareholders.

Convertible securities have advantages under some circumstances over rights issues, according to Michele Crisostomo, partner at Clifford Chance, Milan. He notes that in a rights issue, shares are normally issued at discount and this increases the cost of the capital raising. Rights issues always have a dilutive impact on existing shareholders. There will be more shares to be paid out of the same pot. Profits are diluted and what is paid on the new shares cannot be deducted for tax purposes.

Convertible securities, however, may allow core capital generation while, at the same time, dilution can be deferred until conversion according to Crisostomo. In certain circumstances, there is also the benefit of the tax deductibility of coupon payments to securities holders.

Open offer

An open offer is similar to a rights issue in that it is an offer of new shares to existing shareholders on a pre-emptive basis *pro rata* to shares already held. It is underwritten in the same way but the timetable is shorter. Shareholders cannot sell their right to buy new shares in the open offer, as they can in a rights issue. If they do not take up the share entitlement, they will lose the discount at which the open offer is made. The maximum discount to the market price is 10 per cent.

There is usually a conditional placing (see below) of shares to institutional investors, but these are clawed back where shareholders take up their rights.

The Rights Issue Review Group's report recommended an open offer with a compensation structure by which shareholders who did not take up their entitlement would receive cash for them; the discount should be allowed to extend beyond 10 per cent if this structure is used.

Placing

A company may place shares with institutions, raising up to 5 per cent of share capital in one year, the permitted disapplication of pre-emption rights. Companies commit easily to placings because they are small.

Accelerated book build

The accelerated book build can similarly be used to raise a maximum of 5 per cent of share capital, and can be done at less of a discount to the closing price than an open offer because it is finished fast, so reducing the risk of adverse share price movement. The bank takes a selling company's shares in a listed company onto its books, and offers them to its investor clients. It will sell the shares in the course of one day or, exceptionally, over two or three days. This compares with several weeks for a conventional book build, and allows less time for market conditions to deteriorate. In a declining market, institutional investors respond favourably to this form of capital raising.

Bought deal

The bought deal is where a bank buys securities itself from an issuer and resells them in the market. The bank will have assumed all the risk and so must have confidence in the deal. Issuers are often attracted to a bought deal because it gives instant liquidity.

Other

Other forms of capital raising include a cash-box play, which gets around the 5 per cent limit by structuring the deal for a non-cash consideration. Otherwise, a company may raise cash from strategic investors via Private Investment in Public Equity, commonly known as PIPE.

Bond issues

In a low-interest-rate environment, listed companies may find it cheaper to raise money through corporate bonds than through equities. Fixed-income underwriting accounted for 19 per cent of global investment banking fee revenue in 2007, down from 23 per cent in the previous year, the decline was due largely to a recovery in M&A and equity underwriting income according to the IFSL 'Banking 2008' report.

If a company issues bonds, it may have to pay a coupon of only 6 per cent, but, if it issues equities, it may have to give shareholders a 10 per cent return.

In the United Kingdom and some other developed economies interest on bonds issued is tax deductible against the issuing company's profits, which is another advantage. Companies sometimes issue bonds and use the cash raised to buy back shares from investors.

The downside of bond issuance is the risk of taking on too much debt in relation to equity, which is known as *high gearing* and gives the issuer a riskier profile with the credit rating agencies. Generally, banks have easier access to capital than companies and are more highly geared. Debt issuance is likely to be the second largest liability on a major bank's balance sheet, behind cash deposits.

The bond issuer cannot skip paying the coupon, as is possible with dividends on shares, and must repay the principal on maturity, although it can refinance by issuing new bonds.

Banks, like companies, invest cash in bonds, across the risk spectrum and in all major market currencies. Some bonds will be included on the asset side of the balance sheet, where in terms of risk weighting under Basel II, they are more attractive than loans.

Issuers of bonds usually offer a fixed rate of return, as investors prefer. If the bonds fall in value, however, investors may feel they have lost out. This is why investors use the swaps market, which enables them to swap fixed for floating rates.

8

Credit derivatives and asset-backed securities

Introduction

Asset-backed securities and related credit derivatives have contributed significantly to the credit crisis of 2007–09. In this chapter we will see how they work.

Securitisation

The credit crunch has demonstrated the risks of exposure to collateralised debt obligations, which package pools of debt, including residential mortgage-backed securities. Financial institutions insured this exposure through credit default swaps, which are the most popular form of OTC derivative. It is the writing of credit default swaps, or speculating by means of them, that has been much of the problem in the credit crisis.

The pooling of products that become insured by credit default swaps is part of the process of securitisation, which transfers risks from a bank's balance sheet into capital markets. In this way, it frees up the bank's balance sheet to enable more lending. In addition, securitisation meets the demand for capital. Matching supply benefits with demand is a powerful impetus to continue securitisation.

If Wall Street had been less reckless in its trading, could the market itself have averted the near collapse of our global banking system? Perhaps, but the banks alone are not to blame. The rating agencies had given erroneously high ratings to mortgage-backed securities and regulators had left OTC derivatives

Eurex Clearing risk management.
Sees more. Misses less.

Opportunity can come from nowhere. Then again, so can trouble. Eurex Clearing's proven risk management lets you monitor and manage your post-trade activities in real time. Across multiple asset classes. Our processes keep up with trading trends, which means we're continually setting the industry standards. And every improvement we make, we make sure everybody benefits. So nobody needs to miss a thing – and everyone is c l e a r t o t r a d e **www.eurexclearing.cc**

Eurex Clearing:
Keeping You Clear To Trade

The derivatives segment is without doubt the largest[1] and arguably the most important and most innovative sector within the financial marketplace. It is integral to the financial system and plays a vital role within it. However, owing to some problems in one sector of the market – the over-the-counter segment – derivatives have become widely misunderstood, and recently given rise to alarm and suspicion in almost equal measure. This should not be the case; at their root, derivatives – and most especially exchange-traded and/or centrally cleared derivatives – are simple risk management instruments that are vital to banking, investment and trading practices around the world.

Derivatives – such as swaps, futures and options contracts – were developed to allow banks and investors to hedge risks in financial markets. They enable the provision of mortgage, student, car or home improvement loans, as well as long term financing or revolving credit facilities for corporations. They are also used by investment providers to structure and guarantee pension and life insurance payouts; by governments to manage debt and foreign currency liabilities; by oil and energy companies to defray the price impact of potential falls in production or rises in consumption; and by manufacturers and distributors to hedge out moves in raw material prices.

Therefore, derivatives are thus essential, not just to the financial marketplace, but to consumers and corporations each and every day. Without derivatives many aspects of our domestic and business lives would be more expensive and, undoubtedly, more restricted.

The market can broadly be divided into two areas. Firstly, the OTC derivatives market which is where many of these instruments are developed. The OTC market is a wholesale market, in which instruments are conceived and incubated, and where banks can tailor products to meet each individual customer's – corporations, governments, pension funds etc – very specific requirements, instantly, and on demand.

Secondly, there is the exchange-traded market, which is where Eurex, the world's largest derivatives exchange[2], has traditionally operated and which is the most 'mature', standardised and transparent sector of the derivatives business.

---

1   The Bank for International Settlements estimated that the amount of notional principal derivatives risk outstanding at the end of June 2008 totalled $711.6 trillion, including $683 trillion of over-the-counter (OTC) derivatives risk and $28.6 trillion in listed derivatives.
2   By traded contracts in Q1/2009.

Exchanges like Eurex are efficient, centralised trading venues with strong and proven risk management capabilities, on which standardised, highly liquid instruments are traded. Trading in Eurex-listed derivatives is fully transparent and is monitored and regulated by the national regulator in much the same way as securities trading is on a stock exchange. Once trades are agreed, a central counterparty (CCP), Eurex Clearing, Europe's leading clearing house, immediately steps in, becoming buyer to every seller, and seller to every buyer.

Both segments play important roles in the development and deployment of derivatives but whilst the listed segment is proven and robust, the OTC area has weaknesses, some of which were brutally exposed during the recent credit crisis.

Key to the OTC market's problems is the lack of transparency and bilateral credit risk. When Lehman Brothers went bankrupt last year, for example, no one knew exactly how much was at risk in the OTC marketplace, with whom and why. This generated such a level of mistrust that suddenly no banks wanted to trade with each other, or indeed with their customers. Conversely, exchanges and CCPs such as Eurex and Eurex Clearing were able to manage out Lehman's risk swiftly and transfer the bank's customers' positions to other member firms, willing to accept the positions, whilst ensuring that trading activity was able to continue and that other members' funds remained untouched.

In the case of American insurer, AIG, it would appear that OTC derivatives were misused. The insurer sold large amounts of insurance-like protection through OTC credit derivatives, without apparently setting aside sufficient capital for the payouts it might have to make. Had AIG been trading on exchange, or using a CCP, its activity would have been fully visible to regulatory authorities. Crucially, AIG would also have had to provide collateral and margins to the CCP for the risks it was taking on, thus limiting its ability to over-extend itself.

The policing function undertaken by exchanges and CCPs is now likely to be extended to as many corners of the $683 trillion[3] OTC marketplace as it can reach. Entities such as Eurex Clearing will increasingly be used to 'clear' OTC business, stepping into the middle of the OTC trades once they have been agreed. In doing so, they will substantially reduce or minimize the bilateral credit risk between the derivatives buyers and sellers, thereby ensuring lower risk exposure and better capital treatment. They will also remove the element of doubt that has hitherto surrounded OTC pricing and risk assessment, by

3   Bank for International Settlements OTC Derivatives Market Survey, published September 2008. Figure refers to notional outstanding in OTC trades at June 2008.

centralising these functions and ensuring the safe and wholly unbiased oversight of the market. The introduction of CCPs such as Eurex Clearing to this segment of the business will lessen the chances of misreporting or mispricing; strengthen market integrity and efficiency; and ensure robust and independent risk management and transparency.

Senior regulators around the world are pressing for this transition. The G20 leaders agreed in London in April 2009 that supervisors and regulators should speed efforts to reduce the risks in the OTC market as a matter of urgency, ensuring that the infrastructure for OTC derivatives can support growing volumes. A key part of US Treasury Secretary Timothy Geithner's intended financial market reforms include a comprehensive framework of oversight, protection and disclosure for the OTC derivatives market, "moving the standardised parts of those markets to central clearinghouses, and encouraging further use of exchange-traded instruments". In Europe, both the European Commission and the European Central Bank have echoed these demands, as has the UK's Financial Services Authority's chairman Adair Turner, who has stipulated that in the future, "clearing and central counterparty systems should be developed to cover the standardised contracts".

Eurex and Eurex Clearing are expertly poised to help the industry meet these calls. The exchange's existing listed and cleared marketplaces are large, robust and proven and it is already a one-stop-shop for trading and clearing in everything from equity and credit derivatives, to commodity, inflation, interest rate and property derivatives. The group's reach will undoubtedly grow further in the future, but by mid 2009 Eurex Clearing will offer a cleared credit derivatives service, and by the end of the year, subject to regulatory approval, Eurex together with its wholly-owned subsidiary, the International Securities Exchange will also be able to offer its members seamless trading and clearing in all the US-listed equity options, becoming the first truly transatlantic derivatives exchange.

In line with their growing remit, Eurex and Eurex Clearing of course have to continue to upgrade their risk management capabilities. Both entities continually demonstrate their commitment to this principle – most recently by offering the first ever real-time risk management capabilities to their member firms, the most advanced globally.

We look forward to working with you to ensure the integrity of the financial marketplace to become your preferred partner for a sounder, better place in which to do business: Eurex Clearing keeps you clear to trade.

www.eurex-clearing.com

trading largely unsupervised. The products themselves are sound, provided that their devisers and traders are prepared for the risk exposures.

The problem with securitisation, as we shall see in this chapter, has been a lack of transparency, and perhaps of understanding by regulators as to what is involved. In securitisation, products are packaged and sold on, with a lot of information lost through the use of intermediaries, who retain no risk but just take a fee. In the credit crisis of 2007–09, nobody wanted to buy, the system jammed up and restructuring of individual loans became problematic when global dispersion made them difficult to recognise. Securitisation uses structural subordination, which is complex and difficult to model.

Let us retrace the process of securitisation that led to the credit crunch. I have drawn on research from the US SEC in some of the following explanations and would recommend visiting its website (www.sec.gov) to check out its analysis of all areas related to the credit crisis and how it has affected the securities industry.

Investment banks created residential mortgage-backed securities by packaging thousands of mortgage loans into a pool and transferring them to a trust.

In its turn, the trust will have bought the loan pool, which means that it gains the interest and principal payments made by the borrowers. The trust finances the purchase by issuing residential mortgage-backed securities to investors, paying them interest and principal from the payments received from the loan pool.

The trust issues different classes of residential mortgage-backed securities, known as tranches, and pays interest as coupons at a rate adjusted for the credit protection given to the security. Such credit protection aims to protect the tranche securities from losing interest and principal due to loan defaults within the pool.

A trust may issue securities in eight tranches. There is credit enhancement based on subordination. Any loss of interest and principal from the loans in the pool are allocated first to the lowest tranche until it has lost its entire principal amount and then to the next lowest, and so on.

Another source of credit enhancement is over-collateralisation, which is the extent to which the principal balance of the mortgage pool may exceed that of the tranche securities, creating an additional equity tranche below the lowest tranche security, to absorb losses. A third type is the excess spread, which is the amount by which the trust's monthly interest income exceeds its monthly liabilities.

The collateralised debt obligation is created similarly to the residential mortgage-backed security. It consists of about 200 debt securities, and uses their interest and principal payments to pay investors in the securities issued by the trust. The trust is structured to provide varying levels of credit enhancement, through subordination as well as over-collateralisation, excess spread and bond insurance.

Unlike the residential mortgage-backed security, the collateralised debt obligation may be actively managed. Collateralised debt obligations have been major buyers of sub-prime residential mortgage-backed securities.

The credit default swap has played a part in the growth of both these products. This is a contract where the seller agrees to pay the buyer if a specified credit event such as a default, bankruptcy or restructuring should arise on an underlying entity in exchange for payment. Investment managers have bought credit default swaps, paying annual premiums to protect their bond portfolios, and have also sold such insurance. The credit default swap has been used to replicate the performance of sub-prime mortgage-backed securities and collateralised debt obligations, so meeting investor demand when the cash products become scarce. Some collateralised debt obligations made use of both cash positions (ie non-derivative) and credit default swaps.

The credit crunch arose in August 2007 after financial institutions across Europe and the United States had invested in collateralised debt obligations backed by asset-backed securities, including mortgage-backed securities. Another growth area was collateralised debt obligations referencing leveraged loans, known as collateralised loan obligations.

Between 2005 and 2007, the issuance of collateralised loan obligations tripled, with their backing increasingly consisting of residential mortgage-backed securities, a product whose cash flows come substantially from sub-prime mortgages, which are those lent to high-risk borrowers.

High-grade asset-backed securities are collateralised loan obligations invested in collateral rated highly by the rating agencies. Some financial institutions accepted these ratings uncritically, which was to prove a mistake. The credit crunch proved that the agencies had it wrong and that even the top-rated collateral was not safe.

Investors

Investors, including banks and pension funds, who bought the collateralised debt obligations, taking income from their assets, are exposed to the risk of default. If a default is big enough, it cascades up the scale to include the higher classes of bonds in which they are invested.

Investors in corporate bonds can buy a credit default swap as a hedge against default by the bond issuer. They will pay quarterly premiums to the financial institution selling protection, which could be a bank or a monoline insurer (see page 93). If there is a default, the buyer will give their bonds to the seller of protection and will receive their full value.

The biggest users of the credit default swap are the banks, who use it to hedge their own loan books. Hedge funds use the credit default swap to take a short position on markets, which is to profit from the market's decline, or to hedge their positions, or in arbitrage, meaning to profit from a price difference in the same product on different markets.

Time of reckoning

By mid 2007, investment banks that lent money to hedge funds to buy collateralised debt obligations had been raising their margin requirements. At about this time Florida-based United Capital Asset Management suspended redemptions in its Horizon funds, which were significantly invested in US sub-prime mortgage assets.

Two hedge funds owned by US bank Bear Stearns came close to collapse because they failed to meet margin calls on collateralised debt obligations made up of risky US sub-prime mortgages. Some banks that were their creditors threatened to sell off at auction the underlying sub-prime mortgages that they had held as collateral, but it became clear that a quick sale would fetch poor returns. In June 2007, it was announced that Bear Stearns had agreed an emergency US$3.2 billion (£2.1 billion) loan for one of the funds.

The crisis at the Bear Stearns hedge funds has led to widespread concerns about how collateralised debt obligations of asset-backed securities are priced. The market for collateralised debt obligations is not particularly liquid, and huge sell-offs of bonds can cause a significant re-pricing. This can be triggered by downgrades from the credit rating agencies, a process that was starting to happen in mid 2007.

Large banks, including the investment banking division of insurer AIG and monoline insurers, had used credit default swaps to insure financial institutions against losses on collateralised debt obligations. As it turned out, the collateralised debt obligations backed by sub-prime mortgages were loss making on a huge scale. They were supposed to have had some protection against default by the atomisation of risk but, even so, the losses were massive enough to hit investors.

Regulation and transparency

In an October 2008 Congressional hearing, Alan Greenspan, who had been chairman of the Federal Reserve until three years earlier, admitted that he had put too much faith in free markets and their ability to correct themselves, and had not anticipated the damage that irresponsible mortgage lending could cause. In 1994, Greenspan had successfully opposed more regulation of derivatives. At the hearing, he said that risk spreading through the use of derivatives had since gone out of control.

Credit default swaps

Since the credit crunch there have been calls to introduce transparency and regulation into the credit derivatives market, which has been largely unregulated. In September 2008, the New York State Insurance Department said that, starting in January 2009, it would regulate as insurance the covered swap, where the buyer owns the underlying security on which they are buying protection. Such swaps, which are about 10 per cent of the total, would be subject to regulation for the first time. The 'naked' swaps, which are the remaining 90 per cent, are bought by speculators who do not own the underlying bond, and the New York State Insurance Department said that these products are not insurance.

The department later delayed the regulatory proposal in favour of a holistic approach to regulating OTC derivatives, which was under discussion in the United States. Lawyers had pointed out problems in the department's plan, including that it was difficult for a seller of a credit default swap always to know whether it was covered or not, which made it uncertain whether the product would be an insurance contract for regulatory purposes.

More regulation of OTC derivatives, including credit default swaps, is inevitable. US and European regulators are working together in an uneasy way on this. There is competition between the jurisdictions and there is awareness that, if there is too strict regulation in the United States, it could drive credit default swaps to London, which is already the market leader in OTC derivatives business.

By late 2008, regulators in the United States and the EU and beyond have called for a central counterparty clearing house for credit default swaps. A central counterparty would reduce the impact of default by a large market player. Trades would be novated (transferred) to the central counterparty, meaning that dealers would no longer be exposed to each other's credit risk. The central counterparty could reduce the risk of collateral flows, both by netting positions and through risk controls over its exposure to participants. If the central counterparty led to more trades, this would reduce systemic risk.

By early 2009, the industry was expecting to see multiple clearing houses for credit default swaps, with members putting up collateral and with an auctioning process. LIFFE (London International Financial Futures and Options Exchange), the global derivatives business of NYSE Euronext, and LCH.Clearnet have already launched a clearing house. IntercontinentalExchange in Atlanta has already set up ICE Trust, a proposed clearing house for the credit default swap market. ICE Trust applied to the Federal Reserve Bank of New York to become a member of the Federal Reserve System.

With a pending number of clearing houses, there could be turf battles, and an industry regulator may be needed. By January 2009, talk between Brussels and the industry to create a central clearing system for credit derivatives had broken down but rival US plans for such a system were going ahead.

Freight derivatives and the Baltic Exchange

Freight derivatives, until recently traded over the counter, are a way to hedge exposure to freight market risk through the trading of specified time charter and voyage rate for forward positions. Settlement is effected against estimated prices of routes, which are published by the Baltic Exchange in London, based on assessments of shipbrokers. Forward freight agreements, as the derivatives are known (there are also options based on them), are on the cost of transportation of cargo, on the dry side such as grain and iron ore, or on the wet side, mainly crude oil, along physical routes. This type of derivative is fairly liquid, and is used by ship buyers and cargo suppliers for speculation as well as to hedge positions.

Since about August 2008, freight derivatives took a lead among OTC derivatives in moving almost entirely from OTC trading on a principal-to-principal basis to central counterparty clearing. The International Maritime Exchange in Norway is an exchange dedicated to shipping freight derivatives, and uses the Norwegian Futures and Options Clearing House (NOS) to clear its transactions. NOS relies on the Baltic Exchange to provide it with freight market assessments. Other clearing services are the New York Mercantile Exchange (NYMEX), the London Clearing House and the Singapore Exchange.

This migration of forward freight agreements to central counterparty clearing sets a trend which other OTC derivatives seem likely to follow. It is a direct result of the credit crisis, according to the Baltic Exchange. It reports that there have been recent defaults by counterparties in OTC freights derivatives trades based on, for example, decreased demand for iron ore from the steel industry and banks refusing to provide letters of credit. Freight rates have plummeted in the dry bulk sector due to decreased iron ore demand from the steel industry and banks refusing to provide letters of credit, although they are rising again now.

Freight derivatives are in volume only just over the levels of underlying markets, in contrast with other OTC derivatives which are 7 to 10 times the underlying market levels. But the physical market in freight is huge. There is talk of manipulation going on in the physical shipping market but this would be difficult, partly because of the amount of capital that would need to be deployed.

The Baltic Exchange is not just a price-mechanism provider to the shipping market. It is a community of 560 members, drawn from shipping, but also across P&I clubs (see Chapter 9), banks and lawyers and FSA-regulated freight derivatives dealers. For these members it operates a code of conduct – forbidding a shipbroker, for example, to agree a deal and ditch it 10 minutes later in favour of another at a better price.

The Exchange is self-regulatory and may expel members. With non-members it may post to the market, for example, a failure to stand by an arbitration decision. Such a posting would carry a lot of weight with its members, who include the world's biggest ship owners and ship brokers.

The credit crisis had made irrelevant the main case against regulating OTC derivatives, which was that it was a wholesale market and regulation would make it less efficient.

Monoline insurers

The monoline insurers, also known as financial guarantors, have been downgraded by rating agencies since the credit crunch hit. This caused a downgrading to their products, including collateralised debt obligations, which they covered. The industry has been caught up in a mix of litigation. It has been involved in class actions in the United States – by investors and employees – as well as actions testing the terms of its insurance policies and the involvement with credit default swaps.

In 2009 the New York State Insurance Department plans new legislation on monoline insurers. Among other things, this will limit the amount and type of more complex structural securities, including collateralised debt obligations and asset-backed securities that a financial guarantor can cover. It will require enhanced risk management among financial guarantors, covering how they measure and cover exposure to the products they guarantee, and more robust disclosure on the securities that the companies wrap.

The monoline insurers themselves have proposed that they should back municipal bonds separately from structured products.

Credit rating agencies

Credit rating agencies rate the creditworthiness of a bond. The higher the rating, the better the credit terms a borrower will receive. If an agency reduces its rating on a bond, the price is likely to decline. The rating is a paid-for service, which has long called into question its independence.

In rating a company, the agencies have access to non-public information and they estimate only the default risk. The criteria used vary slightly between agencies, but include social and political risk, the regulatory environment, and the level of Westernisation of the borrower's country. The agencies do not always agree on their ratings.

The rating agencies overrated sub-prime mortgage assets based on the erroneous assumption that house prices would keep moving up; this has brought the industry under serious criticism. Regulation of rating agencies is inevitable, although the industry has argued vociferously against this.

In August 2007, the US SEC started an examination of three major credit rating agencies to review their role in the turmoil in the sub-prime mortgage-related securities markets. Its findings were:

- Significant aspects of the ratings process were not always disclosed and the agencies could better document policies and procedures for rating residential mortgage-backed securities and collateralised debt obligations.
- Arrangers' influence in determining the choice of rating agencies and the high concentration of arrangers with this influence appear to have heightened the agencies' conflicts of interest, and arrangers could have benefited in the ratings process, which they preferred to be fast and predictable.
- Arrangers and their employees are compensated, at least partly, by the volume and dollar amount of deals completed. At least one rating agency allowed deals that were already in the ratings process to continue to use older criteria, even when new criteria had been introduced.
- Arrangers could require more favourable ratings or reduced credit enhancement levels, which would reduce the cost of the debt. And by putting pressure on the rating agencies, the arrangers could influence their decisions on whether to update a model when this would lead to a less favourable outcome.
- High profit margins from rating retail mortgage-backed securities and collateralised debt obligations may have given rating agencies an incentive to encourage the arrangers to route future business their way. The agencies rely upon historical data in order to predict future behaviour, but the performance history of the types of sub-prime mortgages that dominated many of the retail mortgage-backed securities portfolios was very short, and occurred under very benign economic conditions.

Many in Europe have had similar concerns about rating agencies and the flaws in the business model. There is a widespread feeling that regulators have relied too much on ratings. As we saw in Chapter 2, Basel II relies on ratings.

In November 2008, the European Commission (EC) adopted a proposal for regulating credit rating agencies to a higher level. The proposed regulation was based partly on standards in a code of conduct for rating agencies already established by the International Organization of Securities Commissions (IOSCO), but it also included some stricter rules where it found that the IOSCO standards were not sufficient to restore market confidence and ensure investor protection. The IOSCO said in response that the co-running of its code and EU legislation could cause fragmentation.

Under the proposed EC regulation, credit agencies should not provide advisory services or rate financial instruments unless they have sufficiently high-quality information as a basis; they should disclose models and assumptions, publish an annual transparency report and create an internal function to view ratings quality. They should have at least three independent directors on their boards, whose remuneration should not depend on the business performance of the rating agency.

There has been some resistance to regulation from the rating agencies, and an endorsement of the IOSCO code of conduct. Within agencies, there have been moves to revise rating methodologies and introduce oversight measures. So far, there is no cost-effective alternative to the services of rating agencies but, at the same time, some firms and regulators say they have relied on them too much.

9

Insurance

Introduction

In this chapter we will take a brief overview of how the global insurance industry works. We will see how it has survived the credit crunch of 2007–09.

Overview

Insurance is where one party, the insurer, undertakes to pay another party, the insured, money if a specified form of financial risk should arise. For this service, the insured pays the insurer a fee, known as a premium. The category comprises general insurance, and life or health insurance.

The insurance business is global. The largest market is the United States, which is regulated in 50 states. However, Europe as a whole is writing more premiums than the United States and the gap is widening. Insurance premiums in Europe totalled US$1,681 billion (£1,126 billion) in 2007, compared with US$1,230 billion (£824 billion) in the United States, according to an October 2008 report by IFSL 'Financial Market Trends: Europe vs US'. Europe has a 41 per cent share of global premiums, the United States has 30 per cent, and the rest of the world accounts for 29 per cent.

The London market is the largest in Europe, and second in size only to the United States. It covers general insurance and reinsurance business, and is one of the leading providers of insurance and reinsurance to the United States.

How insurance works

In return for providing cover, the insurer takes a premium from the insured and invests it. The investment income can make a significant contribution to profits. The insurer hopes also to receive more in premiums than it pays out in losses, enabling it to make an underwriting profit.

Reinsurance helps insurance to spread risk, and to limit loss exposure. A reinsurance placement is typically shared among reinsurers.

Types of reinsurance

In proportional reinsurance, the reinsurer takes a percentage share of the policy, receiving a fixed percentage of premium income from the original policyholder and paying the same percentage of claims payments. Property insurers prefer proportional reinsurance because the sum insured is known, making proportional divisions practical.

Non-proportional reinsurance is paid only if the loss is beyond the retention of the insurer, which is the amount of the loss it will accept. It is commonly excess-of-loss reinsurance, where the ceding office pays the initial layer of every valid claim, and the reinsurers pay the balance of losses up to a set figure.

The two types of contract are treaty and facultative. Treaty reinsurance is an agreement covering a class or classes of business, and it automatically covers risks written by the insured without evaluation of individual exposures. Facultative reinsurance provides an insurer with coverage for specific risks, typically large or unusual, which are not covered in its reinsurance treaties. Both treaty and facultative contracts may be written on a proportional or nonproportional basis, or as a mixture of both.

Retrocession is where a reinsurer reinsures its own business with another reinsurer, the retrocessionaire.

Financial reinsurance is a form of reinsurance arranged for financial or strategic reasons and there is little or no risk transfer from the insurer to the reinsurer. It is used to smooth the insurer's profits, with the insurer transferring money to the reinsurer in good years. This can be used to offset losses in bad years. Unlike in traditional reinsurance, the level of claims does not affect the premium the insurer pays and the reinsurer's profit. The product has attracted regulatory attention because it has been used to strengthen the balance sheet with increased reinsurance protection, suggesting that the company is stronger than it is.

Underwriters

Underwriters are at the heart of the insurance business. They determine whether to accept the risk for the client and, if so, how much of it and at what price. They issue insurance policies selectively, using gut feel but also modelling, which has become increasingly prominent in recent years. No model is a substitute for the underwriter's judgment, however. Models did not anticipate Hurricane Katrina in 2005. Underwriters have an entrepreneurial approach at Lloyd's, but sometimes less so at composite insurers where the focus is on personal lines insurance that can be priced and marketed electronically.

An underwriter's perspective

For the purposes of this book, David James, a senior underwriter at Ascot Underwriting, an insurer based in the Lloyd's market in London, gives some insights into the underwriting process today, mainly for terrorism risk.

He says that part of the underwriting process is intuitive and subjective, and underwriters' decision making can be affected by their location and local knowledge, providing them with a particular appreciation of risk: 'The underwriter sitting in New York may have a different opinion of risk from his counterpart in the United Kingdom or Bermuda.'

This subjective content is only part of the underwriting process, and ultimately all underwriters are subject to objective checks and balances, notably aggregate controls (how much they are willing to lose in a given event). 'An underwriter aims to write a balanced portfolio. Underwriting an individual risk is relatively straightforward. The greater challenge is to write a portfolio that is balanced, not only geographically but also in terms of occupancy, attachment point and the sources of production.'

Terrorism risk is a non-correlating catastrophe business which, according to James, means it should not suffer losses arising from a natural catastrophe such as a windstorm. As such, it provides a balance, or spread, to an underwriting company that is seeking variation from its exposure to natural catastrophes. 'Terrorism is a unique catastrophe peril because, unlike a windstorm or earthquake, it is carried out by an active intelligent perpetrator. The terrorist will seek out the weakest point with the greatest chance of success.'

James explains that, as part of the underwriting process, underwriters must decide on an appropriate premium and terms and conditions, including how much of the risk they require the insured person to retain (how much of a potential loss they must cover themselves before they can recover anything from the insurer). Increasingly, risk is shared between different underwriters rather than a single underwriter writing and retaining the whole of the risk. This syndication process of sharing risk is particularly common in the London market with its high concentration of brokers, underwriting companies and Lloyd's syndicates.

'When a leading underwriter sets a price, which the following market supports, it is helpful if they have used similar modelling methodologies or pricing systems to arrive at that premium, as this builds consistency within a market place.'

Underwriters need to manage their portfolio within their own protections (reinsurance) and risk appetite. 'This is particularly the case in periods of wider economic uncertainty, with spread of risk and portfolio management as important today as they have ever been. Underwriters will generally seek to write a variety of risks rather than concentrating too heavily in one area, be that geographic or an industry sector.'

This is true not just of terrorism but also other classes of insurance such as property, James says. In its own underwriting portfolio, Ascot uses a tiering methodology to manage risks, allowing it to band its portfolio of risks by perceived threat and the potential to accumulate.

Brokers

The insurance broker is an intermediary between insurance companies and their clients. The broker arranges insurance with underwriters, providing any necessary details, reports or surveys, and may help clients resolve claims.

Commission transparency

Brokers' remuneration has given rise to transparency concerns. Part of the concern has been about contingent commissions, which are where insurers pay commissions to brokers in exchange for steering business their way. In April 2004, New York Attorney General Eliot Spitzer launched an investigation into this area. In the following year, a small number of brokers agreed to pay substantial fines to settle charges initiated by Spitzer, including bid rigging.

Within weeks of Spitzer's allegations, seven global insurance brokers announced that they would stop contingent commissions and, by early 2005, they were presenting revised business models. But others continued the practice.

The EC expressed concerns about the broad issue of broker transparency in a 2007 business insurance sector inquiry report. There is some high-level industry sentiment that there is nothing wrong with contingent commissions provided that there is disclosure, but the issue remains under discussion.

The London market

The London market covers general insurance and reinsurance business and is a leading provider of such business to the United States. It is split between insurance companies and syndicates at Lloyd's. According to IFSL, gross premium income on the London market was conservatively estimated at £24.5 billion in 2007, slightly up on the previous year's total. Lloyd's generated over two-thirds of premiums, with the company market generating 28 per cent and protection and indemnity clubs (known as P&I clubs; see below) the remainder.

London has both non-Lloyd's brokers and Lloyd's brokers. Most of the larger brokers are in both categories and London is a broker-led market.

The London market covers a high proportion of very large or complex risks and has the largest share of premium income in marine insurance. One of the largest types of marine contract placed in the market is for marine liabilities, which is a reinsurance of the International Group of P&I Clubs. The 13 P&I clubs that make up the group insure their ship-owner members on a mutual basis for liabilities such as collision and pollution. The P&I clubs pool their claims, in excess of retention by each club, through the International Group. The reinsurance contract is in excess of the US$50 million pool retention.

Lloyd's is a specialist insurance market with a large global licence network. Lloyd's underwriters write business in 200 territories and countries. In the early 1990s, the Lloyd's market came close to collapse after an influx of insurance claims from employees of US companies who had contracted diseases from exposure to asbestos. Since then, Lloyd's has reinvented itself, focusing on disciplined underwriting. Lloyd's consists of over 70 syndicates, each a collection of individuals and companies that underwrite insurance risks at Lloyd's.

A syndicate is a series of annual ventures. The members of Lloyd's include companies, which may underwrite through only one syndicate, and individuals, known as Names, who typically underwrite through several syndicates. Lloyd's members are not responsible for each other's losses, but a member may pay for another member's losses through its annual contribution to the Central Fund, which is part of the Lloyd's chain of security.

The syndicates, which have consolidated in recent years, cover specialist classes of business such as marine, aviation, catastrophe, professional indemnity and product liability. Reinsurance makes up more than half of Lloyd's income. A closing syndicate year passes its portfolio of policies and reserves covering claims forward to future years in a procedure known as reinsurance to close. This way, each annual venture is brought to an end, normally after three years, crystallising the liabilities of participating underwriting members.

The Lloyd's managing agent employs underwriting staff and manages one or more syndicates on the members' behalf. There are 47 managing agents, most of which are now owned by listed companies or backed by insurance-related capital. The Corporation of Lloyd's runs the market. If it does not consider that a syndicate is acting in a prudent manner, it can terminate its right to trade at Lloyd's and that of its managing agent. In supervision of the market particularly, Lloyd's plays a significant regulatory role, although the FSA has responsibility for the market's overall regulation.

Bermuda

Bermuda's insurance reinsurance market has attracted substantial reinsurance business away from London in recent years, offering the advantages of lighter-touch regulation and a nil tax rate. Lloyd's underwriters, however, cover a far more diverse range of risks than underwriters in Bermuda. There is an argument that Bermuda is not large enough to support writing a large diversified book of business, which would require an enormous number of workers, including underwriting and claims staff.

Bermuda's insurance and reinsurance sector has a large number of captive insurers – owned by the company that insures through them – and specialises in reinsurance of catastrophe risk. The industry experienced a boom period in 2001–03, and reinsurers emerged relatively unscathed from 2004 hurricanes and typhoons. However, the reinsurers were hit hard by losses arising from exposure to hurricanes Katrina, Rita and Wilma in 2005. Bermuda's reinsurers made a net loss of US$2.8 billion in 2005, compared with a US$5.5 billion profit the previous year. Bermuda paid 60 per cent of losses arising from hurricane Katrina in that year.

The 2005 hurricane season created a global reinsurance capacity crunch, which was an opportunity for capital providers. In the last three months of 2005, almost US$18 billion was raised by carriers in Bermuda, including a significant proportion from start-ups. A 'Class of 2005' of Bermuda insurance carriers was created, including start-ups such as Amlin Bermuda, Hiscox Bermuda and Cyrus Re. This echoed the establishment of the Class of 1993 after Hurricane Andrew or the Class of 2001 after the 11 September terrorist attacks. Bermuda's procedures for setting up an insurance carrier with proper capital backing and a sound business plan are much faster than London's.

Looking to the future, the Bermuda Monetary Authority has developed a new risk-based approach and focus on capital adequacy for insurers. In the past it has required minimum solvency margins. It is now looking at the total risk of the companies, including what risk they are writing and what type, and gives them credit for having a good risk-management programme. This is in line with international developments.

In February 2009, Fitch ratings said in a special report that its rating outlook for the Bermuda insurance and reinsurance market remains negative and that it expected downward rating activity globally and across all of its insurance ratings in 2009. Fitch said it believed that Bermuda reinsurers in aggregate were less likely to face widespread rating downgrades primarily because of their comparatively low asset leverage and high-quality investment portfolios. It noted that potential changes in the US tax code may threaten the Bermuda market's tax advantage over US rivals. If a major catastrophe event caused heavy claims, current market conditions would make it far harder to recapitalise than after the 2005 hurricanes or the events of 2001.

Capital markets convergence

Traditional reinsurance has converged with the wider capital markets to meet demands for capacity and to achieve capital relief for regulatory purposes. According to Lorraine Mullins, group compliance officer at insurer Catlin, regulation should support insurance securitisation because capital markets 'diversify the capital base to provide a bulwark against systemic shock'.

As yet, capital markets provide only a small proportion of capacity in the reinsurance field, but the potential is vast. A 'side car' is a reinsurance company reinsuring one insurance company. This type of company is registered perhaps in Bermuda or, less often, in the Cayman Islands. It became popular in Bermuda after the 2005 hurricane losses. This type of vehicle commits itself only short term, for one or two years, to a reinsurance transaction. The premium from the reinsured and the equity capital from investors are typically paid into a trust account which collateralises each policy written by the side car. This form of capital is less needed now, and many side cars have not been extended by mutual agreement.

There is more use now of catastrophe bonds, known as cat bonds, which are another form of alternative risk transfer but aligned to a market event, unlike a side car, which is aligned to a specific event. Cat bonds are seen as more flexible and less risky. They have been around since 1997. Cat bonds are debt that works as insurance cover. An insurer covering a catastrophic risk, such as an earthquake, makes regular payments to a vehicle, which receives cash from investors and pays them regular interest. If the earthquake occurs, the vehicle pays out to the insurer, which means that investors lose their cash. In the credit crunch of 2007–09, both AIG and Lehman Brothers were involved in cat bonds before they ran into problems; this has dampened the appetite for these products.

Changing times

The insurance industry is becoming more uniform globally, more innovative and more computerised. It is extending to developing countries. In countries such as India and Egypt, the growth is in micro-insurance. This is insurance for low-income people; it charges low premiums and provides low coverage. At the time of writing, Egypt is drafting laws and regulations in accordance with international standards to encourage micro-insurance. The insurer Allianz runs the only micro-insurance project in Egypt, and promotes death-and-disability insurance to 30,000 people.

Challenges facing the development of micro-insurance include the lack of a distribution system and reliable data, inadequate training for providers, the lack of consumer recourse methods and support infrastructures, and a complete absence of reinsurance.

As mentioned in Chapter 3, another growth area is Takaful insurance, an Islamic form of mutual insurance where participants appoint a Takaful company to administer a trust in their best interest. The fund complies with Sharia requirements. The Takaful market started in Sudan and then moved to Asia. It is growing fast in Malaysia and has also developed in the Gulf. Among large insurers moving into the Takaful area are AIG, Allianz, Aviva and Prudential.

In the developed world, catastrophes have taught insurers and their regulators that disciplined underwriting matters. In the London market, there appear to be some current exceptions, such as aviation, where there has recently been plenty of capacity and some indemnity at lower rates than some consider realistic, all in an obvious effort to gain market share.

Generally, the 11 September 2001 attacks on the United States had encouraged insurers to make less use of reinsurance as a substitute for quality underwriting. They give brokers less choice of reinsurer. This is particularly so for long-tail business, where the liability may be discovered and claims made many years after the loss.

Reinsurers set aside loss reserves for incurred-but-not-reported claims, which are an estimate of future loss. There is increasing use of downgrade clauses by which, if a reinsurer's rating with credit agencies falls below a trigger level, the primary insurer may void the contract or require collateral.

Through these downgrade clauses the insurance industry has given the rating agencies extra power over it. The rating agencies have a significant impact on consumer confidence in insurance companies and, for some products, a firm cannot be a legitimate player in the insurance industry without a certain rating.

By early 2009, some rating agencies were reviewing how they treated certain insurance assets and liabilities, and a significant change in methodology could have a bigger effect on some companies' ratings than others.

The credit crunch

Some insurance industry professionals liken the recent packaging and selling on of toxic sub-prime mortgage-backed debt in collateralised debt obligations and the way it all went wrong to the LMX spiral experience at Lloyd's. In both cases, risk, sliced and diced, remained risk; and turned out to be real.

In the 1980s and early 1990s, Lloyd's experienced a boom-to-bust period. Catastrophe claims were a major issue. Lloyd's ran into trouble partly because the London market excess of loss (LMX) was used to reinsure catastrophe risks; it led to what became known as the LMX spiral. Syndicates and insurance companies would pay a first slice of a loss, and would pass the next slice onto a reinsurer. A third slice would be passed to another reinsurer, and the spiral would continue through the market, sometimes winding back to the original insurer or reinsurer that would take another slice, effectively reinsuring itself.

Major catastrophes happened. In 1988, the Piper Alpha oil platform caught fire and fell into the North Sea. In 1989, Hurricane Hugo struck Puerto Rico, St Croix, South and North Carolina; and in the same year, oil tanker Exxon Valdez ran aground off the Alaskan coast. In 1990, there were storms across Europe.

Lloyd's Names ended up paying many of the claims. In 1988–1992, overall losses at Lloyd's were £8 billion, partly arising from LMX activity, and commentators had started querying whether the market could survive. This led to litigation. In the event, Lloyd's made a £3.2 billion settlement offer to Names.

Newly established reinsurer Equitas closed all the 1992 and prior years of account of Lloyd's syndicates writing non-life business by way of reinsurance of those syndicates. It proceeded with the run-off of the business, giving Names, at this stage, 'affordable finality'.

The insurance industry says it has learned from the LMX spiral and from downturns in the insurance cycle. Since those days, Lloyd's has manifestly tightened up its underwriting standards and introduced new market disciplines, although implementation remains up to individual syndicates, and there is evidence of recent relaxed underwriting, as in aviation, to gain market share at a time when capacity has been plentiful.

The case is that such experience, coupled with the business model of insurance, which is not based on trading money in the same way as the investment banking model, mean that the insurance industry is better placed to withstand the credit crisis of 2007–09. As capital becomes increasingly scarce for everyone, including insurance companies, so insurance capacity falls and insurance prices rise.

The industry fears, however, that regulators will impose new regulations on it. Life insurers have seen huge declines in the value of their investments. According to the CEA, the European insurance and reinsurance federation, this has not been as bad for European insurers as it could have been, because they have not invested significantly in US assets.

Some in the industry panicked in early 2009 after the FSA demanded that life assurers stress-test their capital reserves against a further catastrophic decline in equity values, another significant widening in spreads and a large rise in bond defaults.

The market for directors, and officers, liability insurance and professional indemnity insurance has been hardening, meaning that premiums are rising. This is because such insurance is now seen as riskier for the underwriters. Claims are clearly being made, with litigation from the sub-prime crisis and, in early 2009, from the Madoff scandal (see Chapter 11) and other cases.

Even with such impacts, the insurance industry has withstood the credit crisis so far better than most areas of financial services and is making continued efforts to present its case. In early 2009, the International Underwriting Association of London (IUA) established a legal and regulatory group to deal more strategically and with greater legal authority with the FSA and government. The IUA wants to be able to demonstrate that the approach to regulating insurers in the United Kingdom today is acceptable, and any regulation of systemic risk should not tear up the existing book of regulation.

Contract certainty

For some years in the London insurance market, there was a lack of contract certainty due to the 'deal now, detail later' culture. In late 2004, the FSA expressed concern and gave the industry two years to find its own solution. The London market rose to the challenge through electronic initiatives implemented with the assistance of The Market Reform Group.

By November 2006, Lloyd's managing agents were reporting 91 per cent of contracts as certain at inception, and some insurance companies were reporting even higher levels. The FSA said that the industry had succeeded, but that the process had to be ongoing.

The United States is following in the same direction but more slowly. In October 2008, the New York State Insurance Department said in a circular letter that insurers and producers doing business in New York had 12 months to develop and implement practices ensuring that policy documentation was delivered to policyholders within 30 days.

The UK approach to contract certainty has run into problems abroad, including in Commonwealth of Independent States (CIS) countries, according to George Grishin, director at Oakeshott Insurance Consultants. He notes that London market brokers often fail to collect premiums due on Lloyd's insurance contracts from CIS clients who make the mistake of thinking they are not bound by them because only limited paperwork is in place. According to Grishin, this is a cultural misunderstanding based on the fact that the insured in CIS countries too often fails to understand that the London market puts a contract in place before a formal policy is issued. London still uses the cover note without the signature of the client to confirm that an insurance policy is in force but, in countries such as Russia, Kazakhstan and the Ukraine, application is inconceivable without full paper support.

Russian companies can make the mistake of feeling free to renege on an insurance contract with a London broker, in order to take up a local cheaper insurance policy instead; and they might not inform the original broker. Grishin adds that in CIS countries, a reinsurance contract is usually in English but the insurance contract is not, and this can lead to translation uncertainties, for example over the word 'hurricane'.

EU regulation

The Reinsurance Directive

The Reinsurance Directive was scheduled to be implemented by all EU member states by December 2007, though not all achieved that deadline. The directive creates a common regulatory framework for pure reinsurers established in the EU. For the first time, such reinsurers can write business through a single entity across the EU, based on one licence and supervised by a home state regulator. They can hold their capital in a single entity, manage it better and save on costs.

Some reinsurers with headquarters outside the EU have decided to take advantage of the directive and establish a presence within the EU. Zurich-based Swiss Re, the world's largest reinsurer, helped to lead the way when it announced a new structure in March 2007. The group would form three legal entitles, based in Luxembourg, as risk carriers for most of its European reinsurance and insurance business, operating through branches in the rest of the EU.

The directive forbids reinsurance-related statutory collateral requirements within the EU. This has gone some way toward encouraging the United States in the same direction. The National Association of Insurance Commissioners (NAIC) has drafted a proposal which envisages that cross-border non-US reinsurers may be allowed to put up reduced collateral, if they come from an equivalent jurisdiction and meet various other criteria including holding certain ratings. This proposal does not become law until implemented into state law. European reinsurers, including Lloyd's, see it as a positive step. They have campaigned for many years to remove the onerous and discriminatory 100 per cent collateral requirements that the United States has required of alien reinsurers.

Under the Reinsurance Directive, EU reinsurers may operate throughout the whole EU, including the Central and Eastern Europe accession states, on a cross-border basis without the need to use a branch or subsidiary authorised locally. This is an opportunity to capitalise on the growth prospects in those regions. These countries now have regulatory frameworks consistent with those of the more developed EU economies.

Solvency 11

The European Commission's proposal for a Solvency 11 Directive is scheduled to enter into force in 2012. It represents a major step forward for some of the newer EU member states, although less so for the United Kingdom, where the FSA has had a stringent system of capital-adequacy assessment in place for several years. The United States, which currently has something of a risk-based solvency regime for insurers, is not involved.

The Solvency 11 regime consolidates the provisions of existing EU insurance deliverables as well as setting new risk-based standards of capital adequacy. Insurers may choose to model this capital requirement either on a standard approach or, subject to regulatory approval, on an internal model. Some large UK composite insurers have already been using internal models for some years.

By early 2009, the main remaining area of discussion was group support, which is about transferability of capital from one operation to another within the same group under the group supervision proposal. The UK insurance industry sees this as an important part of the risk-based approach of Solvency 11.

The critics of group support, originally 12 EU states led by Spain, had two main objections: that the concept was too complicated, and that it gave too much power to group supervisors, depriving solo supervisors. The EC had wanted group support. By early 2009, the European Council had agreed on a proposal in which group support is considerably watered down, but the European parliament had agreed to a version of Solvency 11 with group support, and was in a position to have a second reading.

A compromise solution is inevitable. Group support will probably disappear or be watered down and one possibility is the 'opt in/opt out' option, where certain member states will opt into group support rules, and others will not.

Reinsurers will play a new role, according to Denis Kessler, chairman and chief executive of leading French reinsurer SCOR. Presenting from the podium of the Insurance Institute of London at Lloyd's Old Library in March 2008, he said that primary insurers would be making new demands on reinsurers for solvency relief, and that reinsurers would be providing more risk-management services.

10

Financial services regulation

Introduction

In this chapter we will look at financial services regulation and compliance. With the credit crisis of 2007–09, regulatory initiatives are seen as vital in helping to restore financial stability and to prevent future excess.

Overview

Financial services regulation across the world varies in its sophistication but takes its standards particularly from two sophisticated regulators, the SEC in the United States and the FSA in the United Kingdom, both of which have made significant mistakes in the credit crisis. The pan-European legislation now largely implemented under the Financial Services Action Plan is also a role model for regulatory harmonisation, although far from a perfect one.

The SEC regulates the US securities industry but not commercial banks, which, in the United States, have several regulators. US state insurance departments regulate the insurance industry. The SEC carries out tough enforcement action and levies fines of a size unheard of in the United Kingdom; but since its failure to act on tip-offs in relation to the Madoff fraud revealed in late 2008, a different picture has emerged. Many have accused the SEC of timidity and incompetence, as well as kowtowing to the most powerful figures on Wall Street. The SEC has a rules-based approach, which is an invitation to regulated firms to explore loopholes.

The FSA, in contrast, has a principles-based regime, which gives firms a little more leeway in how they operate than the US regime, but also makes it easier for the regulator to make a case against them. How long this regime will stay in place remains to be seen. There are fears that as a result of the credit crisis it may shift more to a rules-only approach, as in the United States.

The FSA, as regulator, is part of a tripartite system in which the treasury is responsible for banking legislation and the Bank of England is responsible for financial stability. In the aftermath of the Northern Rock scandal, the tripartite system has come under criticism. The Bank of England is seen as unsympathetic to banks and the FSA as insufficiently tough on them. In the Netherlands, in contrast, there is a single regulator that aims to ensure the solvency of the banks and the financial system.

The US and UK regulators are constantly engaged in dialogue. The EU's financial service legislation is a huge bureaucratic burden on the FSA, which is more sophisticated than most other European regulators, and takes up a great deal of its time. It has elements of both the UK's principles-based and the US's rules-based approaches.

Beyond the EU, national supervisory approaches borrow particularly from the US and UK models. In practice, many regulatory regimes have been powerless to prevent market manipulation, fraud and other breaches of regulation, because their sanctions are more limited than they would like. Russia has been rife with market manipulation. But following the credit crisis, the Russian government in February 2009 approved amendments to the criminal code that could jail traders, journalists and officials for up to seven years for insider trading. Separately it was also introducing a new law on insider dealing. There are fears that the inclusion of journalists in the amendments could give the Kremlin greater control over the media.

Some of the newer EU states such as in central Europe have found it easier to adapt to EU legislation than more sophisticated jurisdictions because they start from a clean slate. Countries in continental Europe with a more prescriptive regulatory regime find it easier to adapt than does the UK.

Some EU directives have attracted criticism. The FSA has suggested that the Insurance Mediation Directive is confused and ill thought out. The Markets in Financial Instruments Directive (MiFID), implemented in November 2007, has had at least partial success in achieving its aim of establishing EU standards in some areas of investment business, including transparency, best execution, client classification, transaction reporting and data classification. The MiFID has, however, been slow and expensive to implement and some differences in standards across jurisdictions remain. Dark pool venues (see Chapter 16) have undermined some of the market transparency, and best execution requirements have not seen brokers using all the new trading venues. Fragmentation has made post-trading reporting more complex.

The Capital Requirements Directive is the common framework for the implementation of Basel II rules on capital measurement and capital standards, and there have been problems here. Several broker-dealers in the United States had problems because of high leverage, although, under Basel II, they were well capitalised on a risk-adjusted basis. There are concerns that Basel II does not consider systemic risks.

Lessons from the 2007–09 credit crisis

Compliance failures as well as fraud and sharp practice in the financial services industry serve as a perpetual reminder that our regulators are sometimes inadequate. In 2008, the FSA admitted to faults in the way it had regulated Northern Rock.

International organisations of regulators such as IOSCO and the International Association of Insurance Supervisors encourage members to cooperate and exchange information. This is a step in the right direction but the problem lies deeper – more to do with the ignorance and apathy of the regulators, perhaps linked with their low status and rewards in comparison with those of the regulated community.

The United States in particular has a lot of movement between the public and private sectors, which happens in the financial services regulatory regime like anywhere else. An individual working for the regulator one day could move into a much more highly paid job with a bank the next. In the aftermath of the Madoff fraud (see Chapter 11), the SEC's future role as securities regulator has come under scrutiny. The March 2008 Paulson blueprint for US financial services regulatory reform has proposed putting the Federal Reserve in the role of overseeing risk. The SEC would remain an important regulator focused on disclosure and enforcement but it would no longer be the main body for regulating the securities industry.

If a new super regulator, such as the Fed or another, replaces existing bureaucracies, there will be political controversy. There is a feeling that if authority is transferred to a federal regulator, state regulators would lose power, which would be unpopular politically. The only way to achieve a new structure may be to have an overlay of federal regulation on the existing system; but according to lawyers, this may not work.

Another possibility mooted in the Paulson blueprint is that the SEC should combine with the Commodities Futures Trading Commission (CFTC), the US futures regulator. In December 2008, Barack Obama, US president-elect and a Democrat, nominated Mary Schapiro, chief executive of FINRA, the largest independent regulator for all securities firms doing business in the United States, as chairman of the SEC, to replace Republican Christopher Cox. She is a former chairman of the CFTC. This would make her well placed to oversee a combined CFTC and SEC, which is seen as a likely development despite political pressures against it. In practice, the agricultural committees in Congress which oversee the CFTC will be reluctant to concede power to the banking and finance committees, which oversee the SEC.

With Barack Obama as president of the United States, financial services regulation generally is likely to increase at a time when there is a perceived need for it. Obama's track record gave the first signs of this. In recent years he has proposed various regulatory changes. He has demanded increased oversight of financial services institutions and stronger capital requirements, including in mortgage-backed securities. He had called for hedge funds to come more under federal supervision.

The US regulatory system is very piecemeal and many consider that reforms are long overdue. To add to the confusion, there is both state and SEC regulation of investment advisers. A firm can report as an investment adviser with the SEC or with a state, so the situation can arise where an investment adviser is not registered with either.

In the aftermath of the Madoff fraud, there is some call for a self-regulatory organisation for investment advisers. FINRA is a candidate and is seen as having resources for enforcement and inspection that the SEC does not. One trade body opposes the move on the ground that it would be expensive and bureaucratic.

In Europe, there have also been moves to heavier regulation, although not with the threat of a complete overhaul that has arisen in the United States. The spectre of systemic risk now overhangs the world. In the United Kingdom, Lord Adair Turner, chairman of the FSA, said in *The Economist*'s Inaugural City Lecture on 21 January 2009 that the 'originate and distribute' model of finance lending had a role to play in the future but needed to be reformed, with less opacity. He outlined three key long-term regulatory measures to reduce the probability and severity of future crises. These were: new approaches to capital adequacy, as part of which banks would prepare buffers in good times so that they could draw on them in bad; a new liquidity regime based on market-wide risk as well as in individual jurisdictions; and ensuring the regulation of financial activity according to its economic substance, not its legal form.

In February 2009, the FSA said that its budget, raised from regulated firms, was to rise by 36.5 per cent to £438 million in 2008 as it hired more supervisors and increased pay rates. The regulator has said it will take a more intrusive line with financial services companies, and it has quietly indicated a new approach to regulation, replacing its principles-based approach with outcomes-based regulation. The aim here is that FSA member firms should consider the consequences of what they do.

Money laundering and fraud

Introduction

In this chapter we will focus on money laundering, a crime that is rarely caught. We will also look at fraud, which tends to be practised, and revealed, in difficult economic times.

Money laundering

Money laundering is the washing of dirty money through the financial system to make it clean. It works in three phases. The first is placement, in which the launderer introduces dirty money, the proceeds of crime, into the legitimate financial system; the second phase is layering, by which he or she attempts to separate the proceeds in time and space from the original acquisitive crime by moving them through a series of financial transactions; the third stage is integration, at the end of which the launderer has created a legitimate explanation for the source of these funds, allowing themselves to use them openly as an individual would use honestly acquired assets.

When the conventional banking system seems too risky, some launderers may use the *hawala* system, which works by allowing cheap and unrecorded money transfers. A person pays dollars in the United States to a broker, who informs his partner in another country, who makes an equivalent payment in the local currency. No physical transfer of funds will have taken place, and the broker and partner settle amounts owed through fake invoices relating to, for example, their firm's claimed import–export business.

According to John Cassara, an American expert in terrorist finance, hawala could have helped to finance the November 2008 attack on civilians in Mumbai, widely believed to be the work of Lashkar-e-Taiba (Army of the Good), or LeT, a pseudo Al Qaeda outfit.

Know your customer

Financial services regulation and legislation focus on account-opening procedures, the hope being to detect placement at this stage. Banks and other financial firms must verify the customer's identity, using 'Know your customer' (KYC) procedures, and should recognise and report suspicious transactions.

The processes are far from foolproof and the ongoing shift towards electronic banking and electronic money may debilitate them further. To deposit amounts too small to trigger reports, *smurfers* make small payments to accounts in many banks simultaneously. Money launderers are sometimes helped by corrupt individuals within financial services firms, or by the firms themselves or corrupt officials, politicians, lawyers and other advisers.

Money launderers can easily conceal their identities, for example, by using false passports. The money-laundering reporting officers appointed by financial services firms are not typically trained to detect the fakes.

The official response

At a global level, the Financial Action Task Force on money laundering (FATF) was established by the G7 summit held in Paris in 1989. It was given the task of examining money laundering, reviewing action taken and setting out an action plan. The FATF started with 16 members and now has 34. In April 1990, it published its '40 Recommendations on Money Laundering', which it has since revised.

The Bank Secrecy Act (BSA) of 1970 was the first US legislation to combat money laundering. It requires banks to report cash transactions of US$10,000 (£6,700) or more. The Money Laundering Control Act of 1986 amended the BSA to make it more effective and defined money laundering as a federal crime. To avoid BSA reporting became a criminal offence.

Shortly after the September 2001 attacks on the United States, the US government launched the USA PATRIOT Act (Providing Appropriate Tools Required to Intercept and Obstruct Terrorism) to combat international terrorism. Under the act, financial institutions must make specified KYC checks. US law enforcement has significantly more powers with the purpose of fighting terrorism. The act introduced *reverse* money laundering, the criminal purposes to which money is put after it leaves the bank.

The PATRIOT Act aimed to control foreign banks dealing with US institutions and has led to substantial anti-money laundering activity, much perhaps for form's sake. Non-US financial institutions that fail to comply with the act may be denied access to all financial markets dealing in US dollars.

The first EU Money Laundering Directive was introduced in 1991, in response to the FATF's '40 Recommendations on Money Laundering', and became legislation in member states. Its only predicate offence was money laundering from the proceeds of drug trafficking.

The second EU Money Laundering Directive in 2001 widened the predicate offences to include organised crime, corruption and other serious crimes, and it brought new *gatekeepers* such as accountants into the regulated sector.

The third Money Laundering Directive was implemented by the end of 2007. The directive incorporated the FATF's 40 Recommendations into law and has added terrorist financing to the predicate offences. There were some new definitions, including one for politically exposed persons, and more detail, including a distinction between enhanced and simplified due diligence.

The directive has an explicit risk-based approach written into it, which means that firms must apply a proportionate approach, focusing more on areas of greater risk. The UK treasury has acknowledged industry complaints that some jurisdictions might take advantage of this flexibility, but takes the view that good regulation rather than more EU legislation is the answer.

Laundered funds have often been fraudulently acquired. The financial services industry attracts fraudsters because of its substantial movements of money through various asset classes and its global connections. Let us see how they work.

A hopeless task

In general, money launderers working across borders have been too sophisticated, well resourced and high-tech-savvy for the banks and financial institutions, and for regulators and law enforcement agencies. The result is that few are caught. Regulators do, however, take action against financial institutions that have inadequate systems, controls and procedures to prevent money laundering. To cover their backs, firms file reports and governments introduce new legislation.

Fraud

An unwelcome side effect of the credit crunch is the widely acknowledged upsurge in revelations of past fraud, as companies tighten up their due diligence standards, and in actual current fraud, including by opportunists looking to make quick and easy money in hard times.

The Madoff scandal was a prime example of a past fraud coming to light. It is worth looking at the case in detail as a prime example of how investor greed can overcome common sense. The red flags were there.

The Madoff scandal

In December 2008, news broke that the FBI had arrested investment adviser Bernard Madoff and charged him and Bernard L Madoff Investment Securities, his brokerage firm, with securities fraud. Madoff had told relatives that his investment advisory business was 'just one big lie' and 'basically, a giant Ponzi scheme', according to the SEC complaint.

Madoff once ran a legitimate business, which went wrong, at which point he started the Ponzi scheme, paying existing investors with money coming in from new ones. His victims were particularly among the Jewish community, which was his own, making this an example of affinity fraud, where bonds of trust in ethnic communities make it easier for con men. But the net had spread far more widely across the world, with victims including colleges, charitable organisations, pension funds, banks, hedge funds, funds of hedge funds, and individuals.

The SEC is under investigation for its failure to investigate the fraud despite the fact that whistle-blowers had alerted it to warning signs. The SEC enjoyed cordial relationships with Madoff. Meanwhile, Madoff's niece Shana Madoff, a compliance lawyer at Madoff's firm, is married to Eric Swanson, former SEC assistant director in the office of compliance inspections and examinations. Swanson started his romantic relationship with his wife-to-be only after the compliance team he helped supervise inquired about Bernard Madoff's securities operations.

In 2008, Bernard L Madoff Investment Securities had US$700 million of equity capital and had dealt with 10 per cent of New York Stock Exchange trading volume. A suspiciously small number of employees operated his investment strategy, a warning sign in itself. Madoff claimed that he made 10–12 per cent a year on a consistent basis and he was clever enough to reduce the return slightly in bad years to make it seem more plausible.

Madoff had seemed to achieve the steady returns using what he called the split-strike conversion strategy with options, which is also known as a collar. He sold out-of-the-money call options and bought out-of-the-money put options, both on the S&P 100 index, while holding stocks correlated to that index. The sale of the call options would offset gains in the underlying stock portfolio beyond a certain level and the purchase of the put options would similarly offset losses.

This strategy was a protective put combined with a covered call. Commentators said that it was too expensive for a portfolio the size of Madoff's and, if implemented, would have led to more volatility than his returns suggested. A more obvious warning sign was that Madoff conducted his own custodian and administrator functions, and traded his managed accounts through his own broker-dealer, meaning that there were no independent checks. Bernard L Madoff Securities was family held, which should also have roused suspicions, and was audited by an unknown three-man auditor, ostensibly to save costs. The air of secrecy around the whole business enhanced Madoff's reputation although it kept his investment strategy something of a black box. Investors accepted this, provided the returns kept coming in.

Madoff did not answer questions or see many customers. He acted as if he did not need new customers. He was a former chairman of NASDAQ who hobnobbed with high-level regulators, including at the SEC, and had a sterling Wall Street reputation. Only a few people raised red flags and they were not heeded. Madoff did not provide customers with electronic account access as other brokers do, and he sent only paper tickets, sometimes without time stamps, to the feeder funds that funnelled money to him on behalf of investors.

The feeder funds did not always even reveal Madoff's name to clients. They charged these investors a management fee, typically 2 per cent, and a performance fee, typically 20 per cent, or both, which is standard for hedge funds. Madoff saw none of it. The fact that he was willing to forgo these fees, making money only from standard commissions on the trades, should have been a warning. The feeder funds were audited by major respectable auditors such as PricewaterhouseCoopers and KPMG, staving off suspicion, although these auditors relied, as they are allowed to do, on the audits of Madoff's own firm.

There are a lot of questions with regard to the Madoff case which need further clarification, including whether he had been front-running, which means using information from market making to trade securities ahead of placing client orders, and whether he had been operating alone. One overwhelming issue is how the SEC missed the Madoff scandal and similar frauds. As it turned out, Boston accountant and former money manager Harry Markopolos first told the SEC in 1999 that he suspected Madoff's business was a Ponzi scheme. He had a small team of investigators working on the case and he kept trying to bring it to the regulator's attention – without success.

The SEC is no doubt under-resourced and its staff are not always sufficiently skilled or experienced to recognise a scam, but the legitimate question has arisen whether the SEC has had the will to investigate high-profile Wall Street figures generally.

The fallout from the Madoff scam is keeping lawyers busy. As the Madoff ripple expands from the United States, including into the United Kingdom, parties may stand accused of failing to carry out their due diligence on the scheme. This could include fund managers who involved people in the scheme and auditors accused of not picking up fraudulent activity. In this way, the effect is likely to follow broadly the same pattern as the fallout from the credit crisis, in which ripples are still spreading across the Atlantic.

US auditors are already the targets of claims that arise from the Madoff fraud, and investors in Madoff funds may be asked to pay back profits they had made. The way this works will be very fact specific and ultimately an issue for the courts to decide. In the United Kingdom, unlike in the United States, the unsuccessful party must almost always meet the costs of litigation.

If large enough losses arise from the Madoff scandal, many will make claims, whether or not they have merit. Such claims will potentially be costly to defend. Levels of professional indemnity and directors' and officers' (D&O) cover that are available to meet such claims vary enormously. A D&O policy generally continues to pay defence costs where there is a covered claim for fraud against a director unless and until there is an admission or discovery of fraud.

Other Madoff-style frauds are happening, and that too is an issue. At the time of writing, various allegations are beginning to emerge. In February 2008, the SEC filed civil fraud charges against Sir Allen Stanford, a Texan billionaire, to stop an alleged scheme involving US$8 billion in certificates of deposit sold through Stanford International Bank, his Antigua-based bank which took in deposits but did not, however, make loans. Sir Allen denies any wrongdoing.

According to the SEC complaint, the certificates promised improbable and unsubstantiated high interest rates. These rates were supposedly earned through the bank's investment strategy, which claimed to enable double-digit returns on investments over the last 15 years.

Boiler rooms

Boiler rooms, often operating as pretend stockbrokers, are another form of fraud that regulators have been slow to stop. Phoney share offers, often presented as IPOs, or advanced fee scams, or perhaps high-yield bonds that do not exist and similar are the types of deal that the boiler rooms offer across continents. The boiler rooms are often linked to organised crime. They have plausible websites, sometimes borrowing a bona fide regulator's logo illegally, and their posh-sounding telephone sales people will call investors from hideout offices. The telephone numbers they give out are to switching offices that divert the calls to them. Clients do not know even from which country they are calling. Once a client has been duped, they cannot easily come after the boiler room salespeople, and nor can law enforcement officials.

Typically, the boiler rooms are based in jurisdictions where the police and regulators leave them alone provided they do not sell to nationals. Favourite locations are Barcelona or Marbella, but have also been Costa Rica, Dublin or Eastern Europe, including Croatia.

Behind the boiler rooms is a proven infrastructure. The dealing manager, who is never the main perpetrator, recruits young people, often middle-class dropouts desperate to make money, and tells them to sell shares.

The most aggressive boiler rooms will pay their salespeople – the lifeblood of their business, of course – between 10 and 60 per cent of the money they rake in from gullible investors. The commission rates are so high because it is stolen money. The approach used is high-pressure selling and it is, like any selling, a numbers game. Salespeople will try to shame, browbeat, bully, sweet-talk or simply wear out any likely victim over the phone to send in a cheque for shares in a small company that may be nothing more than a brass number plate offshore. Behind the scenes, a promoter is raking in the money left after sales commissions, with or without honouring other expenses such as office leases, and staving off investigations from law-enforcement officials – with assistance from respectable law firms, which may not be paid.

It is not generally understood that boiler rooms are not always separate from Wall Street and the City of London. They can be one end of a continuum. Respectable regulated broking firms regularly push dubious penny stocks on naive retail investors, stocks in which they themselves may have a stake. They may be using all kinds of dubious techniques to sell the shares but which, unlike those of the continental boiler rooms, stop short of outright lies.

For example, it is against UK regulations for stockbrokers to churn customer accounts, meaning to trade them excessively only for the sake of generating commission. But unscrupulous firms can get around that by leading the customer to suggest selling one stock in order to go into another. If the suggestion comes from the customer, it is hard to present a case that it was at the broker's urgent promoting that the client so proceeded. This is one small weapon in the dubious broker's armoury. Other tactics are to refuse to sell stock for a client by not being available on the telephone to take sell orders, or to persuade the client to wait a few weeks, or to hint at 'big news around the corner' – an invention to persuade the client to continue holding the shares.

Boiler rooms and other dubious stockbrokers proliferated in the late 1980s and, 20 years on, not much has changed. The boiler rooms are still running roughshod over law enforcement and regulators. Certainly these august parties are doing more than they did to address the issues. The SEC sometimes brings an action against individuals running a boiler room and widely publicises it.

This is the tip of the iceberg and it has been argued that the United States, in allowing what are known as 'Regulation S' shares to be sold only to non-US citizens, does not care about boiler room activity outside its jurisdiction. Regulation S allows US companies to sell stock overseas without registration under the Securities Act, which means that non-US citizens are not given the same level of protection as their US counterparts. The boiler rooms often push *Reg S* companies, perhaps quoted on the US Pink Sheets, which are not a stock exchange. These have in the past included some fraudulent companies. To qualify for a Reg S exemption, shares must be sold offshore to a non-US resident and not resold into the United States for a year. There can be an international market in the meantime for the shares but, in practice, they can be very hard to sell.

Regulators are slow to react. They publish lists of boiler rooms, which, as they acknowledge, are quickly out of date. Boiler room promoters change their names in a twinkling, close down websites and start up new ones, and even catch their victims a second time through advance fee recovery firms, which they secretly run themselves.

Nor can the police keep up with the boiler-room fraudsters, although they have a better understanding of how they work than do some of the regulators. Their problem is lack of resourcing. The City of London police are better resourced than most. Operation Archway, established as a City database against boiler-room activity, has had some success in closing down a few operations, including in continental Europe in cooperation with their local counterparts. The Serious Fraud Office (SFO) is also focusing on boiler rooms. None of this is ever enough. Ironically, as surveys by the FSA have shown, the victims are experienced investors.

The FSA may feel vindicated in going after UK advisers, such as lawyers, who help in boiler-room promotions, after it announced in February 2009 that it had appealed successfully against a tribunal hearing by solicitor Fox Hayes, based in Leeds. The regulator had originally acted against Fox Hayes and, in September 2006, had fined it £146,000, noting that the law firm had exploited its FSA-regulated status to approve promotions from overseas boiler rooms that used high-pressure sales techniques to sell US-listed shares to UK investors. It later emerged that Robert Manning, senior partner at Fox Hayes, had personally received substantial commission from the foreign unauthorised overseas companies, on top of fees that his law firm earned for its services.

Fox Hayes appealed to the Financial Services and Markets Tribunal, an appeal body for regulatory decisions. At the tribunal, the FSA argued that Fox Hayes had breached financial promotions rules and had failed to conduct its business with due skill, care and diligence. The tribunal found, however, that Fox Hayes had made enquiries into its clients and had some safeguards in place to protect investors' money. It said that the FSA did not give Fox Hayes adequate advice and help when the firm contacted it, and had failed to give clear warnings and guidance about boiler rooms. The tribunal reduced the fine to £80,000.

The court of appeal then upheld the FSA's decision and increased the penalty levied on Fox Hayes to £954,770, including the £454,770 commission that Manning had earned. Although the earlier tribunal had taken the offer of a research report from the boiler rooms at face value and deemed it not to be a financial promotion, the court of appeal took into account what it judged to be the ulterior motive behind the offer.

Insurance fraud

Fraud can also arise in the insurance industry. Independent Insurance was an award-winning United Kingdom-based insurance company that turned out to be heavily involved in fraud. In October 2007, the SFO concluded a successful prosecution of three senior directors of Independent Insurance. All three defendants were found guilty of conspiracy to defraud various parties by dishonestly withholding claims data from actuaries Watson Wyatt. Two of the three were also found guilty of conspiring to defraud parties by dishonestly making incomplete disclosure of reinsurance contracts.

There are now fewer, however, of the types of reinsurance scam that arose internationally before and during the early 1990s, run by fraudsters such as the late Alan Teale. These were reinsurance companies backed by dubious or non-existent assets, which made money by providing fake reinsurance in hard-to-get lines of business. Some of these frauds were completely outrageous. For example, at least one fraudulent reinsurer claimed to be domiciled in Melchizedek, a fake country named after a biblical figure. The fiction persists even now, discredited though it is, and fools a new generation of victims. Of similar ilk was Sovereign Cherokee Nation Tejas, a phony Indian tribe, which was supposed to hold valuable assets for offshore reinsurers, some consisting of highly valued treasures buried in the ground. The tribe was a scam. Some perpetrators of these frauds are still in business, although they have spent a time in jail, but their operations today are more low key. The world has become more focused on measurability of reinsurance assets.

Claim fraudsters too are finding that the credit crisis of 2007–09 is not necessarily an invitation to make money. Claimants on warehouse fires in Russia have found it difficult to convince major insurers that their claims are bona fide.

The insurance industry has suffered. Organised criminal gangs, often from Eastern Europe, have also run into some problems with their scams based on contrived motor accidents for the purpose of insurance fraud. The United Kingdom's Insurance Fraud Bureau has prosecuted more than 200 such cases over a recent two-year period.

According to Paul Newham, detective inspector at the national terror financial investigation unit at New Scotland Yard, speaking at the Securities and Investment Institute's financial crime and fraud conference in April 2008, these contrived accidents are one of the typically low-key strategies that Al Qaeda uses to raise money for terrorism. He stressed that fraud as a method of financing terrorism could occur across all financial instruments, not just insurance.

Professional fraudsters do not, however, confine their activities to a single jurisdiction. They know that the more borders they can cross with a scam, the more likely they are to get away with it, and the more difficult it is for law enforcement and the regulators to act quickly.

UK fraud investigation

Overview

In the UK, financial services fraud is investigated by the City of London police, or, if it is large and complex, perhaps by the SFO. The SFO's cases tend to have a four- to five-year gestation period, and the cumulative conviction rate stands at about 70 per cent a year. The SFO has had some high-profile successes, including the BCCI investigation, which led to six convictions, the latest in April 1997, and the Barlow Clowes case, where the principal defendant Peter Clowes was sentenced to 10 years in February 1992. The SFO's failures have been no less publicised. One was the Blue Arrow trial, which cost taxpayers an estimated £40 million. Another was the 1996 indictment of Ian and Kevin Maxwell, sons of Robert Maxwell. They were found not guilty of fraud charges after a trial that had lasted eight months and cost taxpayers £25 million. This is one of the cases that led to government proposals to scrap jury trials in complex fraud cases on the basis that juries do not understand complex fraud. The House of Lords has so far rejected the proposals.

In recent years, the SFO has become better resourced, although critics say that it still does not attract the best investigative staff because it cannot afford to pay private-sector rates. The SFO has a budget of around £40 million a year, funded by the treasury, to cover the normal run of operations and has the ability to make applications for more.

Recently the SFO has increased its speed of operating and efficiency, taking into account criticisms made by Jessica De Grazia, a former senior prosecutor in the United States. She was commissioned in March 2007 to report on the working practices of the agency.

One of her criticisms was that it took the SFO six months on average to decide whether there was a case. The SFO has reduced this to a month, placing less reliance on referrals. In February 2009, an example of an early preliminary inquiry was into the UK operations of AIG Financial Products Corp, the non-insurance subsidiary of American International Group. The US government had to rescue AIG last September as a result of the subsidiary's heavy losses from insuring securities backed by toxic mortgage debt.

This particular investigation is an example of how the SFO is now working closely with the US authorities, including daily contact with the FBI and the Department of Justice. The SFO has talked of moving towards a new globalised system in which investigators could deal with UK and US authorities together instead of speaking to each separately.

The SFO has revamped its operations to be more efficient, with more shared work, so that lawyers are working on several cases rather than just one, and resources are spread across three domains: City fraud, overseas corruption and bribery, and share marketing fraud, including boiler rooms. The SFO does not make deals that guarantee immunity from prosecution, but wants people to come forward and talk.

As part of its new-look approach, the SFO has appointed Vivian Robinson QC as general counsel from April 2009 to have oversight over the office's operations, sit on the board and supervise every case. De Grazia noted a SFO conviction rate of 60 per cent, which the SFO is looking to build on. Problems remain, including lack of overseas cooperation in some cases. The SFO focuses on complex frauds and pursues not just convictions but confiscations, of which, unlike some law enforcement agencies, it gives back a large proportion to the victims.

The FSA takes an interest in fraud if it is linked to system and control failures. For example, in December 2007, the FSA announced that it had fined Norwich Union's life and pensions business a record £1.26 million for putting its customers at risk of fraud by failing to protect confidential information.

The Fraud Act 2006

In the United Kingdom, The Fraud Act 2006 came into force in January 2007, replacing the complicated array of over-specific and overlapping deception offences. It established a new general offence of fraud, comprising false representation both by failing to disclose information and by abuse of position.

The Fraud Review, commissioned by the UK government and published in July 2006, was followed by public consultation and, in March 2007, the government launched its response, 'Fighting Fraud Together'. It proposes steps such as setting up a National Fraud Strategic Authority to lead and coordinate fraud-prevention activities, and a National Fraud Reporting Centre to gather intelligence and measure fraud.

The idea is to provide a one-stop shop for fraud victims and to prevent duplication in fraud reporting, providing a more sophisticated sharing of data between different areas of financial services, government and non-government agencies. The proposals include encouragement of early guilty pleas through a safe legal framework, which protects defendants' rights but also improves the experience for victims.

Electronic fraud

Fraud has increasingly penetrated cyberspace. Data breaches can have a major impact on brands, and electronic information assets are often more critical to business than data centre buildings and hardware. In January 2008, employment website Monster.com revealed that hackers had accessed personal information of millions of job seekers. While it was unclear what financial loss might follow, experts said that there was a major potential impact on the business's reputation.

Canada, Australia, Thailand and Korea are among the countries that have enacted data protection legislation. For credit cards, there is the Payment Card Industry Data Security Standard (PCI DSS), which is a global set of requirements for merchants and credit card processors. The credit card companies are expected to follow rules but this does not mean security in the case of, for example, a novel attack. Insurers expect security to be in place if they are to cover data security breaches.

Cybercriminals now seek a slice of the money changing hands in e-commerce. They commit identity theft or extortion, or distribute malware (malicious software) on the internet as an intermediate measure, according to Dr Neil Daswani, security engineer at Google. His 2008 presentations on the topic are available on YouTube. The attacker profile has shifted from amateurs to professionals, including organised criminal networks, and the biggest 'attack goal' is stealing sensitive information such as credit card numbers. There are black-economy networks where, for example, stolen credit card numbers may be swapped for a number of infected computers, or simply sold for say US$10.00 per credit card number.

Criminals may hack into a website using SQL injection. This has been defined as a code injection exploiting vulnerability in security arising in the database layer of an application. A malicious code is inserted, making up a database command such as 'Delete all information about users from the database.' This enables the criminals to steal information. Another way to break into a website is the cross-site-request forgery, which is a malicious exploitation of a website in which unauthorised commands are transmitted from a user that the website trusts.

Daswani notes that cybercriminals can infect machines and have them connected to a server they control. A few years ago, a virus or worm would infect first one computer, then other linked computer users. Now the crooks find the web a better way to distribute malware. They break into websites and add a snippet of code, sourcing in extra content from perhaps Russia or China; when a user visits the web page, the code will infect their computer. The crooks have automated the attacks. They make inquiries of search engines and request lists of vulnerable websites for this purpose. A group of malware-infected computers is known as a botnet, and may be used to attack other computer systems. It is a way to steal identities, or data for ransom. The crooks send out e-mails that appear to come from a respectable source, and with exciting news items and a click-through link that leads to an infected site. Once malware is installed on a computer, it can log all the user's keystrokes.

There are ways to prevent the attacks. As part of his advice, Daswani cautions users against using WEP (wired equivalence privacy) as a protocol, and instead recommends WPA (Wi-Fi protected access). Perhaps the largest cyber attack of all time, revealed in early 2007, was the theft of 45 million credit card numbers from TJX, a US holding company for stores. This was a direct result of the vulnerability of WEP protocol. To avoid using cables, the TJX stores used Wi-Fi technology to transmit credit card numbers from the point-of-sale station to back-end servers. They attempted to protect the process using the WEP protocol but had not upgraded it. The attackers found that they could gather wireless traffic and, thanks to the vulnerability, reverse engineer the encryption, figure out the key and decrypt the traffic. They had been doing this for months, stealing credit cards for transactions since 2002.

If you are interested in finding out more about how cybercriminals work, visit Neil Daswani's website at www.neildaswani.com, where there is a link on the front page to one of his YouTube presentations.

In the United States, notification to an affected group is required when sensitive personal data has been accessed. This does not apply in the EU, but there are strong regulatory requirements to prevent unauthorised sharing or marketing of data. In many countries, including in the United Kingdom, data owners or collectors are responsible for data transferred to outside vendors, which covers outsourcing.

12

Corporate governance and accounting

Introduction

Corporate governance has never been perfect. Just when the worst problems in this area, such as Enron and WorldCom, seem to have disappeared, new ones, such as at Satyam Computer Services (see Chapter 18), arise. In this chapter we will look at how corporate governance and accounting work.

Overview

Corporate governance is about how a company conducts its corporate affairs and responds to stakeholders, employees and society. It covers ethical, legislative and other rules specifying how a company should act.

Most countries in Europe have a *comply or explain* code. The concept is now recognised in EU law in the 4th Company Law Directive. The EC has said that it sees no need for a single corporate governance code across the EU and that, in most cases, rules should be left to each member state. But it has introduced some common requirements to be implemented.

Under the revised 4th Company Law Directive, all EU-registered companies listed on an EU stock exchange must include in their annual reports a statement on how they have complied with the relevant national code, and describe their internal controls related to financial reporting.

In the United Kingdom, the FSA's principles-based regime, with its emphasis on management responsibility, makes corporate governance a major issue. Regulators, senior management, listing authorities, analysts and investor-related trade bodies have an interest.

The United Kingdom's Combined Code on Corporate Governance sets out standards of good practice in, for example, board composition and development, remuneration, accountability, audit and relations with shareholders. The code requires boardroom practice to be clearer and more formal. All United Kingdom-listed companies are required under the listing rules to report on how they have applied the Combined Code in their annual report and accounts. Overseas companies listed on the main market are required to disclose how their corporate governance practices differ significantly from those set out in the code. Recently, a revision to the Combined Code has removed a restriction on an individual chairing more than one FTSE 100 company.

In the United States, corporate governance is more rules-based than in the United Kingdom, and enforcement powers rest with the SEC.

Recent history

Corporate governance has made significant progress globally since the business excesses of the late 1980s, including the Polly Peck collapse and Robert Maxwell's theft from the pension funds of Mirror Group Newspapers. In the United States, corporate governance standards tightened up after the WorldCom and Enron scandals, and there has been a ripple effect into other jurisdictions.

Enron

Enron, a now infamous US energy company, saw substantial growth but then collapsed amid an accounting scandal. Enron had been created from the merger of Houston Natural Gas and InterNorth, a Nebraska pipeline company, following which it had substantial debt. Following federal deregulation of natural gas pipelines, Enron had lost exclusive rights to its own pipelines. It found a new way forward, which was to trade energy like stocks and shares. Enron founder Ken Lay hired Jeff Skilling, the consultant who had come up with the idea, to run a new division, Enron Finance Corporation, to implement the plan.

Between 1985 and 1999, Enron's net income rose from US$125 million (£87 million) to US$893 million (£624 million) amid frenetic talk of the new economy and the internet boom. Enron had moved from distributing gas to a role as a first mover in trading energy. At one time, Enron was by stock market value the seventh-largest US company.

Enron had developed a ruthlessly competitive trading culture and by 1992 had become the largest buyer and seller of natural gas in North America. Skilling had told staff at Enron that it was only money that motivated people. He rewarded traders with uncapped bonuses but, through his employee ranking system, the performance review committee, employees were rated on a scale of one to five, with fives typically fired. In 1996, Skilling became Enron's chief operating officer, and soon the company started trading electricity as well as gas, and subsequently moved to trade broadband.

Enron had benefited from the decision in 1993 by the Commodities Futures Trading Commission not to regulate OTC futures transactions in energy, and also from loopholes in the accounting rules. The company exploited mark-to-market accounting, which the SEC allowed in 1991. This form of accounting requires assigning a value to an instrument based on its current market value or that of similar instruments. In energy forward contracts, there was often no active market, and in such circumstances, mark-to-market accounting required marking to model, which has scope for different assumptions. Enron used assumptions that would maximise accounting profit, even when this did not reflect economic reality. In addition, Enron benefited from wash trades. These were situations where only money changed hands, providing the equivalent to a bank loan but which could be booked as working capital rather than, as for a conventional bank loan, long-term debt. This strengthened the company's image of creditworthiness.

Enron also ran off-balance-sheet partnerships, which enabled the company to shift poor performing assets off balance sheet, thus helping to maintain the image of a dynamic growth company. This was done under the leadership of Andrew Fastow, Enron's chief financial officer. He did not break the accounting rules but there was a lack of disclosure and some concealment of the company's true financial state.

The problems became more widely known when Enron made substantial losses from investing in the broadband market. The company had to write off a US$1.01 billion (£0.69 billion) asset impairment, connected with both broadband investment and an off-balance-sheet partnership. This led to its downfall. In December 2001, 10 months after Lay had announced his retirement and named Skilling president and CEO, the company went into Chapter 11 bankruptcy protection amid allegations of accounting irregularities. It became clear that Enron had used off-balance-sheet offshore firms to hide losses. Many executives had gained from the company's high share price by cashing in stock options, but employees who had put their pension money into Enron shares lost all their money.

Arthur Andersen, Enron's auditors, were blamed for not auditing the accounts properly, for destroying evidence of its dealings with Enron, and for taking more money for consultancy fees than for auditing. In 2002, the firm voluntarily surrendered its licences to audit in the United States after it had been found guilty of criminal charges related to its destroying of evidence in connection with Enron. The Supreme Court overturned the verdict but Andersen has not returned as a viable business.

In May 2006, Lay and Skilling were found guilty of fraud, conspiracy and other charges. They had both pleaded not guilty and denied knowledge of fraud schemes, putting the blame partly on Fastow, but the jury had not believed them. Lay died of a heart attack in July, and Fastow was sentenced to six years in jail after pleading guilty to charges of securities fraud and agreeing to testify against his former bosses. In late October, Skilling was sentenced to 24 years in jail but he has maintained his innocence.

WorldCom

Then came news of a US fraud that in financial terms would dwarf even Enron. WorldCom, a large and heavily indebted US telecoms group, had expanded by acquisition, linking up with 75 companies, and at its height had 850,000 employees in 65 countries. Its competitors had reacted by reducing costs, which squeezed profits and left less money for investing in growth.

In June 2002, WorldCom revealed a US$11 billion (£7.6 billion) accounting scam. The company said that its profits between January 2001 and March 2002 had been inflated by US$3.8 billion (£2.6 billion). WorldCom said that its chief financial officer had improperly booked expenses as investment to make the company look healthier than it was. The company had capitalised its long-distance line costs, which are the largest expenses for telecoms capacity. These were represented as an asset instead of being charged to the income statement. This flattered the income. Arthur Andersen, auditor of WorldCom, signed off annual reports to say all was well and did not apply the checks and balances it should have done.

A month later, WorldCom made a Chapter 11 bankruptcy protection filing. It was the biggest bankruptcy in US corporate history. WorldCom shareholders had lost about US$180 billion (£125 billion) and 20,000 workers lost their jobs. In 2004, WorldCom emerged from bankruptcy protection as telecoms group MCI, which, in January 2006, merged with Verizon Communications.

In March 2005, WorldCom boss Bernard Ebbers, a self-made businessman, was found guilty of fraud and conspiracy and seven counts of filing false documents, and in July was sentenced to 25 years in jail. He surrendered substantial assets to settle with WorldCom shareholders.

There have been other major accounting frauds globally, which have been compared with Enron and WorldCom. In December 2003, Parmalat, the Italian food and milk products company, almost defaulted on a small bond issue. Shortly afterwards, it was discovered that the group had falsified its accounts to conceal losses and that substantial sums had been embezzled, mainly by Calisto Tanzi, the group's former chairman and chief executive. In December 2008, Tanzi was jailed for 10 years in the €14 billion (£12.3 billion) scandal, which the press dubbed Italy's Enron.

The Sarbanes–Oxley Act of 2002

Legislative developments were inevitable. The United States Congress phased in the Sarbanes–Oxley Act of 2002 shortly after the Enron fraud as emergency legislation, based on reforms agreed with the New York Stock Exchange.

This act met the recognised need for stricter auditing controls. At Enron, the Arthur Andersen team in charge of the company audit was found to have destroyed documents to conceal the truth, which showed a need for greater controls. The act reinforces the independent status of external auditors and requires procedures that stamp out creative accounting. Financial reports should be auditable and supported by data, as well as protected against alteration, with systems in place to detect this.

Under Sarbanes–Oxley, accountants cannot mix auditing with certain activities, including actuarial or legal services and bookkeeping. Auditors are supervised by a Public Company Accounting Oversight Board that is answerable to the SEC. They are required to maintain audit records for five years. Failure to comply may be punished with a fine and up to 10 years' imprisonment. The company's audit committee must pre-certify all other non-audit work.

The act increases corporate responsibility for any fraudulent actions taken, and there are criminal and civil penalties for securities violations. Controversially, the chief executive and chief financial officer must sign off financial statements to confirm compliance with the provisions of the Securities and Exchange Act, 1934. If the statements turn out to be incorrect, the signatories can be held criminally liable under Sarbanes–Oxley, even if they had not intended deceit. They can receive a fine of up to US$1 million (£0.7 million) and up to 10 years' imprisonment. If they certified the inaccurate statements wilfully, the fine could be US$5 million (£3.3 million) and the prison sentence 20 years.

In addition, significant extra disclosure is required in the report and accounts, as well as ethical guidelines for senior financial officers. Guidelines are required on analysts' conflicts of interest. There is a ban on personal loans to executive officers and directors. Accelerated reporting of trades by insiders is required, with no such trades allowed during pension fund blackout periods.

Sarbanes–Oxley requires organisations to introduce adequate internal control systems and assess their adequacy annually. To assist the process of justice, whistle-blowers are protected. Civil penalties are added to disgorgement funds to relieve victims.

US listings have become less attractive to foreign companies as a result of the Sarbanes–Oxley Act, and the London Stock Exchange has gained. The act applies to those companies that issue securities in the United States, which includes about half of those included on the United Kingdom's FTSE 100 index. It also applies to companies that own a US subsidiary or are required to file reports with the SEC. The company's physical location is not significant, although the national rules of a non-US country will prevail should they conflict with the act.

By early 2007, the United States was starting to soften some of the requirements of Sarbanes–Oxley. Commentators have taken this to be an admission that the legislation has had adverse impact on the competitive position of US financial markets. In March, the SEC published new rules for deregistration by foreign companies, eliminating conditions that had been considered a barrier to entry. Until this point, a foreign issuer could exit the registration and reporting regime only if it had less than 300 resident shareholders. This was a difficult requirement for a foreign issuer to meet, given the increasing globalisation of financial markets.

From March 2007, the criteria for exiting this regime changed, and the new main condition became that the US average daily trading volume of the securities had to be no greater than 5 per cent of the average worldwide trading volume for a recent 12-month period. The SEC said that the amended rules would encourage participation in US markets and increase investor choice. In April, SEC commissioners endorsed measures to improve Sarbanes–Oxley implementation, to ease small company burdens.

Critics say that the act, even in its original form, has not worked well, as the credit crisis has shown. They point out that it has failed to prevent bad oversight of risk by financial institutions that the US government has had to bail out, such as Citigroup and AIG. How far government involvement in the firms will help their corporate governance remains to be seen.

International Financial Reporting Standards

Creative accounting has been a problem in many jurisdictions, not just the United States. In Europe, International Financial Reporting Standards (IFRS) have gone a long way toward stopping this by introducing uniformity and clarity.

For financial years beginning on or after 1 January 2005, IFRS came into force for the consolidated accounts of all listed companies in the EU. They have since been spreading worldwide, albeit in some countries more slowly than in others. The rewards of IFRS implementation are that accounts should reflect economic reality and that the uniformity of accounting should lead to cost savings for multinational groups.

XBRL

XBRL (Xtensible business reporting language) is a computer language that enables additional data to be attached to financial information, such as currencies and accounting concepts, so that when the data is transferred from one system to another, it is recognised, eliminating the need for re-keying or pasting in data.

The concept, backed by the SEC, will enable analysts to do their job faster without the burden and accuracy risk attached to re-keying or without outsourcing such work, and will benefit regulators in preventing another Enron or WorldCom accounting scandal. That, at least, is the idea. At present, some large companies are voluntarily using XBRL data to report to the SEC. Meanwhile, interest in XBRL is spreading to other countries such as India.

The case for IFRS is beginning to convince even the United States. The SEC has voted unanimously to seek public comment on a potential mandatory adoption of IFRS from 2014. Qualifying domestic users may have an opportunity to use it earlier. In the meantime, according to the SEC proposed roadmap for IFRS adoption, IFRS must be improved and XBRL, the international tagging system (see the case study), must be enhanced to accept IFRS data.

In emerging markets, IFRS has made headway. Malaysia expects to amalgamate its accounting standards with IFRS by 2012. In Japan, outright adoption of IFRS is increasingly under consideration at the highest level, which is a change from the previous focus on converging it with Japanese Generally Accepted Accounting Principles (GAAP).

The initial main changes under IFRS are as follows. For the first time, the cost of stock options estimated at the date of grant is expensed to the income statement. Many companies have restructured their remuneration schemes to avoid calculating the expense, which requires option valuation models.

Goodwill must be recognised and tested annually for impairment, and there must be significant disclosure of key assumptions and sensitivities. Accountants say that valuing intangible assets such as brands has proved more complex than anticipated.

Dividends are no longer accrued, unless they are declared before the year end. Deferred taxes are calculated on revaluations as well as on timing differences and feedback suggests that this broad area of accounting has been as challenging as was predicted. There are many methods to apply in accounting for actuarial gains and losses.

The classification of leases into operating or finance accounts has had to be reassessed. Hybrid securities such as preference shares are classified as debt rather than as equity, as was formerly the case. This is because there is a focus on the substance of the transaction which, in this case, may resemble a debt instrument. Pension deficits under IFRS appear on the balance sheet and must be valued, with key assumptions disclosed. Changes in value to investment property must now be reflected in the income statement.

Derivatives must be put on the balance sheet at fair value and marked to market through the income statement. This became an issue in the credit crisis of 2007–09. The question arises as to what should be done when there is no genuine market to mark to. Subjective models have been used, contributing to huge bank write-downs. According to a September 2008 policy paper, 'Climbing out of the credit crunch', published by the Association of Chartered Certified Accountants (ACCA), this can pressurise other players into using the new lower benchmark. The ACCA still believes that the fair-value accounting approach, as part of IFRS, is the best model available.

By the end of 2009, there is likely to be a new international financial reporting standard on consolidation accounting, which will introduce considerably more transparency around structured vehicles, as were used in shadow banking, and will discourage financial engineering. A US initiative is running on its own but roughly in parallel with this consolidation-accounting focus, and has broadly the same disclosure requirements.

This is one example of convergence of regulatory changes across the world. Another is the political pressure to reduce or eliminate huge bonuses for bankers, particularly when they have brought their banks almost to ruin.

The future

In a speech focusing on challenges for EU corporate governance at an October 2008 conference in Paris, Charlie McCreevy, European commissioner for internal markets and services, noted, among other things, that over the past 10 years or so, corporate governance codes had either been adopted or modernised in many European countries and had served EU countries well. This did not mean, however, that codes were always the right solution, and in some situations binding rules might be necessary.

He said that the role that credit rating agencies played in the market turmoil by greatly underestimating the credit risk of structured credit products meant it could no longer be left to them to assess these risks. He proposed an external oversight regime.

McCreevy also noted that some incentive schemes within companies had led to excessive risk taking. He said that compensation incentives should focus not only on short-term gain, but on overall shareholder interest and long-term, firm-wide profitability.

Executive compensation

In some cases, senior executives and others have not been scrutinised enough by boards of directors, and their compensation has reached unacceptable levels. In a London presentation in February 2009, Matthew Fosh, CEO of insurance group Novae, who previously worked in stock-broking and derivatives, said that banks had for years paid bonuses and dividends based on profits that proved fictional and, in the end, had to ask for the money back from shareholders via rescue rights issues.

In early 2009, many people were angered that RBS, now majority owned by the UK taxpayer, was preparing to pay £1 billion in bonuses. The political pressure is on banks to reduce or eliminate bonuses for high earners and UK Chancellor Alistair Darling said that the government was limiting the bonuses that RBS would pay its staff. The Treasury has ordered an investigation into the management of UK banks, and also into the pay and bonuses of top banking executives. This is to be led by Sir David Walker, a former City regulator.

In the United States, President Barack Obama has said that top executives in banks bailed out by the government's TARP initiative would have their salaries capped. France has banned bonuses at banks that receive state aid, and Germany plans the same approach. Other countries such as Switzerland and Russia are discussing salary caps.

In some cases, bankers have contractual arrangements to receive their bonuses, and have hired lawyers to argue that the payments should go ahead.

The *profitability* of best practice in corporate governance is a different issue, and remains uncertain. McKinsey's 'Global Opinion Survey' (2000, updated in 2002), widely quoted opinion-based research, found that 80 per cent of respondents would pay a premium for well-governed companies. Other studies have supported this finding, but scepticism lingers.

Consultants say that, over time, there will be pressure from stock markets, environmental and other groups, and league tables to promote good standards. How far companies see corporate governance as red tape, and how far they apply it in spirit, remain up for discussion.

In Russia, the negative financial trends of 2008 put governance mechanisms of many Russian companies to the test, according to S&P in a December 2008 country governance study. Companies in Russia have exploited legal loopholes to avoid obligations to minority shareholders. The study reports that many Russian companies are satisfied with attaining moderate corporate governance standards in the absence of specific national regulations and in view of the relatively mild governance requirements that most international exchanges present to foreign issuers. With some exceptions, this does not extend as far as establishing effective checks and balances at board level or building a strong independent internal audit.

In India, there has been a widespread perception that companies have corporate governance broadly along US lines, requiring accountability to stakeholders. The fraud revelations at Satyam Computer Services in early 2009 refuted some of this belief.

The general view is that China has a more closed and biased system of corporate governance than India.

Foreign Exchange and You

Adam Evans, edited by **Gretchen C. Mathis,**
Global Public Relations, IBFX / Interbank FX, LLC

The foreign currency trading market, in conjunction with the Off-Exchange Foreign Currency Market, also known as the Forex market, is often considered to be the largest financial market in the world. As such, the market is broken into two distinct parts, institutional and retail.

The institutional side of the Forex market consists of large companies, hedge funds and the central banks of nations. For example, if a British company were to build a factory in a foreign land, it would need to exchange large amounts of British pounds for the currency of the country in which it were to build its factory. The vast majority of activity in the Forex market takes place on the institutional side. It would also be through the institutional side that Soros tries to break the Bank of England again...

The retail side of the Forex market consists of brokers, small banks who sell currency and airport kiosks—any entity that deals in foreign currency exchange at the individual level. At the retail level, an individual that buys or sells foreign currency through a small bank or airport kiosk typically will not get the best price available, as there is normally a large difference between the price at which such entities are willing to sell a currency and the price at which they are willing to buy it back.

In recent years, however, trading in the foreign exchange market via a retail broker has gained much attention among speculators, or individual investors, who are drawn to the market for various reasons.

Leverage

Perhaps the most important reason that investors are now turning to the Forex market is because of the significant leverage that it offers. In its most basic form, leverage makes it possible for a trader with 200:1 leverage to have $50 in margin controlling a $10,000 position in the market. Some brokers offer as much as 400:1 leverage and it is precisely for this reason that foreign currency is considered to be one of the riskiest asset classes available to the retail trader.

The leveraged nature of FX trading means that any market movement will have an equally proportional effect on your deposited funds. This may work against you as well as for you. The possibility exists that you could sustain a total loss of initial margin funds and be required to deposit additional funds to maintain your position. If you fail to meet any margin call within the time prescribed, your position will be liquidated and you will be responsible for any resulting losses.

Liquidity

The Forex market offers traders unmatched liquidity and trading opportunity. At any given moment during trading hours, there are hundreds of thousands of people online trading currencies. This makes it easy for an investor to open and close trades at any time during the day or night.

Volatility

The foreign currency market is a very volatile market, which means that trading can very quickly be lucrative. The great potential for monetary gain, however, is matched by an equal potential to suffer a large monetary loss.

Decentralization

Many traders are also attracted to the market because it is decentralized, meaning that no one person or economy can control the market. Plus, because there is no physical central exchange, the Forex market doesn't operate during fixed hours. In fact, it is open for trading 24 hours a day, 5.5 days a week. This allows people who work during the day, anywhere in the world, to trade in the evenings or at their leisure.

Low Barriers to Entry

Most anyone can open an account with an online broker within just a couple of days and with a minimal investment. In fact, nowadays, most brokers offer mini accounts, which can be opened for a couple hundred dollars. Moreover, the fees that an investor pays to trade are low, relative to other financial markets. In Forex, the trader typically pays only the spread (the difference between the bid and ask prices).

In the world of Forex, there are two types of retail brokers, a market-maker broker and a straight-through-processing broker.

It has often been said that some 85% of retail traders lose all of the money they invest within the first few months of trading. A market maker brokerage understands this and operates by selling foreign currency the same time its clients buy it, essentially trading against its clients. At first glance, this may not seem unfair, as Forex is a net-sum-zero market. In other words, when a trade is placed, one party necessarily gains, while the other party necessarily loses, so it shouldn't matter whether or not the party on the opposite side of the trade is your broker. However, there are additional factors that come into play when a broker trades against its clients. First, the broker keeps the trades in-house, rather than passing them onto a bank. In this instance, the broker itself takes the other side of its client's trade—that is, if the broker is willing to assume the risk. Often, if an individual trader is skilled and has been profitable in the past, the broker may not wish to assume the risk and may even reject the trade altogether. This is all done by a dealing desk, where traders at the broker monitor all client trades and decide what trades to accept, or what trades to decline.

Second, because Forex is off-exchange, they have the ability to manipulate prices, and they engage in the act of 'stop hunting'. Because the dealing desk can collectively see where all stop losses are set, they have the ability to push prices up or down to hit customer stop losses.

In short, there is a conflict of interest with the market maker business model: it is in the broker's best interest for the client to lose money.

The other method removes the dealing desk, and has all trades processed straight through to a bank or someone providing liquidity (hence the name Straight Through Processing). Because this method removes broker intervention – and conflict of interest – from the client's trades, it may be a better way to go for investors.

Bid			Ask		
Provider	Amount	Price	Price	Amount	Provider
Bank 1	2,500,000	1.3391	1.3393	3,000,000	Bank 5
Bank 4	3,000,000	1.3390	1.3393	2,000,000	Bank 2
Bank 3	1,500,000	1.3389	1.3394	3,500,000	Bank 4
Bank 5	4,000,000	1.3389	1.3395	1,500,000	Bank 1
Bank 2	2,000,000	1.3388	1.3395	2,500,000	Bank 3

Here we see an example of different banks offering different prices. The best bid and best ask prices are taken, and clients would trade with those banks offering the best price.

Some brokers will have a network of banks or liquidity providers to pass trades onto. Because Forex is off-exchange, there is nothing to prevent one party from offering a different price on a currency than another party. This system allows the broker to pool together all of the prices being quoted by the providers, and offer the best bid and ask being offered at the time (though, the broker will add a little to the spread or charge a commission, as this may be their only source of income).

Choosing a Broker

Most brokers offer free demo accounts, and investors new to the Forex market should take advantage of them – not only to refine a trading strategy, but to try out the tools and services that brokers have to offer. Feel free to research the industry; open demo accounts with a few brokers, research their marketing material, call their customer service to see if they are helpful and friendly, and choose a broker that fits you.

Trading in the off exchange retail foreign currency market is one of the riskiest forms of investment available in the financial markets and suitable for sophisticated individuals and institutions. The possibility exists that you could sustain a substantial loss of funds and therefore you should not invest money that you cannot afford to lose. Nothing in this presentation is a recommendation to buy or sell currencies and Interbank FX is not liable for any loss or damage, including without limitation, any loss of profit which may arise directly or indirectly from the use of Interbank FX tools or reliance on such information.

13

Foreign exchange

Introduction

Foreign exchange is an international market where currencies are traded. In this chapter we will see how it works and how currency rates have been affected by the credit crisis of 2007–09.

The market

The foreign exchange market is unregulated and has no physical location. Business is conducted around the world. A trader who has bought into a currency will often invest the amount in securities, which means that foreign exchange has a knock-on effect on other markets. The market is driven by speculative flows and by trading from governments, central banks and companies. Foreign exchange, like derivatives, is used for hedging.

There are 170 currencies in use worldwide, but most are not very liquid. The US dollar is by far the most widely traded currency, partly because the United States has the biggest and most liquid bond markets, and commodities are priced in dollars. The US dollar is the global reserve currency and an invoice currency in many contracts.

The euro, introduced at the start of 1999, is the next most important currency. It has enabled euro-zone member countries to trade with each other directly without the need to exchange their currencies. Following the euro's introduction, London was able to increase its share of foreign exchange markets because transactions in sterling no longer had to compete with those in a variety of European currencies.

Traders focus on the exchange rate, which is how much a foreign currency costs outside its country of origin. Currencies may be expressed against the dollar, although sterling is the exception and it is normal to talk of dollars to the pound. In recent years, cross rates, where the US dollar is not included as one of the benchmark currencies, have gained in significance. Cross trades in liquid currencies take place without reference to the US dollar exchange rate. Currencies can be expressed against a basket of currencies. If the pound rises against the dollar, it may fall against the basket, gaining its strength relative only to a weakened dollar.

At the time of writing, China, Japan, and some other Asian countries have an exchange rate that is formally or otherwise fixed against the US dollar, which gives them an international trading advantage over countries with floating rates, such as the United Kingdom.

Among the most widely traded currencies after the dollar, sterling and euro are probably the Swiss franc, sterling and yen, and perhaps then the Australian dollar. Next in priority come the New Zealand dollar and the Norwegian kroner, followed by emerging-market currencies and those in the Arab countries.

Average daily turnover of traditional foreign exchange has grown by an unprecedented 69 per cent between April 2004 and April 2007 to US$3.2 trillion (£2.1 trillion), according to the triennial survey of foreign exchange and derivatives market activity conducted by BIS in 2007. The growth was broadly based across instruments. The currency composition of turnover has become more diversified over the past three years, although the US dollar and the euro continued to be the most traded currency pair. The Hong Kong dollar, linked with the economic expansion of China, and the New Zealand dollar saw significant increases in share, and the share of emerging market currencies rose by almost 20 per cent.

Over the three-year period, Singapore, Switzerland and the United Kingdom gained market share while the US share dropped. The United Kingdom had a 34.1 per cent share of reported foreign exchange market turnover in 2007, up from 31 per cent in 2001, while the United States had a 16.6 per cent share, down from 19.2 per cent.

The survey found that Europe was the largest market for foreign exchange trading, accounting for 56 per cent of trading worldwide.

The cost of not joining the euro

The credit crisis of 2007–09 has brought home the message that not to have joined the euro may have been an expensive decision. Denmark has had to raise its main interest rate three times to defend the krone, and its population narrowly favours joining the euro. Poland's zloty fell as a result of the credit crisis and the government plans to join the euro by the start of 2012. In Hungary the forint became volatile, which prompted political and business leaders to put forward an urgent case for joining the euro.

Sterling fell sharply in the currency crisis. No doubt the United Kingdom could survive alone, as now, although this could mean borrowing money from others if, however, it were to join the euro it could lock in at a competitive exchange rate and would have the support of the ECB, and the safety of the common currency at a time of exchange-rate fluctuation that has arisen since the start of the credit crisis in 2007. But there would be disadvantages too. The ECB acts for the euro zone and not individually for its member countries, for which its rates are often inappropriate. In Italy, for instance, costs and prices have risen higher than the euro-zone average, but as a euro-zone member the country has not been able to devalue its currency to compensate.

The United Kingdom's budget deficit is an obstacle to joining the euro. In the next few years, this deficit is likely to be 8 per cent of GDP or higher. Even when the economy was strong, the United Kingdom had a budget deficit over the 3 per cent limit set by the Maastricht treaty, signed in 1991 in the Netherlands with the aim of establishing a single European currency and creating economic cooperation in Western Europe.

The credit crunch and the dollar

As the credit crisis rapidly worsened towards the end of the third quarter of 2008, there was a flight to the dollar, which regained some of the strength it had lost previously against the pound and the euro. A stronger dollar helps European companies that make substantial sales into the United States. In this way, European exports into the United States become cheaper than comparable US products, and the stronger dollar converts product sales into more revenue in euros for the companies.

In the credit crunch, drug companies saw their shares decline in value by far less than some sectors partly because they benefited from significant sales in the United States and the strengthening dollar. Oil companies also benefited, given that crude oil is priced in dollars. Retail companies in contrast have high dollar costs, which has had a negative correlation with the US dollar's rising strength.

dbFX.com

The Professional Online Foreign Exchange Trading Platform for Individuals

More Investors and Money Managers around the world choose to trade Foreign Exchange with Deutsche Bank than with any other provider*. dbFX now brings Deutsche Bank's renowned expertise in FX to the retail market with a platform tailored specifically to meet the needs of individual traders and small institutions.

Why Trade Foreign Exchange

Massive Liquidity = Massive opportunity

The Global Foreign Exchange market, the largest market in the world, is experiencing rapid growth. Nearly $2 trillion is traded on the FX market each day, more than 20 times the NY stock exchange and 3 times that of the US government bond market.

Manage Your Risk by diversifying with FX

The FX markets can offer consistent returns and is proven to have a low correlation to Bond and Equity market returns, making it an excellent portfolio diversifier. Technical traders, in particular, find the FX market follows the same technical principles as Futures and Equities markets plus the ability to trade 24 hours a day makes FX an attractive asset class for technical traders.

Correlation of FX Strategies Low Compared to Equities and Bonds						
	Bond	Equity	DBCR	Carry	Mom.	Valuat.
Bond	100%	26%	−21%	−16%	3%	−25%
Equity		100%	5%	4%	−2%	7%
DBCR			100%	74%	38%	66%
Carry				100%	−6%	40%
Momentum					100%	−25%
Valuation						100%

Source: DB Global Markets Research
DBCR (Deutsche Bank Currency Returns index)

Transparent Markets and data

Information and News on Foreign Exchange Markets is widely available, enabling you to keep up to date, tic-by–tic on market knowledge and form an opinion on the markets.

Identifiable Beta

There is evidence that positive returns can be generated by pursuing a combination of trading strategies. What is less widely known is that the introduction of FX in a properly constituted portfolio of other assets can actually reduce the probability and severity of drawdowns. This means that many participants in the FX market trade to hedge exposures rather than to generate investment profit.

FX Trading Strategies

There are three common FX trading strategies - Carry, Momentum and Valuation.

Carry

This strategy exploits the widely observed "forward premium puzzle" which suggests that systematically buying high interest rate currencies and selling low interest rate currencies may be profitable. This opportunity exists because of a risk premia, the use of different models used to forecast currencies by rational market participants and the differing constraints and objectives faced by market participants.

Momentum

Currencies appear to trend over time which suggests that using past prices may be useful when investing in currencies. This is due to the existence of irrational traders (such as institutions that are trading FX in order to hedge their positions not to generate an investment profit). Other factors are the possibility that prices provide information about non-fundamental currency determinants or that prices may adjust slowly to new information.

Valuation

In the long-run, currencies tend to move back to their fair value based on Purchasing Power Parity (PPP). However, in the short to medium term, currencies can deviate from their PPP values due to trade, information and other costs. This allows traders to potentially profit from currencies as they revert back to their fair values over the long run.

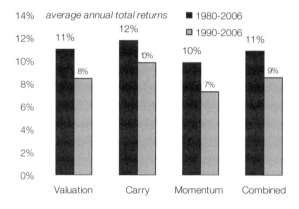

How can I trade FX

You can trade FX with Deutsche Bank via our state-of-the-art electronic trading platform dbFX, available to any individual or small institution, subject to security and credit clearance checks. The prices available on dbFX are updated automatically and are real-time prices that can be traded at the click of a button. dbFX is open 24 hours a day six days a week, and is supported by an exceptional client support team. The margin requirements on dbFX are as low as 1% of the value of the trade, with a minimum funding account of $5000. Clients of dbFX can go long or short individual currencies. They can also access on-line news and research and real time charts and charting tools.

Trading FX with Deutsche Bank on dbFX

- Streaming real-time executable rates
- Funds are deposited directly with Deutsche Bank AG, London
- Account funding starting at $5,000 or the equivalent in GBP, EUR or JPY
- Margin as low as 1% for qualified clients, one simple margin level
- Minimum trade size of 100,000 units
- Optional, Long/Short Position Management Tool, allowing you to have simultaneous long and short positions in the same currency pair
- Online news and research
- Real time charts and charting tools

Customized Solutions

dbFX offers customized solutions for active traders:

- Managed Accounts: Managers have the full power of trading with dbFX and investors have the comfort of investing with dbFX.
- Introducing Brokers: dbFX offers a full end to end offering for IBs and their clients
- API trading: dbFX has several APIs for algorithmic traders.

For more information visit www.dbfx.com/TT or call 0808-234-4650

Deutsche Bank

Transactions

The spot transaction is the most common type of currency transaction. Two currencies are exchanged at once, using an exchange rate agreed on the day. Dealers quote spot rates as a single unit of the base currency against units of the variable currency.

There is a different rate for buying the currency than for selling it; this difference is the spread. The spread is the market maker's gross profit. The transaction, with some exceptions, takes two working days for cash settlement (T+2). The spot market is not always liquid, although liquidity is boosted by automated trading where it might otherwise be lacking.

Among derivatives, forward contracts in currencies provide for the sale of a stated amount of currency at a specified exchange rate and on a specified future date or within a given time period. If you will need dollars in six months, you can buy them now in the forward market. Generally forwards are non-standardised contracts traded over the counter. They are not anonymous like futures contracts but are similar in that there is a contractual price, which in this case is the forward price.

Currency futures are traded on exchange in multiples of fixed-size lots, and delivery dates are standardised. Unlike in OTC market trades, there is price transparency and resulting market efficiency, and the futures are accessible for all types of market participants, including retail. A currency exchange is the counterparty to transactions, which effectively removes counterparty credit risk. Traders must put up margin which, if necessary to keep their position covered, they will maintain.

Options can be in currencies, and are traded over the counter. Besides straightforward – known as *vanilla* – currency options, there are exotic options. One of their uses is to trade against the volatility of volatility. There are also options on currency futures, which are traded on exchange.

A currency swap is where a company may raise an amount in the currency which it can borrow most cheaply, and then swap the proceeds and fixed interest payments with those for an equivalent-size loan in a target currency. This is the most common type of swap after interest-rate swaps, and the two types can be combined. Many currency swaps are traded on organised exchanges. The original purpose of currency swaps was to circumvent exchange controls, which are regulations restricting convertibility of one currency into others.

Dealers and customers

In foreign exchange, the sell side consists of banks that make a market or conduct foreign exchange business for their clients, with dealers working for them. The buy side consists of their customers. The banks have access to the primary markets, whose activity heavily influences prices in secondary markets.

The dealers buy and sell currency for clients, quoting competitive real-time spreads on portals, which are online markets. They may hedge exposures, and will take speculative positions for themselves. Dealers of one bank will deal directly with those in the trading room of another. They make money from the spread.

Dealers may use a voice broker, who operates as a go-between for dealers, but this method of broking foreign exchange transactions has been increasingly giving way to electronic interbank broking platforms. Some large banks promise to sell a given amount of currency at a given price any time, and this means that supply and demand no longer entirely dictate exchange rates.

Investment funds do most of the foreign exchange business, and they invest real money. The fund manager may manage foreign exchange risk through a currency-overlay programme, which hedges currency exposure from overseas investments, or seeks to generate return for assuming extra risk, known as Alpha.

Foreign exchange has developed into an asset class (a type of investment, such as equities or bonds) over the past decade. According to IFSL, this is partly because it is uncorrelated to any other asset class. Pressure on fund managers to deliver greater returns from their assets has led them to look outside traditional asset classes. Many foreign exchange trading platforms allow very high gearing (borrowing in relation to cash put up as margin), which is barred from derivatives exchanges: for example, positions of 100 times capital.

The hedge funds do up to perhaps half of all foreign exchange trading. They operate as the buy side in posting their own prices and, in some cases, are effectively making a market, which is contributing to a blurring of the dividing line between the buy and sell side. They can drive a currency further up or down than it would otherwise go.

On 22 September 1992, George Soros initiated his most famous transaction. His hedge-fund vehicle, the Quantum Fund, took a US$10 billion (£6.7 billion) short position in sterling on a bet that it was overvalued. The UK government raised interest rates to prop up the currency, but Soros only increased his position. The Bank of England eventually withdrew the pound from the European Exchange Rate Mechanism (ERM), and sterling plummeted in value. Soros made an estimated US$1 billion (£0.7 billion) from his bet.

The central banks are major customers in the foreign exchange market, trading their reserves in a process known as *reserves adjustment*. They may sell their reserves in a foreign currency to support their own. They regularly adjust their massive US dollar reserves, and so become significant buyers and sellers of sterling, the yen and euro, as well as of dollars. They can trade anonymously through BIS, which serves as a bank for central banks.

Sometimes, central banks work together internationally to keep exchange rates at an agreed level, but this practice is less common than it was. Open intervention by central banks can fail, as when the pound was withdrawn from the ERM.

Companies are heavily involved in foreign exchange, although their participation has dwindled compared with the capital flows of speculators. If, for example, a UK firm is selling into another country, sterling could become stronger, and make its goods more expensive. The firm can hedge against the risk of such currency fluctuations; it can also speculate on foreign currencies.

As it turns out, companies have not always managed foreign exchange wisely or prudently. In the 1980s, Japanese companies were involved in a scandal where they traded more in currencies than was justified by their business. Disgraced US energy company Enron had also done a lot of foreign exchange business. Retail traders deal through retail foreign exchange platforms, and have sometimes been abused.

Default risk

Default risk arises in foreign exchange, and any party to a transaction needs to exercise due diligence in checking out their counterparty. There are settlement and pre-settlement risks. Settlement risk arises because one party has paid out before the other. This risk was greater in the past because settlement was manual and used paper transactions, a process that was expensive and left wide scope for errors.

One solution has been netting, by which two parties offset trades, making it necessary to pay out only net amounts. The risk is that if one of the party defaults, a liquidator could challenge the netting agreement, forcing the non-defaulting party to join a queue of creditors in claiming for losses.

Entities engaging in larger trades may be required to put up collateral, otherwise known as margin, for these trades, adding to this where necessary to cover their open position. Straight-through processing, where the journey from trade inception to trade inception is electronic, has replaced manual and paper-based processing. This has gone a long way towards cutting costs and errors.

The Society for Worldwide Interbank Financial Telecommunication (SWIFT) has provided the foreign exchange market with connectivity and standards through its electronic network. Continuous linked settlement (CLS) provides a payment-versus-payment model, enabling both sides of a foreign exchange trade to settle simultaneously.

Some credit risk remains, particularly pre-settlement, and participants in the foreign exchange markets must have reciprocal credit agreements in place, with limits based on the counterparty's credit risk.

14

Commodities

Introduction

Commodities are a volatile asset class, and are negatively correlated to stocks and bonds, which feature can be useful for diversifying an investment portfolio. They are of interest to investors and speculators. In this chapter we will look at how they work.

Overview

Commodities are now a derivatives-driven market, with only precious metals normally owned physically. Commodity derivatives are largely unregulated. There are commodity futures, which are traded on exchange. There are also commodity forward agreements, which are traded over the counter. Let us look at each.

A futures contract is an agreement to buy or sell a commodity at a specific price on a predetermined future date. The futures market was originally invented to smooth fluctuations in the price of agricultural products, enabling farmers who sold the products and companies that used them to hedge their price risk. The market has since spread to precious metals and energy as well as financial instruments. Speculators try to profit from this risk.

Commodity futures are traded on exchange, which means that the products are standardised, and parties do not trade with each other directly but rather with a clearing house, generally a highly rated financial institution, so reducing default risk. An exchange is a centralised market place, providing liquidity. This means that there are many other people to trade with, and an efficient market.

Commodity futures prices are ultimately aligned to the commodities in the underlying industry, but the basis differential – the difference between the futures price and the underlying commodity price – will fluctuate during the contract's life.

There are also commodity contracts traded over the counter, which is off exchange, and these are known as forward agreements. The deals are customised, but there is a lack of efficiency in matching up two people with the same needs. The lack of a central counterparty means that the two parties are trading directly with each other, and there is some significant default risk. There is a lack of price transparency, meaning that buyer and seller cannot see prices of other deals to check that they are dealing at a fair price.

Trading

Commodity futures, like any futures, are used primarily for hedging, but are also used for speculating. The trader may buy a commodity future and if its value rises above the price paid, the trader will benefit from closing out the position with the opposite contract. By trading before expiry, the trader invariably avoids physical delivery of the underlying commodity. Otherwise, the trader may sell short, seeking to gain from a downward valuation of the future's price.

The trader in commodity futures may pay the full amount at the start, as when buying a stock, or may pay on margin, which is when the trader pays only a small amount of the amount traded but will top it up if the position goes against the trader to a level not covered by the initial amount plus margin. For example, a car manufacturer may buy futures contracts on the London Metal Exchange to lock in the price that it pays for metal as a buyer. Once the futures position is financially closed out, a hedge investment will offset any adverse price movements that may have arisen in that physical purchase of the metal. A buyer may also hedge sales of metal.

The prices for some commodity futures are included in tables under 'Commodities', a section in *The Times* published Tuesday to Friday. The spot price, which is the present delivery price, is sometimes given. For futures prices on commodities, delivery months vary. For example, crude oil has 12 contracts a year and cotton has six.

The futures price on the earliest of the delivery months, called the front-month contract, is closest to the spot price, but will be slightly higher to include interest, dealing charges and, where relevant, the cost of storing the underlying commodity. If the gap between the futures price on the front-month contract and the spot price should become too wide, trading arbitrage would reduce it.

The number of derivatives contracts traded on the exchanges has mush-roomed in recent years, partly due to electronic trading, but exchange trading

Safety and balance in gold

By John Mulligan, World Gold Council

Over the last eighteen months or so, the financial markets have experienced unprecedented levels of turmoil, with the value of equities and other assets plummeting to lows not seen in over a generation. Not surprisingly, gold's value as an investment in times of duress has again attracted considerable media attention and, more significantly, the attention of a growing number of investors. At the end of February 2009, the price approached record highs, buoyed by unparalleled investment demand as investors sought out the safe haven qualities and security that gold offers. But there are substantial additional investment benefits to gold beyond its well known role as the asset of last resort, and these are rooted in the supply and demand dynamics and unique structure of the gold market.

Gold has, of course, been valued as a thing of beauty, a precious commodity and as money for many centuries, but as an asset for consideration by the contemporary investor, it has really only featured on the radar of the financial community for less than a decade. It can be argued that during the latter part of the twentieth century, the exploding financial markets and the pursuit of rapid returns, which in turn fuelled a boom in the further development of new financial products, left gold languishing and neglected as an asset. But severe mishaps in specific markets and more recent and extreme deteriorating economic conditions have caused many to reassess how they view the risk-return balance of their investments, and this has led them to examine the value of alternative assets, such as the commodities complex and, more particularly, gold.

Informed investors have been emphasising the importance of a diversified investment strategy for some time. Holding diverse investments of varying risk/return characteristics can balance a portfolio, protecting it against falls in the value of any specific asset class or set of assets that tend to react in a similar fashion.

Whilst there has been much written of the shift to investment in commodities in recent years, it is worth noting that, at the institutional level, this is still only a very minority trend. The vast majority of funds still consist largely of a very narrow band of assets. Recent estimates suggest that the global pension fund industry, worth an estimated $28.2 trillion in 2007, whilst having increasingly invested in alternative assets beyond equities and bonds, still only allocated an average of 15% to all other asset classes, and this alternative space largely consisted of hedge fund, private equity and real estate (*Fund Management 2008*, IFSL, October 2008). Whether these alternatives represented sufficient diversity to offer balance and protect portfolios from the corrosive market conditions of the last year or so is highly questionable.

Although the move to diversify via commodities may still be limited to a relatively small percentage of funds, it is not insignificant that those that have done so have proved themselves to be both thought-leaders and amongst the best performers in their field. A World Gold Council case study of the Missouri State Employees'

Retirement System, one of around 80 US funds to have invested in commodities, showed that its decision in 1998 to make the allocation on the basis of the added diversification it would bring to the fund helped it become one of the best performing funds in its peer group, posting an impressive annualised return of 9.2% in the 10 years to June 2007.

Once the validity of portfolio diversification is recognised, investors then need to identify assets which exhibit little correlation with their existing investments. Whilst it is noted above that the commodities complex, via investment in leading commodity indexes, represents one such solution, it can be argued that an examination of gold's characteristics as an asset make it an even stronger candidate as a diversifier.

Adding gold to a portfolio introduces an entirely different class of asset. Gold is unusual because it is both a commodity and a monetary asset. It is a particularly effective diversifier because it is exhibits little or no correlation with other markets or instruments; that is, it tends to move independently of other traditional asset classes and also, although to a lesser extent, of other commodities.

Gold's geographically and sectorally diverse demand base is a key factor in its independence from general market trends and the tendencies of other assets. Typically, around two thirds of global gold demand comes from the jewellery market and discretionary spending, unlike most other commodities which are reliant on industrial demand and heavily tied to economic cycles and consumption patterns in the developed world.

On the supply side, mine production has remained relatively flat or on a slight downward trend for several years. Mining is an extremely lengthy and complex process. Long lead times to production mean the supply-side cannot easily respond to exploit an ascendant gold price. Unlike several other key commodities, such as oil, supply is also spread across the globe and can draw upon relatively accessible above-ground stocks to alleviate temporary shortages, reducing the immediate impact of supply shocks on the price.

Volatility is also a pressing concern when selecting portfolio components, with considerable urgency behind the need to find ways to minimise it and mitigate risks within portfolios. Many commodities are extremely volatile when compared to more mainstream assets. However, this is not the case with gold. Investment professionals are frequently surprised to learn that, over the long term, gold is less volatile than most blue chip equity indexes, such as the S&P 500. Since 1984, the average monthly volatility of gold has been around 13.7%, compared to 15.3% for the S&P 500, one of the world's most liquid stock market indices. And looking at more recent movements, whilst the current market turmoil has raised the level of volatility across a range of asset classes, gold has maintained its relative stability, with far lower volatility than other commodities, and been generally less volatile than most stock markets.

Gold also helps address the other concerns of investors, much heightened in the current environment, regarding liquidity risk and counterparty risk. Gold is one of the most liquid assets, traded around the world, around the clock, and gold, unlike many other liquid assets, has no default risk; there is no risk that a coupon or a redemption payment will not be made, as for a bond, or that a company will go out of business, as for equity, or that savings will be lost through a bank that is going out of business.

Whilst gold is generally viewed as performing best when other assets are declining in value, a recent study by World Gold Council, 'Gold as a Strategic Asset for UK Investors', shows that a strategic allocation to gold can be optimal, irrespective of the stage in the economic cycle or market sentiment, and can enhance portfolio optimality across the risk spectrum.

The study suggests that an optimal allocation to gold does not necessarily require a major shift in investment strategy or portfolio composition. The amount of gold required to achieve expected returns in an optimised portfolio varies depending on the level of risk tolerance. In fact, a small allocation to gold can improve stability of returns when combined with a portfolio of more conventional assets - as little as 4% in a low / medium risk portfolio through to 10% in a higher risk one. Furthermore the study shows that gold's unique diversification qualities mean an allocation to gold can be justified even when other alternative assets, such as commodities indexes, are introduced to the portfolio. In other words, gold's role as a diversifier is not easily substituted.

Gold's other beneficial properties as an asset are perhaps more familiar. It has long been valued as a hedge against inflation and currency weakness. Looking at the latter a little more closely, via the World Gold Council study, Commodity Prices and the Influence of the US Dollar, gold's particular potency as an independent asset is again evident, offering greater hedging capabilities against US dollar weakness than any of the other commodities analysed in the study.

The flight to quality currently being witnessed can be perceived as part of a broader reappraisal of gold's strengths as an asset. The corresponding growth in investment demand since the turn of the millennium has also been mirrored by development of new routes to investment, such as the launch of bullion-backed exchange traded funds (ETFs), and new gold products to suit a range of investor profiles. These have helped to further simplify investor access to gold.

Increased investor interest in gold over the course of 2008 contributed to total annual dollar demand for the yellow metal being pushed to $102bn, a 29% increase on year earlier levels. According to the year-end edition of World Gold Council's Gold Demand Trends report, shares on stock markets around the world lost an estimated $14 trillion in value, whereas identifiable investment demand for gold, which includes exchange traded funds (ETFs) and bars and coins, was 64% higher in 2008 than in 2007, equivalent to an additional inflow of $15bn. The most striking trend across the year was the reawakening of investor interest in the holding of physical gold. Demand for bars and coins rose 87% over the year with shortages reported across many parts of the globe.

has yet to catch up with the OTC derivatives market, a market strictly for professionals, which has an 85 per cent share of the total market. The OTC trades are carried out by telephone, often using interdealer brokers. According to BIS, the notional amount outstanding of OTC commodity derivatives globally in December 2007 was US$9 trillion (£6 trillion), which had risen steadily from under US$5.4 trillion (£3.6 trillion) in December 2005.

Investors

Pension funds are the main institutional investors in commodity derivatives. In the United Kingdom, they are less keen on commodities than, for example, in the Netherlands and Germany. Many commodities investors put their money in commodity futures index funds, which have significantly contributed to the growth of the industry (see Chapter 19). The largest is the Goldman Sachs Commodity Index (GSCI), which S&P acquired in February 2007. In addition, there are exchange-traded commodities, which are stock market-listed vehicles like exchange-traded funds (see Chapter 19) but the index is based on the price of a commodity or basket of commodities, not on listed companies.

Retail investors have limited exposure to commodity derivatives, but they can invest in exchange-traded funds or in managed funds that invest in underlying companies such as energy or mining companies, or directly in the companies themselves. This does not always achieve the same result as investing in pure commodities because many corporate factors unrelated to commodities must be taken into account. Spread betting is a way in which retail investors can trade commodity derivatives.

The investment case

The case for portfolio diversification by investing in commodities is strong. In their 2006 paper, 'Facts and Fantasies about Commodity Futures', professors Gary Gorton, then of Wharton School, University of Pennsylvania and K Geert Rouwenhorst of Yale School of Management show that between 1959 and 2004, a portfolio of 34 commodities made returns negatively correlated with stocks and bonds, suggesting that commodities are an ideal form of diversification. Already some pension funds and insurance companies have embarked on this diversification journey.

Within a basket of commodities, investor feedback suggests that the correlation is not enormous, although it has seemed so at times in the credit crisis of 2007–09, when energy and food prices were out of kilter.

The case that commodities generate high returns is more controversial. It is agreed that commodities are driven by supply and demand and that, when they are out of synchronisation, investors can make a profit, whether from long or short positions. The long-term commodities portfolio scrutinised by Gorton and Rouwenhorst generated only an average return and volatility compared with stocks.

But over a shorter, more recent period of years, it is commodities that have overpowered stocks. Commodities are as prone to speculative bubbles today as they were in the tulip mania of 17th-century Holland.

Types of commodity

Hard commodities

Hard commodities are the product of extractive processes. They include energy, the largest market in commodity derivatives, and metals.

Energy

The energy market has grown in recent years, partly due to the deregulation of electricity generation in the United States and Europe, and to the increasing range of energy-related financial instruments. Banks and hedge funds are now active in the market, as well as oil and gas producers and consumers.

Energy contracts are traded on exchange as well as OTC. ICE Futures, which was known until October 2005 as the International Petroleum Exchange, is Europe's leading futures and options exchange for energy products. Nearly three-quarters of its worldwide business is in Brent Crude. Also traded on this exchange are gas, oil and, from February 2006, West Texas Intermediate crude contracts.

Non-ferrous metals

The London Metal Exchange (LME) is the world's leading non-ferrous metals market, and its three core services are hedging, pricing and physical value. The exchange provides futures and options contracts for metals and futures contracts for plastics, which enable the physical industry to hedge against movements in the prices of raw material.

The exchange's largest contract is for primary aluminium. Of the six metals traded, the second-largest contract is for copper (grade A), which has applications in housing, construction and many other areas. In recent years there has been an increased demand for copper from China, India and other developing nations. Chile and the United States are the major producers.

The other contracts traded on the LME are zinc, tin, lead, nickel, plus two aluminium alloy contracts. There is also a metals index future. Futures contracts can be set for any duration, from cash (two days forward) to three months ahead; they can then be traded weekly, followed by monthly.

Precious metals

Precious metals, unlike non-ferrous metals, are often owned physically. They are traded away from the LME. The most prominent one is gold, which is a basic store of value against inflation, depreciating currencies, revolution and war. Gold differs from other metals in that it does not have industrial uses. It is mainly bought for jewellery, and its volatility has proved to be limited compared with most commodities. Gold is a dollar-denominated currency and, should the dollar weaken, it increases in demand, although it becomes more expensive for buyers holding other currencies.

Most global gold trading is through OTC transactions, although there are also standardised exchange-traded futures and options, including through London terminals of the COMEX division of the New York Mercantile Exchange.

London is the main centre for the 24-hours-a-day OTC market in gold, but there are other major OTC markets, including New York, Zurich, Tokyo, Sydney and Hong Kong, with smaller levels of OTC business taking place in Asia and the Middle East. In the large OTC markets, the transaction size has high minimum levels, which means that the main players are gold market professionals and institutional investors. Trading is done by telephone and electronically. The market is most liquid in the London afternoon, which is morning in New York and when both markets are open.

Most OTC trades are cleared through London, and most major bullion dealers around the world are members or associate members of the London Bullion Market Association. The basis of settlement is delivery of a standard London Good Delivery Bar. The clearing process is a system of paper transfers, avoiding the security risk and cost of physical movement. The lack of physical delivery enables the market to be used by speculators and for hedging as well as for investment.

The gold price quoted in the international market (in US dollars per troy ounce) is the spot price – for delivery during the two days after the transaction date. Other forms of transaction in gold, notably forwards, futures and options, will be settled against a date further in the future than the spot settlement date. The forward or futures price is a function of the underlying spot price and the prevailing interest rate in the money markets plus insurance and storage.

The forward premium will usually be quoted as a percentage of the underlying price. Gold is nearly always in a *contango* (an upward-sloping forward curve), meaning that the forward price is at a premium over the actual price, because of the ready availability of above-ground stocks, which can be borrowed at low interest rates. A *backwardation* is when the forward price is lower than the spot. This may happen during a price squeeze, but is extremely rare.

According to IFSL, futures and options trading of gold on exchanges rose by more than 80 per cent in 2008 to reach a record US$5.1 trillion (£3.4 trillion), up by 10 times on the value traded six years earlier. Trading of silver rose by 60 per cent to a record US$1.2 trillion (£0.8 trillion). In addition, IFSL found that exchange-traded gold and silver funds have been the strongest source of growth in demand for the metals since their introduction in 2005.

Silver is a more practical metal than gold but is similarly a store of value. The metal has been used as money for longer than gold, and in more countries. The metal is in demand from investors, including hedge funds.

Among other precious metals, platinum is used in industry and, to a lesser extent, in making jewellery. It is a rare metal, mostly from South Africa. However, supply is at least equal to demand. Platinum is volatile and trading in the metal has attracted speculative traders, including a few hedge funds.

Palladium is derived from nickel mining in Russia and Canada, and is also produced in South Africa. The metal has attracted trading from hedge funds. Unlike for gold, there are no significant above-ground stocks in palladium, which means that supply can run scarce, driving up demand.

Soft commodities

Soft commodities are those such as cocoa, sugar and coffee. Others such as orange juice and cotton are sometimes included in this category. Manufacturers use soft commodity futures to ensure that farmers deliver raw material such as sugar or wheat at a fixed price when required. Farmers also use futures.

Soft commodities are affected by climate issues and by factors such as drought and frost. Like hard commodities, the price benefits from strong demand for the underlying goods from China and elsewhere. The price in the developed world tends to be inelastic, which means that price fluctuations make little difference to demand.

On Euronext.liffe, the London-based international derivatives arm of NYSE Euronext, the markets in soft commodities are much smaller than in crude oil futures. But cocoa, Robusta coffee and white sugar futures on the exchange set the global price benchmark for the underlying physical markets, and are actively traded by managed funds, other institutional investors and a range of short-term investors.

The products are also traded on the Coffee, Sugar and Cocoa Exchange in New York, owned by the New York Board of Trade, in contracts sometimes strongly correlated to Euronext.liffe, which provides arbitrage opportunities.

FINE

RETURNS

FROM

FINE

WINES

The Fund works with institutions, private investors and financial intermediaries worldwide

THE WINE INVESTMENT FUND

www.wineinvestmentfund.com

THE WINE INVESTMENT FUND

Chris Smith,
Investment
Manager

Andrew della Casa,
Director

Fine Returns from Fine Wine

At a time when market volatility has hit other asset classes hard, an investment in fine wine holds several specific advantages. The Wine Investment Fund, the granddaddy of the publicly offered wine investment funds, has been successfully managing wine assets since 2003. Here's how and why.

Risk
Investment is all about risk and good investment choices are made when risks taken are clearly understood.

Risk is best expressed in terms of price volatility, with greater volatility bringing higher exposure to timing risk. Measuring a combination of absolute performance with price volatility, therefore, is useful for those looking to assess and maximise return on risk. The Sharpe ratio does exactly this and from the chart below it can be seen that fine wine outperforms the other asset classes shown. It has recorded not only attractive average annual returns (15%+ per annum), but has done so with lower price volatility than most investments.

Supply/demand
The underlying supply and demand dynamics reinforce the attractive qualities of wine as an investment.

Bordeaux (and we consider only fine wine from Bordeaux as 'investment grade' for our purposes) is a finite geographical area in which are to be found a finite number of wine producers. Therefore, the wine produced by these producers, the 'Châteaux', will also be finite.

But there's more. The quantity of any given wine from any given vintage can only decrease over time as it is consumed. Moreover, and uniquely, while supply is decreasing, demand is increasing because as fine wine matures it actually improves.

Demand for fine wine is now global, encompassing both the traditional markets of Europe and North America, and the newer markets such as Russia and the Far East. As the emerging economies become wealthier, the number of consumers grows.

With decreasing supply of each given wine, and increasing demand as both the quality improves and the number of consumers increases, prices should rise. This

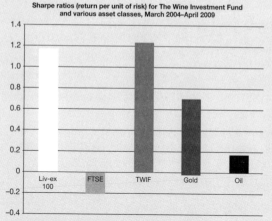

Sharpe ratios (return per unit of risk) for The Wine Investment Fund and various asset classes, March 2004–April 2009

The Liv-ex 100 Index is the traditional benchmark for fine wine market returns and is produced by Liv-ex, the fine wine exchange.

'TWIF' is The Wine Investment Fund.

Sources: www.liv-ex.com; London Stock Exchange; www.kitco.com; US Energy Information Administration; and calculations by The Wine Investment Fund

is borne out in practice: the long-run growth rate of wine prices has been around 15.5% per annum. Despite recessions and economic downturns, the very top end of the fine wine market has never fallen dramatically in value (even in 2008, the market as measured by the Liv-ex 100 index fell 'only' 14.6%, and has recovered more than a quarter of that fall since).

Investing in fine wine

Of all the world's wines, only some 2% come from Bordeaux. However, only the top 40 to 50 of the 4,000 Châteaux in Bordeaux achieve the standards required for their production to be considered investment grade – less than 0.1% of the world's wine stock, and worth in total about £6 billion.

The key issues for any wine investor are 'what to buy?' and 'how much to pay?'. In deciding what to buy, concentration on any single producer or vintage should be avoided, and a decision made on whether to buy en primeur (i.e. wines at the pre-bottling stage of their life) and/or small production 'trophy' wines. In our own case we have limits on the concentration in any producer or vintage and we do not buy en primeur or trophy wines.

We then turn to the specific selection of châteaux and vintages. During their period of aging, many great wines have quick short bursts of prices increases, interrupted by price plateaus of varying lengths. The trick is to judge which wines and vintages are nearing a significant rise in value at the end of a plateau. The key factor is the state of maturity of the wine, which determines when larger quantities of it will begun to be drunk.

We then also look at the relative price of each wine (say Château Lafite 2000) in the wider market. This is complex as we know that Lafite generally commands a premium compared to most other Châteaux, and that the 2000 vintage also has a particular standing. Finally, there is the issue of critic's ratings – most famously the American writer Robert Parker. A wine with a higher score will typically trade at a higher price. So we strip out all of these factors to estimate a 'raw' price for the wine, which we can compare across potential purchases.

Once the difficult 'what to buy' issue has been resolved, we move on to 'how much to pay?'. Key here is to be able to look across the whole market, including London and Bordeaux, for the cheapest price (for stock in excellent condition and with sound provenance). This is a critical advantage of wine investment funds over brokers or merchants, as the latter will use only their own stock at the price they themselves set – an inherent conflict of interest.

Top tips

Here are some tips to consider when selecting a portfolio of fine wine where the emphasis is on managing an investment portfolio (rather than laying down a wine cellar for drinking).

First, pick stock predominantly from the most famous wines of Bordeaux and from the best vintages. This minimises liquidity risk, as these wines are regularly traded on a mature secondary market. In addition, data is available to allow analysis of trends and price fluctuations.

Second, remember to take into account the costs of storage and insurance. For wines below the top tier, these can be high. A £250 case of wine might increase in value by 50% in 4 years, but the cost of storage and insurance over this time would, to a private investor, be about 5% of the asset value per year (trade storage could cost half this amount). The net return of around 30% is less impressive. But storage and insurance costs do not vary with the value of the wine, so this effect can be minimised by maintaining a high average price. Our average cost is around £2,500 per dozen bottles, meaning annual storage and insurance costs are only about 0.3% per year.

Third, price differentials, or bid/offer spreads, of a given fine wine may be as much as 30% in what is still an imperfect market. This can make private investment hazardous, but professionals will use multiple sources to ensure we are only buying at the lowest prices (amongst stock in excellent condition and with sound provenance) at any given time.

Fourth, the spread of prices in the market means that when selling it is vital to get as close as possible to the end consumer, who pays the highest price. Commissions on selling might be between 10% (the minimum at most merchants) and 25% (for example at an auction, including the buyer's and seller's premiums). Just as we buy from across the market, we also use a variety of sources to sell wines so as to maximise returns.

Fifth, provenance is an essential consideration when buying and selling fine wine. Buying 'under bond' offers reasonable security that the wine has been correctly stored since original shipment from the Château to the bonded warehouse. Wines that have additional ('strip') labels may have endured lengthy journeys and should be avoided - perfect storage is in dark, cool cellars, not on ships or planes or indeed in most private homes. The bonded warehouse system also provides a low risk, secure storage facility, reflected in the very low premiums paid for all risks insurance at full replacement value. By contrast try taking home five cases of Chateau Petrus 1990 (current value £25,000 each) and asking for an insurance quote!

Impact of the credit crisis

In 2008, most commodities fell sharply in value. The price of crude oil declined from a peak of US$147 a barrel in mid July 2008 to below US$50 in December of that year. Between March and August 2008, steel fell by 68 per cent, wheat fell by 67 per cent and ethylene dropped by 50 per cent.

On a positive note, gold and silver saw record trading activity and soaring prices. In March 2008, IFSL reported that gold recorded an all-time high of US$1,011 per ounce before easing back in the second half of the year, partly due to a strong dollar and deleveraging by short-term investors. Gold closed 2008 at US$870 per ounce. The gold price in 2008 was on average up 28 per cent on the previous year, which IFSL attributed partly to its safe-haven appeal but also to such factors as rising industry supply costs, high commodity prices and central bank easing. Gold has no credit risk because it has no counterparty. This makes it attractive to investors during financial instability, according to IFSL, which noted some level of inverse relationship between gold prices and other investment returns such as on shares.

Silver reached over US$20 per ounce during 2008, a level not reached since the 1980s, and its average price was up by 12 per cent on the previous year.

The future

The bull run (rising market) in commodities has come to a halt. Specialist intelligence company Exclusive Analysis in its yearbook *Foresight 2009* anticipates that commodity exporters to the United States or Western Europe will be hit hard in 2009 by a decline in commodity prices. Countries exporting base metals that will suffer include Cuba, Peru and Chile, and, in Africa, Guinea, Zambia and the Democratic Republic of the Congo.

The long-term prospects are perhaps not so gloomy. In late 2008, Jim Rogers, commodities guru and investor, said on Bloomberg TV that commodities remain a highly promising investment and would emerge from the recession as unimpaired assets, unlike, for example, General Motors or Bank of America. Rogers said he was buying all commodities, including gold, but he expected to make most money from the agricultural type. He noted that the trading price of sugar, for example, was down by 80 per cent from its peak, or more if inflation was taken into account. His commodity investments hedged a short position in financial stocks.

Investor exposure needs to be proportionate to the risk profile. In future, says the World Economic Forum in 'Global Risks 2009', an annual report, corporate commodity risk management needs to be more responsive to changing risk levels and higher than expected volatility.

15

Derivatives for retail investors

Introduction

This chapter is about derivatives products traded on exchange, which means they are accessible to retail investors. We will cover options, futures, covered warrants, spread bets and contracts for difference. Read in conjunction with Chapter 14 on commodities. OTC derivatives are for institutional investors, and so outside the scope of this chapter. For more about these, see Chapters 6 and 8.

Overview

This chapter is about the nuts and bolts of derivatives for retail investors. I include it because younger retail investors, particularly those working in the City of London, are showing a growing interest in derivatives speculation as well as hedging. Spread betting firms offer user-friendly access to derivatives, and are more accessible than many stockbrokers. Derivatives are a more liquid market than, for instance, small stocks. Furthermore, derivatives can be traded on almost anything, from stocks and indices to wheat and oil, energy and even the weather.

Traders can gain exposure to derivatives on margin, which means putting up only a small proportion of the trade in cash, basically to cover initial losses. This may appeal to those who are strapped for cash. Of particular interest in the credit crisis of 2007–09 has been the fact that derivatives trading offers opportunities to take a short position, which means seeking to profit from a declining market. Some investors have shorted the banking sector, where this is allowed, or have taken long positions in gold and similar, making a good profit. Many more, unfortunately, got their timing wrong. The opportunity to take short positions is, nonetheless, desirable in volatile markets. It is not now realistically available to retail investors buying equities due to the standard short standard settlement period.

Let us look at the rich array of derivatives products available to retail investors.

Products

Options

A traded option enables you to bet on the movement of individual shares, or of indices, currencies, commodities or interest rates, or it may be used for hedging. Through an option, you have the right to buy or sell a security at a predetermined price, known as the exercise price, within a specified period.

The option is geared, which means that the underlying share or other asset is under control for the comparatively small upfront cost of the premium, which is the market price of the option. The premium is a small percentage of the option's size. For every buyer of an option, there is a seller, also known as a writer.

An option buyer on completion will pay an initial margin, which goes to the writer of the option. Initial margin is calculated to cover the worst loss in a day that could arise, although it may not prove enough. The option buyer must regularly top up the initial margin to any extent that their position has declined in value to an uncovered level.

If the investor does not exercise the option, the premium that they have paid will be lost to the writer. But if it is exercised, the writer must provide the underlying financial instrument at the exercise price. One side will gain and the other will lose, but neither has the odds intrinsically in its favour.

You can buy a call option, which gives you the right, but not the obligation, to *buy* the underlying security at the exercise price. If the asset price is more than the exercise price of the option, the difference represents the option's value, and the option is *in* the money. If the asset price is less, the call option is *out of* the money. If you buy an option *deep out of* the money and the underlying price moves a lot, the premium could move in absolute terms much less, but in percentage terms significantly.

As the buyer of a call option, you will make money if the price of the underlying share moves up so that it becomes higher than the exercise price plus the premium that you paid. In this case, you could sell the option and realise the profit on the options trade, but it is usually simpler to trade it at a profit.

You can buy a put option, which gives you the right, but not the obligation, to *sell* a security at the exercise price. If the exercise price is higher than the underlying security's current market price, the option is in the money. If it is lower, the option is out of the money. You will make a profit if the option price falls to below the level of the exercise price plus the premium that you paid.

The extent to which the underlying asset's value surpasses the option's exercise price is known as intrinsic value. An option only has intrinsic value when it is *in the money*. The time value of an option is its total value less intrinsic value. The more time an option has until it expires, the higher this figure is likely to be, as the price of the underlying stock has so much more of a chance of changing in the option buyer's favour.

The premium consists of both intrinsic and time values, each of which can change constantly. These are factors used in the Black–Scholes model, which was developed in 1973 and is widely used in financial markets for valuing options. Other factors used in the model are volatility, the underlying stock price, and the risk-free rate of return. Black–Scholes has proved far from perfect, and makes key assumptions that are not always tenable, including a constant risk-free interest rate, continuous trading and no transaction costs. The hedge fund Long Term Capital Management (LTCM) relied on the Black–Scholes model and, in 1998, it lost US$4 billion and had to declare itself bankrupt. The company's strategy of trading volatility, through buying when option prices were above underlying value, as calculated by Black–Scholes, and selling when they fell below it, did not work. The problem was that market fluctuations were not, as the model assumed, normally distributed. In addition, LTCM had between 25 and 30 times leverage, which had raised the stakes.

Equity options tend to come in the standard contract size of 1,000 shares. To find the cost of an option contract, multiply the option price by 1,000. If a call option is priced at 70p, the cost will be £700 per contract. The contract size may vary if the underlying company is involved in a capital restructuring such as a rights issue.

The leading equity derivatives exchanges in Europe are Euronext.liffe and Eurex. In December 2007, Eurex, which is owned by Deutsche Börse and SIX Swiss Exchange, completed the acquisition of International Securities Exchange, which created the largest global derivatives market place.

The options on Euronext.liffe, the London-based exchange, have expiry dates grouped three, six or nine months ahead. A first group of companies has the expiry dates of January, April, July and October; a second group has February, May, August and November; and a third group expires in March, June, September and December. In any given month, options for only a third of the relevant companies will expire. When, for instance, a contract expires in March, a new one is created for expiry in June.

Options on stock market indices, known as index options, are essentially contracts for difference (CFDs) (see below). They are riskier than equity options as they often trade for larger amounts, perhaps several thousand pounds per contract against several hundred pounds. They are also more volatile.

The interest-rate option enables traders to speculate on or hedge against interest-rate risk. The price level of a contract is derived by subtracting the interest rate from 100. An interest rate of 5 per cent means that the contract is $100 - 5 = 95$ per cent. Settlement is on a value per fraction of a percentage change in interest rates. Because of the price structuring, the higher the interest rate rises, the further the contract price declines, and the reverse.

Futures

We looked at commodity futures in Chapter 14. Futures in financial products are the same concept, which is a binding agreement to buy or sell a given quantity of an asset at today's price by a specified future date. The market has become increasingly open to private investors and has made available some small-sized contracts and packaged futures products.

Futures can be on commodities such as cocoa or coffee (see Chapter 14) or, since the 1970s, on financial futures.

Financial futures are based on a financial instrument such as a bond, share, index, interest rate or currency, and the agreement is to exchange a cash sum reflecting the difference between the initial price of the underlying asset and its price on settlement. Interest-rate futures enable buyers to hedge against adverse movements in interest rates by buying a future to offset it. Contracts on indices or on interest rates cannot go to delivery, and any buyer or seller who does not close the position is closed out by the clearing house. Most major bond futures contracts can go to delivery.

In theory, a trader can run a futures contract to expiry, but in practice, will usually trade it. If you have bought a contract, you will sell it, or if you have sold a contract, you will buy.

The trader who goes long or short on a contract will put up an initial margin rather than the entire value of the contract, and this may have to be topped up, on the same principle as for options or spread bets. The trader can place a stop loss to sell an off-setting contract at a specified price or as near to it as possible.

In the United States, leading futures exchanges include CME Group and IntercontinentalExchange. Other big exchanges include Euronext.liffe and the National Stock Exchange of India, as well as JSE Limited in South Africa.

Warrants

Covered

Covered warrants are an exchange-traded packaged derivative mainly for retail investors, which have been popular for some years in continental Europe. The covered warrant is a security and not a contract. As with options, traders in covered warrants pay a small premium, which is how much they pay for the right to buy or sell the underlying asset. The warrants are split into calls and puts.

As time passes, the covered warrant becomes less valuable, which is reflected in a declining premium. Every covered warrant is normally traded before its maturity date and is *covered* because the issuer covers its position by simultaneously buying the underlying stock or financial instrument in the market. Covered warrants are expensive compared with some equivalent derivative products and cannot be shorted, but the spread (the difference between the buying and selling price) is often narrow, and the packaging is user friendly.

Unlike in financial spread betting or CFDs (see below for both), the trader cannot lose more than 100 per cent of his or her money, and at the end of the term, covered warrants that are *in the money* are automatically closed out on the investor's behalf. No stamp duty is payable on purchase, and owners will receive no dividend from the underlying shares. Capital gains tax is payable.

Conventional

The covered warrant should not be confused with the conventional warrant, a product that may be used to buy a specified number of *new* shares in a company at a specified exercise price at a given time or within a given period. Companies like to issue conventional warrants because they do not need to include them on the balance sheet. They are not part of a company's share capital and so have no voting rights. Sometimes the warrants are packaged as a sweetener to accompany a bond issue. They tend to rise and fall in value with the underlying shares, sometimes exaggerating the movement. Capital gains tax is payable on profits.

Spread bets

The spread bet is a way to trade on the movement of stocks, indices or other financial instruments. It is a derivative, and is sometimes a derivative of a derivative. The most popular instruments on which bets are placed are stocks and indices. The range of stocks available on spread betting has greatly expanded in recent years and now includes American Depository Receipts, which are certificates issued by a US bank representing shares in a foreign stock traded on a US exchange, and some popular pending new issues (a grey market). In addition, bets are available on foreign exchange, treasuries, commodities and other products. Multiple exposures are allowed.

You may bet on futures, or sometimes on the underlying cash products. The spread betting firm may hedge its own portfolio, using futures or CFDs. Spread bets are accessible even to the least sophisticated traders, and on small sums of money. The market is OTC and the party issuing the bet is always the counterparty. The financial bookmakers are execution-only, which means they cannot advise on how, or whether, to bet, although they may offer data and working examples.

As a trader, you may place a bet based on your belief that a share price, an index, or interest rates will move up or down. Spread betting, like CFDs, makes it possible to take a short position, which means a position that will profit if the underlying instrument goes down. Short selling is effectively closed to private investors in conventional share trading due to the short standard settlement period.

As a trader, you may nominate a unit stake which, on a small transaction, is typically £2–£5 for a single point. Spread bets are geared and, as a trader, you need to put up only an initial margin, perhaps 10 to 15 per cent of the underlying value, but will need to top up the amount should the trading position move against you, on the same principle as for options or futures. You will gain or lose as a percentage of the underlying instrument. Because of the gearing, price movements can quickly wipe out the margin or more, or can make a large profit. Some spread betting firms have increased the margin required from August 2007 onwards as a result of the credit crunch and to protect them against the risk of default.

The difference between the price at which you place a bet and that at which you close it out is your profit or loss. If you have made a gain, the firm will deposit it into your account.

Traditionally, spread bets have been on futures and options which, by anticipating movements, are likely to move faster than the underlying share price. In 2002, CMC Markets started rolling spread bets where the basis for pricing a spread bet is the cash price of the underlying instrument. Other large bookmakers now offer a similar product, at least on large stocks and indices.

Rolling cash bets have a much tighter spread – the difference between the buying and selling price – than forward bets, ie bets on futures, and it can be the same as when you buy directly in the cash market. A rolling cash bet on Vodafone has a spread of a quarter of a point at the time of writing, which is the same as on its shares.

Spreads, even as narrow as this, are one way in which spread betting firms make their money. A second way is through overnight lending charges to traders on rolling cash bets, which are based on 100 per cent of the underlying money. The daily charge is typically LIBOR plus perhaps 2 or 3 per cent, which is divided by 365, representing days of the year.

This is a small daily sum but, on an aggregate basis from all customers, it makes a profit for the spread betting firm. If you take a short position, it is the *firm* that pays interest on overnight positions. The firm pays no interest on deposit accounts where the margin is placed, or perhaps, if the margin is sizable, a low rate, which means it can use the money so saved more profitably.

If you take a spread bet on futures rather than on the cash price, you will not have to pay overnight borrowing charges, but the spreads are larger, covering *cost of carry* as well as expenses and the firm's profit margin. If the underlying shares will go dividend before the forward dealing date, the forward price is reduced accordingly.

Spread betting, like other derivatives, may be used for hedging but it mostly attracts speculators. You cannot enter a bet with one firm and close it with another, but you can enter two bets simultaneously with different firms. Canny speculators have two or three accounts with financial bookmakers in an effort to get the keenest prices.

In all cases, you will pay neither fees nor commissions to the spread betting firm, but spreads are at its discretion. Critics say that spreads on futures bets are too opaque and enable dealers to change them as it suits them for individual trades. Professional advice is that, when you ask for a two-way quote on the telephone, you should not reveal whether you are a buyer or seller.

Contracts for difference

The CFD is a contract between two parties to exchange the difference between the opening and closing prices of a contract, as at the contract's close, multiplied by the specified number of shares. It provides you with exposure to the price movement in, among other things, a stock or index without ever owning the underlying instrument. If the price of the underlying shares goes up or down, you, as a trader in the CFD, will make or lose money on the movement.

Like spread betting, CFDs are an OTC market, which means that the counterparty is the product issuer. But unlike spread bets, the CFD aims to replicate all the financial benefits of share ownership except for voting rights. As a trader, you are entitled to dividend payments and, depending on your broker, will have full access to corporate actions, including rights issues and takeover activity.

CFDs are offered by spread betting firms, CFD market makers, specialist brokers and online dealers. The market now accounts for more than 20 per cent of trading by volume on the LSE. CFDs have expanded their coverage to include almost any market or any kind of asset. There are CFDs based on indices, currencies and commodities and in all UK stocks with a market capitalisation (share price multiplied by the number of shares in issue) of over £50 million, in many US and European stocks, and in all major world indices.

The market attracts institutional investors, particularly the hedge funds, who can take a position in equities without revealing their identities. By direct market access through brokers, the traders often obtain keener prices than through spread betting firms acting as market makers, but the deal will have to be of a specified minimum size.

In recent years, private investors have become increasingly involved in CFDs, but, unlike spread bets, this product is open only to experienced investors. As with other derivatives, the CFD is traded on margin, which is required to be high for stocks outside the FTSE 100, and low for indices. As a trader with a long position in a stock, you will pay a financing charge (perhaps LIBOR plus 1.5 per cent) for the outstanding amount above the margin, pro rata to the annual rate. If you have a short position, the firm will pay you the interest (perhaps LIBOR minus 2.5 per cent). If you close out the CFD intraday (within the day), financing payments will not apply.

The CFD has no settlement date, unlike futures and spread betting where the contract on expiry must be rolled over to the next one. As in spread betting, no stamp duty is payable on a CFD purchase but, after it has been held for about 60 days, the amount saved this way compared with owning shares is eroded by interest payments. From this point, it makes no economic sense to continue holding a CFD unless it is significantly increasing in value.

Unlike in spread betting, you are liable for capital gains tax on profits beyond the annual exemption level (£9,600 in 2008–09), but you may offset losses against future liabilities.

Regulatory developments

In October 2008, the FSA said that from 1 January 2009, investors holding 3 per cent or more of a single company through aggregated shares with CFD holdings must disclose their position. The aim is to prevent secretive stake building. Several European markets are reviewing their rules on similar lines.

The FSA's proposed disclosure requirements are expected to hit hedge funds, which may build up shares in companies. An example of what can arise, perfectly legal when it does not break disclosure requirements, was when German car maker Porsche announced publicly in October 2008 that it controlled 74.1 per cent of car maker Volkswagen and planned to raise this to 75 per cent in 2009, at which point it could launch a bid. This came as a shock because Porsche had only just over 40 per cent of voting stock, controlling 31.5 per cent of Volkswagen shares in cash-settled options like CFDs. If someone holds a position in CFDs, the CFD provider may buy the physical shares to hedge against the position, and the CFD holder may at any time convert the options into shares. In this way, it is possible for investors to build up a shareholding in companies without disclosure.

The way forward

If you are going into the derivatives game, you will need a thorough understanding of the products. This chapter, in combination with the rest of the book, has given you a start but you should read further books or do a course. I would steer you clear of expensive face-to-face seminars, but would direct you initially to books. You may like to consider my own books, *The Complete Guide to Online Stock Market Investing*, or *How to Win as a Stock Market Speculator*, both published by Kogan Page. I only wish I had room to include all the text of these books here, but all I can do is suggest you read them.

In addition, you will need to cultivate a trading mentality, which is based on money management, including a willingness to cut losses and run profits. It is easy to say but hard to carry out. You will need a trading system. This should include stop losses, meaning that if your investments drop below a given level, say 10 or 15 per cent below the latest price or what you paid, you will automatically sell out. Do not set the level too high because you must allow for sometimes substantial temporary fluctuations.

Spread betting firms will organise a stop loss for you. As a derivatives trader, you will be interested less in the fundamentals of the underlying financial instruments and more in what is driving short-term change. You may find that technical analysis – following trends and assessing the future from past performance by analysing charts – works for you. I touch on the basics of this in Chapter 20 but if you are really interested in this subject, in which I take an enormous but impartial interest, check out the coverage in another of my books, *The Times: How to Understand the Financial Pages*, also published by Kogan Page.

As a derivatives trader, you should also keep an eye on relevant news flow. Please check out the website of ADVFN (wwww.advfn.com). You may also like to sign up for free access to the message boards at Trade2win (www.Trade2win.com). And naturally the web gives you plenty of alternatives to these.

Bear in mind that the same firms may offer trading facilities in spread betting, contracts for difference and foreign exchange (see Chapter 13), and more.

The firms will typically help you understand the products and how their markets trade, although it is best to know a good deal before you open an account with them. Some firms offer free courses, which can impart valuable techniques on spread betting or CFDs and technical analysis, although the aim will be to sign you up as a client.

In derivatives, as in any other financial products, a simple rule applies. If you do not understand something, do not touch it. What the experts present as a safe product may have hidden complexity and risks. This is particularly true of structured products, including those which increase their coupons by the sale of derivatives. The way it works is that part of the investment is held as principal and part is used to sell – for example, options or credit default swaps – taking in premiums to boost the coupon. The risk is that the derivatives written give rise to losses, which would be met by payment from the principal sum. The price of higher coupons is risk to principal.

From late 2008, it has transpired that in Hong Kong and Singapore, retail buyers of structured products linked to Lehman Brothers had not understood the risks of the products they bought. That at least is their case. Some of these investors claimed they thought that the Lehman mini-bonds they were buying were a safe investment, although the product was linked with complex derivatives. The value of these credit-linked notes, which depended on Lehman as underwriter or reference counterparty, is now uncertain.

16

Exchanges and trading systems

Introduction

In this chapter we will look at how exchanges and alternative trading systems work in the United States, the United Kingdom and across Europe. Trading can take place on an exchange, between two parties off exchange, or through an alternative trading system.

Stock exchanges

A stock exchange provides a quotation for securities in public companies. It is also a market place where members can trade securities and it provides price information for each security listed on the exchange. In the last 16 years there has been a trend toward demutualisation, which is where stock exchanges convert from non-profit-making organisations owned by members to organisations run for profit. Exchanges have seen demutualisations as a better way to manage conflicts between market participants, including through the introduction of a new corporate governance framework, and a way to gain access to capital they need for new technology investment.

The Stockholm Stock Exchange was the first to demutualise in 1993, followed by others, including, in 2004, the London Stock Exchange. Demutualisation gave the LSE the freedom to invest in SETS, its electronic trading system (see page 185).

Another trend is for stock exchanges to become increasingly internationalised by attracting foreign companies to list their shares. Investor demand for access to a wider variety of company shares on a single platform, with lower trading costs and greater liquidity, has led to cross-border stock exchange mergers and cooperation agreements, including with alternative trading systems, which offer similar trading functionality to stock exchanges.

Stock exchanges started back in ancient Rome, where stockbrokers worked from a temple within the Forum. Let us look in detail at the main exchanges in the United States and London.

New York Stock Exchange, NASDAQ and ECNs

The New York Stock Exchange (NYSE) is the largest stock exchange in the United States. It started in 1792 and later benefited from the New York Securities Law of 1812, which liberated rules for companies to trade on the stock exchange. It established limited liability, which meant that if a listed company was sued, its shareholders could not be held liable. Similar securities laws were enacted later in Europe.

Until 1964, the NYSE used the ticker tape, which printed out stock symbols and prices of trades. Different exchanges had different prices for the same listed security. Under the Securities Act of 1975, securities brokers were required to establish an electronic system enabling trading at the best price across exchanges. The Intermarket Trading System filled the role and, in June 2007, was replaced with the more modern National Market System linkage.

NASDAQ, meanwhile, was set up in 1971. This was split into NASDAQ national market and NASDAQ small cap, the latter being for companies with a relatively small market capitalisation. NASDAQ is an OTC market, distinguished from on-exchange dealing by the organisation of a multiple dealer system. Dealers for NASDAQ stocks would compete for investor orders to buy and sell shares of companies for which the dealer agreed to make a market. A broker would look for the best price quote from dealers before buying or selling a stock for a client. In addition, some institutions traded off the exchanges and outside NASDAQ.

In the 1990s, with the progress of internet technology, market practitioners established entities known as electronic communication networks (ECNs), such as Instinet, to compete with the exchanges and NASDAQ. At this stage, the NYSE was floor based only.

Traders can post, buy and sell orders on the ECNs. They are considered to be a more open and flexible version of stock exchange order books, aiming to increase automated trading in the OTC markets. In addition, they provide an authorised, after-hours trading venue.

In the mid to late 1990s, ECNs were boosted by new rules under which dealers' quotes had to reflect limit orders, which are orders to a broker to buy a given amount of stock at or below a specified price or to sell it at or above a specified price. Limit orders from this point had to be executed immediately at the specified price when a counterparty was found to deal at that price, or had to be forwarded to another dealer or ECN. Before 1994, dealers had been able to ignore limit orders and so could post prices that made extra profits for them at the expense of investors. ECNs also benefited from a 1997 rule that dealers had to display their most competitive price quotes.

By 2007, ECNs were taking retail orders and were handling 30 per cent of trading volumes on NASDAQ. They were in the early stages of an electronic revolution, one that continues today. It is not just about faster trading, but also about accessing capital across international borders.

Electronic trading has reached even the NYSE, which has now merged with Euronext. Most exchanges have abolished a trading floor in favour of electronic trading, but NYSE Euronext has kept it as part of a hybrid model.

For each listed company stock, the NYSE has traditionally retained a specialist, who physically stands at a post on the exchange floor and maintains an inventory of orders in the stock, acting as both agent and dealer for the stocks in which it specialises. As an agent, the specialist matches buy and sell orders and makes a book of limit orders, placed with brokers. Brokers and dealers walk about the floor freely, trading stocks both with each other and with the specialist. They sometimes form a crowd at the specialist's post when there are peaks in demand for one or more of the shares the specialist represents. As a dealer, the specialist sometimes posts its own price quotes for shares in their books and may trade from its own inventory if order flow has dried up. The specialist must always provide a market for a security to trade, even if on its own account and even if the share price plummets. In a market crash, however, this has not always stabilised prices.

Under rules approved by the SEC in October 2008, the NYSE Euronext has retained specialists, to be renamed Designated Market Makers (DMMs). Each stock has a specialist/DMM, who matches up buyers and sellers and is rewarded for adding liquidity and taking incoming orders when markets are volatile. Floor brokers continue to represent buyers and sellers, and meet at the trading post, which is the location of the DMM. However, the DMM does not see the broker's order book in advance, a practice which has given the floor brokers an unfair advantage over competing firms. Nowadays, a DMM is involved in 1 in 10 trades or fewer. Most trading on NYSE Euronext is done electronically.

NASDAQ OMX now operates the NASDAQ stock exchange in New York City. The group competes with NYSE Euronext for listings and is the largest electronic screen-based equity securities market in the United States.

The London Stock Exchange

The London Stock Exchange evolved from an informal market trading government debt that started in the late 17th century. Brokers sold securities to clients on commission and jobbers acted as counterparties, taking turns on the bid–ask spread. In the early 19th century, a governance structure was implemented in the exchange.

Over the next few decades, the exchange expanded as a result of interest in foreign mining shares and, in particular, railroad securities. Members were asked to pay more fees and eventually new members joining were required to become shareholders in the exchange. The proprietors and members then had joint control.

During the First World War, the LSE suspended trading in July 1914 until the start of 1915, in line with other European exchanges. In 1918, the British government introduced a successful series of 'Victory bonds', a type of savings bond used to help fund the war effort and to control inflation in an economy affected by war. Trading on the LSE became busy again.

During the Second World War, the exchange helped the Treasury to market Treasury issues. Committees of LSE proprietors and members were combined into a council, which was dominated by members. This gave effective control to the government, and the exchange became a quasi-regulator.

Dual control by proprietors and members ended in 1948 and the exchange was tasked with providing services to members. In 1974, the LSE merged with domestic exchanges across the United Kingdom. The International Stock Exchange, as the combination of exchanges became known, was bigger and could regulate the securities industry better, but was less able to fend off foreign competition. In 1979, Margaret Thatcher's government abolished exchange controls, which meant that financial institutions could invest abroad easily.

The Thatcher government held that London banking had declined in competitiveness due to over-regulation and the dominance of old boy networks, and saw open competitive markets as the solution. 'Big Bang' was the term used to describe the deregulation of the London stock market on 27 October 1986. This was part of a broader government move to reduce the influence of the LSE as a private club that controlled its members according to its own rules, and to stop a flight of capital from London.

Following Big Bang, overseas securities firms could for the first time become members of the LSE. Trading on the floor was replaced by a screen-based system. Fixed stockbroking commissions and single capacity were abolished. The jobber who had quoted wholesale share prices to the stockbroker gave way to market making. The main difference from the old jobber system was that market makers were part of the wider group. Big Bang strengthened London's competitive place in the world, making it arguably the world's most significant banking centre. Some critics said that the deregulation was responsible for subsequent city scandals but others saw the problem as the continued existence of old boy networks.

In 1995, the LSE created the Alternative Investment Market (AIM) for small and start-up companies. Some rival small-cap markets across Europe were to follow, particularly in the dot-com boom for internet companies in 1999 and early 2001, although many subsequently failed. In late 1999, the LSE introduced TECHmark, a new market for technology companies.

SETS and market making

In 1997, the LSE introduced the Stock Exchange Electronic Trading Service (SETS), which offered electronic trading alongside market making.

Since then, almost all main market stocks, as well as an increasing number of AIM stocks, have been tradable on SETS, which has now developed into a hybrid model that offers electronic execution alongside quotes displayed by market makers. Where there is a suitable level of liquidity in a security, trading on an order book can be more efficient. Prices on an order book are more transparent than those advertised on the quote-driven market-maker system, the alternative, because they are firm and based on orders from the entire market and not only on the decision of a small group of market makers.

The LSE opens and closes trading on SETS each day with an auction. Anybody who trades the order book has access to the auctions. By concentrating liquidity at a set point in time, the auctions set the opening and closing prices for each security. Some might use the auctions to balance their books, and others to fulfil a trade they want to execute. During the auction, market participants can enter limit buy and sell orders, and the LSE automatically calculates and displays the real-time *uncrossing* price (the mean price at which the bids and offers can be matched). In London, market makers still take part in quote-driven trading that runs parallel to the order book. They provide liquidity and price formation in those shares in which they choose to make a market. They are wholesalers of shares and may specialise. It is mainly in small-cap stocks that market makers are seen as useful. But even in larger-cap stocks, buyers and sellers may go to a market maker rather than SETS in order to achieve trade immediacy, in size.

Every stock has a notional minimum of at least one market maker, but in practice has at least two and mostly five or more. Competing market makers display continuous buy and sell prices on terminals globally. The market maker has a responsibility towards the client companies in whose shares it makes a market, but also to brokers and share dealers.

Through the quote-driven system, market makers are committed to providing a share price and to dealing in a minimum deal size throughout the trading day. They set their own prices based on their anonymous proprietary position and their knowledge of order flows, as well as their perception of supply and demand.

The market maker makes its money on the spread, which is the difference between the bid and offer price. Bid is the price at which customers can sell, and offer is the price at which they can buy. A bid-offer spread of 8–10 means that you can sell to the market maker at 8p or buy at 10p.

If one market maker has dealt with another anonymously, or otherwise privately through interdealer brokers (IDBs), the screen price is altered accordingly. Market makers may use IDBs to balance their books. If one market maker has bought a lot of shares, it may unload some, perhaps through an IDB, onto other market makers. But according to the LSE, most market makers now use SETS to balance their books because it offers greater liquidity.

Users of LSE trading systems

Users of the LSE trading systems include retail service providers (see below), hedge fund managers, market makers and sell-side brokers, including retail to a small degree, and member firms trading on their own account. The retail service provider (RSP) network was developed by Merrill Lynch and other financial institutions. This is an interface between retail brokers and the wider equity markets. Brokers use RSPs for the vast majority of the 10 million-plus retail trades they execute each year.

When asked by a customer for a stock price, the stockbroker relays the request electronically to the RSP, which will send back the best price it has determined, with reference to both the order book and quote-driven market makers.

The RSP is itself a market maker in some stocks to a size limit, beyond which it will refer the trade to its own market makers, which provide a service in both quote-driven and order-book securities. Brokers choose how many RSPs they poll; it could be three or a dozen.

Hedge funds often prefer DMA (direct market access) to the traditional model whereby they pay a broker to execute trades on their behalf. The trades still go through the broker's system, but the fund itself controls the trading, and pays much lower commissions as a result. The LSE takes the view that the price improvement so obtained offsets the cost of setting up the appropriate technology, and that private investors could benefit from trading in a similar way. Some day traders remain unconvinced of this.

If hedge funds cannot spare the cash outlay for the positions in shares they would like to take, or if they want to keep their holdings opaque, they will use CFDs (see Chapter 15). This will impact the share price because the shares are held as security against the CFD trades.

Tokyo Stock Exchange

The Tokyo Stock Exchange is the third largest in the world, behind New York and London. It has separated its listed stocks into a 'First' section for large companies, a 'Second' section for mid-sized companies and a 'Mothers' section for start-ups.

The exchange started trading in 1878 and, in 1943, was combined with 10 other Japanese exchanges to form one, later shut down. The Tokyo Stock Exchange reopened in May 1949 and, by 1990, was the biggest in the world by stock market capitalisation. In 1999, it switched to electronic trading.

Share trading venues

In Europe, shares have traditionally been traded on exchanges such as the LSE or Deutsche Börse. After the MiFID directive came into force in November 2007, multilateral trading facilities (MTFs) have been established across London and continental Europe. MTFs have been introduced partly because with the prospect of trading across all the different European markets there is a far greater incentive to start up and a better chance of turning a profit. The MTFs are broadly equivalent to the US ECNs although, unlike these as start-ups, they have had to compete with established electronic trading systems. The MiFID also provides an additional incentive to competition through its new rules on best execution.

Best execution broadly means that brokers must find the best price although, beyond retail investors, there are other key criteria such as the cheapest route for clearing and settlement of trades. The concentration rules across many European states, requiring shares to be traded on the national exchange, have been abolished. In London, the LSE competes with newcomers, such as MTFs, as well as other exchanges for listings and trade orders.

A stock exchange has as its main function bringing together buyers and sellers through a centralised trading system. Unlike the MTFs, it also has other functions such as launching new issues of securities and the dissemination of listed company information, whether prices or company announcements. The MTF tends to focus on blue-chip stocks. An exchange will tend to provide trading functionality for a far broader range of stock, including small-cap securities, and may operate a number of other businesses such as post-trade services or derivatives platforms or, in the case of the LSE Group, fixed interest trading.

The MTFs have an advantage over exchanges in being able to set up operation from scratch at low cost. They can offer other advantages such as faster trading speeds and access to pan-European share trading. So far it has proved difficult for MTFs to gain significant market share from Europe's main exchanges, although Chi-X (see below) has a 12–14 per cent market share. The established exchanges have long experience of competing with other exchanges, although this can work both ways. The NYSE has seen a major hit to market share from competition. Faced with new competition from MTFs, the European exchanges are cutting fees, as far as their staff and legacy infrastructure costs allow, and speeding up trade execution. For example, the LSE has been upgrading its £40 million TradElect electronic trading system.

The MTFs boast that they have lower staff costs than exchanges and not the same legacy infrastructure costs. The LSE Group has around 1,000 staff across centres in London, Milan and Rome to carry out its various functions. According to one MTF chief executive, this will limit the fee cuts it can implement.

The speed of trading is an area where the MTFs can beat the exchanges. This is important, because high speeds attract the algorithmic traders. These trade a number of orders simultaneously, responding to economic or market developments with computerised efficiency based on complicated mathematical formulae. They are major liquidity providers.

In the speed stakes, Chi-X, launched in March 2007 as the first of the MTFs, trades around 800 blue-chip stocks. Trading a share on its platform takes 1–2 milliseconds, provided that clients put servers right at the Chi-X data centre, which can be achieved by leasing space on Chi-X's server rack. At the time of writing, trading takes significantly longer on the LSE's platform. Chi-X was established by Instinet, a subsidiary of Japanese broker Nomura, and operates in the United Kingdom and Canada, offering a cheap fee structure with a rebate model, in which liquidity providers are rewarded with a larger rebate than liquidity takers. The market data feed it provides is free, while exchanges sell data to the market. In February 2009, Chi-X was awaiting regulatory approvals for planned expansion into Japan, Singapore, Hong Kong and Australia.

Starting up in September 2008 was Turquoise, a pan-European trading platform backed by a consortium of seven investment banks. The plan was to launch it earlier and run it on a non-profit-making basis, but there were substantial delays.

Among other trading venues looking to start up is Börse Berlin Equiduct Trading, which aims to be an exchange rather than an MTF, and NASDAQ OMX Europe, which operates as an alternative equities trading venue in Europe. In the United States, BATS Trading went live in January 2006 and BATS Europe was launched in London in October 2008. At the time of writing, NYSE Euronext is planning to launch NYSE Arca Europe, an equities trading venue.

Systematic internalisers

Trading firms have the option of becoming a systematic internaliser (SI), which is effectively a mini-exchange. The MiFID directive has defined a systematic internaliser as an investment firm which on an organised, frequent and systematic basis, deals on its own account by executing client orders outside a regulated market or an MTF. The SI must comply with pre-trade transparency requirements for liquid shares and must make trades public in both liquid and illiquid shares within three minutes of execution. Each regulator must maintain and publish a list of SIs.

In theory, the SIs can pose serious competition to the exchanges and MTFs. However, the small number of registered SIs so far, amounting to about a dozen, including several from one banking group, suggests that the business model is unattractive.

Dark liquidity pools

Dark liquidity pools are electronic trading venues where institutional investors can buy and sell large blocks of shares without the user's order being displayed publicly. Like exchanges, they match buyers and sellers. These investors value this form of anonymity, with no publication of the trade until after execution. Because the market cannot see a larger order being placed in a particular stock, other trades are not influenced and so the share price should not be impacted in advance of execution. Dark pools are widely recognised as a method of achieving 'best execution' as required by the MiFID, particularly for large or block orders and trading in less liquid stocks.

There are various types of 'gaming' that exploit the dark pools. One such technique is when traders send a lot of buy or sell orders out into a dark pool. If the traders hit something and get an execution, this gives them an idea of some of the larger orders in the pool, and they can use this information to their advantage. Another technique is to buy small amounts of stock on conventional exchanges and sell them as a block on a dark pool. Small-cap stocks lend themselves most obviously to this type of activity due to their thin markets, which means that the share price changes easily even on marginal trading volume.

Traders usually get away with gaming but it can involve market manipulation. There is some growth in anti-gaming technology in the dark pools, which does not necessarily put off the players. Dark pools have gained in popularity in Europe after the MiFID, which has enabled trading venues to compete with exchanges.

Away from the dark pools, stock prices based on visible trades may not reflect the reality of the price at which a share can actually be traded. In addition, dark pools could absorb the liquidity of small-cap shares, making them harder to trade at a fair price.

The activity of buying stocks in small amounts on conventional exchanges and selling them as a block on a dark pool at a better price is known as 'gaming' and could give rise to market manipulation. Small-cap stocks, with thin markets and prices that change easily with even marginal trading volumes, are the most obvious type of security for gaming. Anti-gaming technology in dark pools is not necessarily putting players off. The number of members of dark pools suspended for practices such as gaming appears to be small.

Dark pools have developed in popularity across Europe since November 2007 when the MiFID came into force, enabling trading venues to compete with exchanges across Europe. Even on the exchanges, iceberg orders, as they are known, have elements of dark-pool liquidity given that traders may have more to trade than is displayed on the trading screen.

Turquoise, the equities trading platform backed by nine banks, announced plans for a pan-European share-trading service in the first quarter of 2009 that would route and distribute orders to connected dark pools. According to a Turquoise statement, the aim is to execute trades with minimum market impact and improved prices. The independent centralised infrastructure offered by Turquoise will provide a meeting point for otherwise fragmented liquidity and a place where institutional size trades will execute securely.

The LSE plans Baikal, its own dark pool, for the second quarter of 2009. NASDAQ has also made arrangements with dark-pool operators and puts some of its own volume through non-display platforms. In early February, SmartPool, an MTF set up by NYSE Euronext, BNP Paribas, HSBC and J P Morgan, launched a dark pool for block trading. It started trading 1,000 stocks from 15 European markets, including Spain, in a phased introduction.

Consolidation

Exchanges are facing up to the new competition partly by consolidating, although there have also been some new exchanges. In April 2007, the NYSE completed a merger with Euronext, which had itself been formed from the union of the Paris, Amsterdam, Brussels and Lisbon exchanges, through which it obtained the London-based LIFFE futures exchange.

In the same month, Deutsche Börse, the German stock exchange, announced it was buying International Securities Exchange, the US options exchange, for US$2.8 billion (£1.9 billion). One month later, NASDAQ, the US high-tech exchange, announced it would buy OMX, the Nordic exchange group, for US$3.7 billion (£2.5 billion). The combined group expects to focus much of its efforts in London.

In London, the LSE has fought for its independence. In 2005, it rejected a £1.6 billion bid from Macquarie Bank and, subsequently, higher bids from NASDAQ. In 2007, the LSE bought Borsa Italiana in Milan for £1.1 billion. This move formed the London Stock Exchange Group, in an all-share deal. In July 2008, the LSE and the Tokyo Stock Exchange announced a joint venture for a new Tokyo-based market based on the AIM.

17

Clearing and settlement

Introduction

Clearing and settlement are the back-office structures that support the trading of securities. In this chapter we will look at how they work.

Overview

Clearing and settlement are the plumbing of the securities industry. Clearing is the link between trading and settlement. Central counterparty clearing is where a neutral central counterparty comes between the buyer and seller of securities to reduce risks and net transactions before they are settled. In this way, the central counterparty helps to manage risk. The facility is available for exchange-traded transactions on electronic order books.

Settlement is the point at which the buyer and seller exchange securities for cash, and vice versa. During the credit crisis of 2007–09, it has been a challenge for the post-trade infrastructure to deal with large swings in transaction flows, including some company liquidations as well as the partial nationalisations of some financial institutions. The infrastructure has stood up to the strain.

Managing counterparty risk has increased in criticality within back offices, alongside service pricing issues. With increased use of central counterparties and as the settlement infrastructures in Europe offer delivery-versus-payment settlement, in which cash and securities are exchanged simultaneously, the risk is eliminated that one of the counterparties to a trade delivers the promised asset, such as cash, without receiving another asset, such as securities, in return. In this respect, the clearing and settlement infrastructure is easing market concerns about counterparty risk.

euroclear

Rising to the challenges of crisis and change

There is really only one market issue today - how to cope with what is the greatest financial crisis in living memory. For most financial firms, the focus today is on two objectives: reducing risks and costs.

MiFID and the Code of Conduct on Clearing and Settlement have created a more competitive trading and post-trading environment. They have prompted the emergence of new trading venues and central counterparties (CCPs) to compete with national incumbents. They have helped reduce fees and improve services, but have also increased fragmentation. This is generating new types of risks, which market infrastructures can help mitigate, for instance through more seamless interaction between clearing and settlement, and links to efficient collateral management solutions.

What is expected from a market infrastructure in a crisis like the one we face today?

Resilience

Crises often generate high levels of volatility, leading to transaction-processing peaks, with which back offices must cope. For instance, Euroclear UK & Ireland recently settled 1.6 million trades in one day, triple its average monthly volume. The ability of an infrastructure to do this is not coincidental. It requires the infrastructure to anticipate and invest in the relevant hardware and software to ensure it can manage such events.

Similarly, infrastructure providers like LCH.Clearnet and Euroclear, which are the post-trading institutions in Europe that have the closest business relationship with broker-dealers, have been able to unwind their exposures to Lehman Brothers with no losses and without market disruption.

Cutting costs

Client pressure to reduce fees in market infrastructures will increase in coming years. Euroclear continues to reduce fees while investing in best-of-class services and service enhancements, as it is clear that the need for expert client support will grow in the current context.

With the recent acquisition of the Finnish and Swedish central securities depositories, the Euroclear group now covers approximately 50 per cent of all European domestic debt outstanding and about 66 per cent of blue-chip equities in Europe. Our Single Platform will soon allow financial firms to access a single, harmonized platform to process the greater part of their European domestic and cross-border settlement activity.

Such solutions are more necessary than ever before, as firms cannot afford to carry the high friction costs of infrastructure fragmentation.

Process automation

Manual intervention is a well-known source of costs and risks in high-volume businesses. An effective way for a market infrastructure to reduce these costs and risks for its users is to automate processes.

In the funds market, for example, the Euroclear group is spearheading an industry-wide initiative to drastically reduce fund-transaction processing fees through increased levels of automation. Euroclear UK & Ireland, together with fund order-routing company EMXCo, which Euroclear acquired in 2007, is automating the order routing and settlement process for UK funds.

Reducing risk

Relying on market infrastructures with a recognized track record in risk management and risk avoidance is particularly important to firms today.

Reducing settlement risk by automating trade matching is a case in point. The automated onward transmission of trade information for settlement has proved to have a major impact on the reduction of settlement risk, especially when it takes place within a few minutes of trade execution. Estimates show that even a 5 per cent reduction in the number of settlement fails could deliver several million pounds of savings per year.

The massive growth in OTC derivative transactions has generated backlogs in back offices and has substantially increased counterparty risk in the market. There is now consensus among regulators and market professionals that, at least for credit default swaps, a CCP is needed.

But CCPs will not solve all issues for all derivatives. Complementary solutions, such as trade and portfolio reconciliation services, and matching services to help identify and manage risk exposures, are needed.

Euroclear has developed its DerivManager tool to help counterparties for all OTC derivatives products to match their exposures and then to collateralize them.

Creating liquidity

The past year has painfully underscored the fact that access to liquidity and the ability to mobilize assets, wherever they are held, is not just a question of efficiency, but may prove to be a matter of survival. Infrastructures often play the role of conduits for liquidity and should, therefore, focus on ways to facilitate liquidity flows. For instance, Euroclear Bank will shortly make it easier for clients to mobilize assets as collateral to access central bank credit.

Infrastructure service providers like Euroclear are in a unique position to take on these challenges successfully. It is their duty to do so in a way that contributes to the stabilization of markets. They are the entities that can provide this combination of lower costs and lower risks so that clients will have a better chance of weathering the credit crunch in 2009 and possibly thereafter.

www.euroclear.com

In the United States, earlier consolidation has led to the existence of only two major clearing and settlement entities, the Federal Reserve System and the Depository Trust and Clearing Corporation (DTCC), a user-owned entity. The Federal Reserve acts as the depository and settlement agency for US government securities; those securities are cleared by DTCC. In addition, DTCC, through its subsidiaries, clears and settles most US market trades in equities, corporate and municipal bonds, mortgage-backed securities and investment funds. It provides settlement services, and has safekeeping and asset-servicing capabilities for various products. DTCC's charges for clearing and settlement are cheaper than any equivalent domestic settlement service provider in Europe, primarily due to economies of scale. DTCC also provides matching and confirmation of OTC derivatives, and is especially strong in providing depository and asset services for credit derivatives globally through its Trade Information Warehouse.

The United States is a single market operating in one language, one currency and under a single fiscal and regulatory regime. Europe has a different challenge to centralise clearing and settlement. Because it is a collection of individual markets, each with its own operational idiosyncrasies, cross-border transactions are complex and often six to seven times more expensive than domestic transactions to clear and settle. There are eight central counterparties in Europe, which some see as good for competition, although others see as too many.

As announced in October 2008, DTCC is planning a combination with LCH.Clearnet, Europe's largest independent clearer, which means that, for the first time, the United States and Europe would be supported by a common infrastructure. This combined service would compete with Eurex Clearing, jointly operated by Deutsche Börse AG and SIX Swiss Exchange, and the other clearing and central counterparties operating in Europe. A consortium of LCH.Clearnet's users also plans to make a counteroffer for LCH.Clearnet.

In addition, DTCC has introduced its own central counterparty clearing and settlement organisation to Europe to support several of the new MTFs created as a result of the MiFID directive. That clearing organisation is European Central Counterparty Limited, or EuroCCP. It is a unique model for Europe in that it operates at cost rather than for profit, is governed by its users rather than shareholders, and leverages the economies of scale provided by its parent corporation to lower its costs. Clearing and settlement are available on a pan-European basis, and as of early 2009 that includes 15 European markets. Trades are cleared by EuroCCP across all MTFs submitting trades to the clearing firm, and settlement is completed by EuroCCP at each of the national market central securities depositories in each of the 15 markets (such as Euroclear UK and Ireland Ltd in the United Kingdom), using Citibank as EuroCCP's settlement agent.

To arrive at the point at which Europe will have cheaper and fewer clearing and settlement service providers, as in the United States, Europe has chosen a competitive model.

In the United Kingdom, equity trades on the LSE may be cleared through LCH.Clearnet or SIX x-Clear, which is part of the Swiss post-trade infrastructure. As we saw in Chapter 16, the LSE now owns Borsa Italiana, the Italian stock exchange, which has its own clearing facility known as Cassa di Compensazione e Garanzia (CdCG). It is widely expected that CdCG will become a third competitor for UK share transaction clearing.

In Europe, there is a push to separate trading from post trading and to encourage competition in both. Some countries operate within vertical silos, where the local stock exchange owns its own clearing and settlement providers, and requires users to use these post-trade facilities when trading on the stock exchange. For example, Deutsche Börse, the German stock exchange, includes trading, clearing and settlement as part of the same business model.

Euroclear UK & Ireland Ltd, previously known as CRESTCo, which was capitalised in October 2004, is the United Kingdom's only central securities depository (CSD). It is part of the Euroclear group, based in Brussels, which also includes the CSDs of Belgium, Finland, France, Sweden and the Netherlands. Euroclear is completely user owned and user governed.

The Euroclear group currently owns 15.8 per cent of LCH.Clearnet and openly expects to retain a similar level of ownership in the future. There are technical synergies and operational efficiencies to be gained from a close business relationship between clearing and settlement service providers.

Euroclear UK & Ireland owns the CREST system, through which there is settlement of money market instruments, bonds, equities, and soon investment funds, but not futures or other derivatives trades. Euroclear UK & Ireland receives settlement instructions from clients of the LSE, as well as netted settlement instructions from LCH.Clearnet and Eurex (the clearing house for the Irish Stock Exchange), and a growing list of MTFs, their clearing companies, and others.

Settlement processing occurs on the CREST system on settlement day, no matter how long the agreed settlement period, which is the time between the trade date and settlement date. It is a real-time electronic process conducted on a delivery-versus-payment basis, which entails the simultaneous and irrevocable transfer of cash and securities. Full legal title of the securities is transferred at the point of settlement.

There have been efforts to force competition in the post-trade area, as the MiFID has accomplished among trading venues. As a result of MiFID and the introduction of MTFs, there are now even more trading venues and central counterparties in Europe. At present, competition is creating greater fragmentation. There will, however, be a shake-out leading to consolidation, which is arguably the only way to get cheaper services.

The challenge is that all EU-based trading, clearing and settlement infrastructure service providers, including those in the United Kingdom, have yet to fully implement a code of conduct approved by the EC. The signatories must meet standards in price transparency, access and interoperability, and service unbundling.

It is the part relating to interoperability, leading to greater competition, that is the biggest challenge. As we saw earlier in this chapter, some parts of the capital market infrastructure operate in silos, while others have operated as near monopolies. Provided there is a business case, interoperability will allow a clearing or settlement service provider in one market to receive feeds directly from the local stock exchange and/or clearing facility in another EU market, respectively, in order to offer users a competitive service.

Post-trade service providers are hesitant about opening up their markets to competition without reciprocal arrangements in place with the part of the infrastructure seeking to offer a competing service. The EC and other authorities are assessing how to unblock the situation, partly by analysing whether some infrastructure service providers are protected by artificial barriers of local regulation, law and market practice. Nevertheless, the cost of cross-border clearing and settlement remains too high.

In 2001 and 2003, the Giovannini Group issued reports on the clearing and settlement environment in Europe. The group said that 15 barriers needed to be overcome, and assigned responsibility to different public- and private-sector organisations to remove them. The recommendations include such measures as harmonising opening hours of settlement systems and establishing a single EU law defining settlement finality. Some have proved easier to overcome than others and, since then, new barriers have been identified.

In a speech at the 2008 Annual Conference in Venice of the Association of Private Client Investment Managers and Stockbrokers, Pierre Francotte, chief executive officer at Euroclear, said that the industry's code of conduct has greatly increased the transparency of pricing for services provided across Europe, encouraged a more competitive spirit among market infrastructures and led to a more open dialogue between users and providers. But he also said that the practical benefits have still to be felt.

Another initiative is TARGET2-Securities (T2-S), which the ECB announced in 2006. This is a programme to build its own euro-zone securities settlement infrastructure, and is backed by the EC. The project aims to create a platform for the cross-border and domestic settlement of securities against central bank money in the euro zone and beyond from 2013. This is similar to part of Euroclear's Single Platform initiative, which will not only settle trades in multiple currencies but will also process custody and other transactions. Two of the three phases of Euroclear's Single Platform have been delivered, and by 2011 the project will be completed.

Under the T2-S plan, the ECB would take over the role of private-sector CSDs as the single provider of settlement processing activities. The CSDs would, however, continue to provide all other related processing services, such as custody, collateral management and issuer services.

The idea is to achieve lower costs and settlement risk. Cross-border settlement may be cheaper with T2-S than any individual CSD can offer today. However, one of the major outstanding issues is the level of fees that end users will pay, as T2-S will charge the CSDs, which in turn will add their service charges on top to the end user. The CSDs also want an appropriate legal framework with the T2-S operator that will govern arrangements for the CSDs' outsourcing relationship. Euroclear is as concerned as the other CSDs about these issues and has set as one of its conditions of using T2-S that each Euroclear client may have the choice of settling transactions in central bank money either in T2-S or in Euroclear's Single Platform.

Euroclear and the ECB are not necessarily competing for settlement. Euroclear's user-choice model provides a safety net for users in the event that T2-S is delivered later than 2013 or does not offer the degree of savings promised. If T2-S is cheaper than Euroclear's Single Platform for settling transactions in euros, Euroclear would outsource the portion of its Single Platform that offers settlement in euros in central bank money to T2-S and share the lower cost benefits with its clients. Its Single Platform would continue to be used for non-euro settlement activity and for all settlement activities relating to Euroclear Bank, the international CSD, which does not settle transactions through a central bank; as a bank, it settles transactions in what is known as commercial bank money.

A third initiative to reduce cross-border settlement costs in Europe is Link Up Markets, a joint venture that will establish links between eight European CSDs to facilitate CSD access to the services of the other participating CSDs across all asset classes except derivatives. Link Up Markets will absorb any differences in communication standards across the markets. Thus, it will route orders between CSDs, thereby eliminating the need for intermediaries to intervene. However, it will not consolidate systems nor reduce the technical running costs of any participating CSD. Euroclear is not among the founding members, but, like every other CSD in Europe, is invited to join Link Up Markets.

In emerging markets, Romania's central depository in January 2009 launched a service giving Romanian investors direct access to Eurobonds traded on international markets through a direct link with Clearstream Banking Luxembourg. The National Depository Center of Russia launched a similar service for Russian investors in May 2008 through Euroclear Bank.

Some economies, such as Russia, have spent years discussing the formation of a single CSD, which would replace the fragmented approach to dealing, settlement and the provision of other back-office services that otherwise prevails. Progress seems always too slow. Such developing economies are the subject of the next chapter.

18

Emerging markets

Introduction

Emerging markets may grow much faster than European and US markets in good times but they are riskier. The economies provide vital exports to the West, including oil, steel and agricultural commodities, but demand may plummet in times of crisis. They are also importers. For Western businesses they provide partnership and merger opportunities, but the price can be high and their cultures are different.

Overview

Corruption and lack of transparency are generally rife in emerging markets. Official statistics are often unreliable and the media may be censored. Business disputes may be settled with shootings. Governments have control of the police, the judiciary and businesses.

The credit crisis of 2007–09 hit emerging markets but later than in the West. Among oil-producing nations, some have been hurt more than others by a plunging oil price, down by more than two-thirds from a July 2008 peak of more than US$147 a barrel. In Venezuela, oil accounts for 89 per cent of exports and the government has put on hold some of its social programmes, including subsidised oil to Cuba, Bolivia and Ecuador.

Over the long term, some specialist investors have profited enormously from emerging markets. From the start of 2003 to the end of 2006, the Morgan Stanley Capital International (MSCI) Emerging Markets Index had a total return of 240 per cent in dollars, making an average annual 36 per cent increase, compared with 106 per cent for the S&P 500 Index over the period.

Even a single year of investment can be startlingly profitable; but it has to be the right year. In 2007, the MSCI BRIC Index (covering the so-called BRIC economies: Brazil, Russia, India and China) rose by 56.1 per cent. Compare this with the 3.28 per cent gain on the United Kingdom's FTSE 100 index in the same year, or, worse still, the 2.63 per cent gain on the S&P 500 in the United States. The wide gap suggested that emerging markets had been decoupled from the West. By August 2008, sharp stock market declines in Russia, China and India suggested that the decoupling theory was mistaken. Nonetheless, it is widely accepted that the economic growth of the countries has only declined, not stopped.

The long-term growth of emerging markets and their ability to save and build up reserves, compared with the heavy borrowing of the US government, are part of a message. The world does not depend on the United States as much as it did. Asian countries learnt from their own 1998 crisis to invest in infrastructure, not to borrow too heavily and to save; they do not have the debt culture of the West.

According to 'Global Trends 2025: A Transformed World', released in November 2008 by the US government's National Intelligence Council, economies such as China, India and Brazil will grow in influence over the next 20 years at the expense of the United States, marking a shift from a unipolar to a multipolar global economy.

Clearly, investors shy away from the burdensome regulations of the United States, including the Sarbanes–Oxley Act and the PATRIOT Act with its anti-money laundering provisions that have put off legitimate investors. The United States has imposed heavier taxes on businesses than Europe and, particularly, Asia.

The US dollar remains strong, however, in times of crisis. Asia and other emerging markets depend on the United States and Europe to buy their exports and so have a vested interest in those countries' economic health. In October 2008, after the credit crisis had heightened, UK prime minister Gordon Brown asked China, Japan and the Middle East, which had significant foreign exchange reserves, to provide money to the IMF to help lend money to countries with problems.

Let us now take a look at the present state and likely future of China, the C in BRIC.

China

'Global Trends 2025' reports a shift from the Western free market model to the state capitalisation model of China, as well as of India and Russia. China accounts for 5 per cent of the world's economy. This is currently dwarfed by the 28 per cent share held by the United States, but China is growing much faster, at an average of nearly 10 per cent a year since Deng Xiaoping came to power in 1978.

China has a stable currency and a vast US$1.9 trillion (£1.3 trillion) in hard currency reserves, a large part of which is in US government bonds. China, more than most of the emerging markets, had seemed decoupled from the West in the early stages of the 2007–09 credit crisis. The Chinese banks did not have major sub-prime mortgage exposure and some of China's slowdown was due to its monetary tightening policy rather than Western influence.

At the same time, China has links with the West through foreign direct investment which, in November 2008, had declined by more than a third in a year. The annual growth rate in China's GDP had slowed to 9 per cent in the third quarter of 2008, its lowest rate for five years, down from 10.1 per cent in the second quarter. Large foreign companies cancelled plans to create new production facilities.

China's growth as a major importer and exporter of commodities has slowed, although from a high level. The country's demand for metals has declined, which has led to a fall in metal prices. In December 2008, Rio Tinto, the Australian mining group which is a major exporter to China, said it would cut 14,000 job and scale back spending plans by US$5 billion (£3.4 billion), as the global crisis reduced demand for metals.

The Chinese stock market was also hit by the global financial crisis. By June 2008, the Shanghai Composite Index had dropped below 3,000 points, which was half its level in mid October 2007, although still well up on its June 2005 level of only 1,000.

The Chinese government had restricted property development to avoid a bubble and, by late 2008, China's property prices were down.

In November 2008, it came as a relief globally when the Chinese government announced a four trillion yuan (£393 billion) stimulus package, including tax cuts and spending on infrastructure following recent disasters, including the May 2008 earthquake in the Sichuan province. Between mid September and late November of that year, the Chinese central bank cut interest rates three times. In the short term, forecasters agree that China faces slower economic growth, although they differ on the expected level of decline.

In the long term, China's prospects look bright. The International Energy Agency (IEA), a Paris-based intergovernmental organisation founded by the OECD, has forecast that China will overtake the United States as the world's largest energy consumer. International oil and gas groups are focused on China. BP, Europe's second-largest oil group, has invested US$4.6 billion (£3.1 billion) in China, a modest sum given the size of the company and the country.

The 'Global Trends' review predicts that, on present trends, China will become the world's second-largest economy, above Europe and behind only the United States, and the world's largest natural resources importer, and will be a leading military power.

Another emerging economy viewed as particularly promising from a Western perspective is India, the I in BRIC.

India

India is the country to which many Western financial services companies have outsourced their call centres. The news agency Reuters, in my time as a stock market journalist working for it, was making extensive use of resources in India, not just for IT help but also for some areas of journalism.

Even after mid 2008, India still had a 9 per cent annual GDP growth rate, although there were signs of slowing. India has high currency reserves and an economy, half based on agriculture, driven by domestic demand rather than exports. Banks and finance play only a small part in the economy.

By late 2008, India was feeling the impact from the credit crisis. Consumer lending was in decline and IT development had slowed. Property investment was declining as US companies were no longer rushing to buy commercial premises.

In November 2008, to protect local producers, India's government imposed a 20 per cent import tax on crude soya-bean oil and a 5 per cent customs duty on steel imports. This was in the face of global sentiment against protectionism.

India suffered a blow to its corporate reputation from the accounting scandal that hit software firm Satyam. The company had won awards for corporate governance but, in January 2009, its founder and chairman, Ramalinga Raju, resigned after admitting that he had falsified the company's accounts. He said that the company had exaggerated its cash reserves by about US\$1 billion (£0.7 billion).This was India's biggest corporate scandal in memory, and although small in comparison with US scandals such as Enron (see Chapter 12), it cast doubt over auditing standards and corporate governance, and on the outsourcing industry in India.

Brazil is the B in BRIC and, like India, it has made money from commodities. Let us take a look.

Brazil

As an emerging economy, Brazil has come a long way. Before July 1994, inflation in the country was topping 2,500 per cent a year but since 1999 it has dropped to below 10 per cent. In October 2002, after a fast victory in the election for a PT (Workers' Party) government, the new president, Luiz Inácio Lula da Silva, promised in a letter to the Brazilian people to retain the floating exchange rate and the central bank's anti-inflation policy. In the same year Brazil received a US$30 billion (£20.1 billion) loan from the IMF and then paid it off early.

Brazil was hit by the credit crisis of 2007–09 but, like some other emerging markets, late compared with the West. In September 2008, Brazil's currency, the real, was swiftly and heavily devalued following an August record high against the dollar. Consumer lending had declined but not stopped. The economy was considered stable and continued to grow. In 2007 and 2008, GDP rose by more than 5 per cent each year. It was the first time in 20 years that it had shown two years of consecutive growth.

At the time of writing, Brazil has around US$200 billion (£134 billion) in foreign reserves, enough to manage the impact of the credit crisis for the short term. The economy had gained from the 2001–08 commodities price boom, and from China's demand for its commodity exports. In April and May 2008 respectively, credit rating agencies S&P and Fitch Ratings gave the country investment grade status.

For the future, Brazil will benefit from its efficient agricultural sector and is the world's largest sugar and coffee producer. It is a main producer of iron ore, and has seen significant ethanol producer growth. The country will benefit from recent major oil discoveries at the Tupi and Carioca fields on Brazil's Atlantic coast.

On a less positive note, the country's debt is as high as 42 per cent of GDP. According to Exclusive Analysis's *Foresight 2009* yearbook, President Lula has not done much to bring about structural reforms. In the private sector, taxation is relatively heavy, in part to fund an unsustainable pension system, and outdated labour legislation increases production costs, while high interest rates constrain investment.

Russia

Russia is an emerging economy with fierce detractors as well as defenders. Speculators have gained from the rise of its stock market in recent years, which has been linked to the oil price boom. Oil accounts for 63 per cent of the country's exports. Even in this boom time, however, investor Jim Rogers was one of those who criticised the country's lack of self-investment and infrastructure.

Until the recent credit crunch put an end to this growth, the LSE was attracting many Russian companies to list in London, initially at an IPO price discounted by 40–60 per cent to reflect Russian risk, including corporate governance uncertainties, state intervention possibilities and general political instability. The Sarbanes–Oxley Act of 2002 drove many Russian and other listing candidates from the United States to London.

As financial markets soared in value, the Russian discount narrowed and eventually disappeared. Emerging market investors tried to forget the 1998 Russian financial crisis when the public had rushed to withdraw money from banks, the country was unable to pay its debts and the rouble went into free fall.

But it was never possible completely to forget the Russian risk. Part of this was the possibility of state intervention, such as hit Russian oil giant Yukos. In October 2003, the FSB, Russia's internal security service, viewed by many as secret police, arrested Mikhail Khodorkovksy, chief executive officer of Yukos, and in June 2005 he was sentenced to eight years in jail on fraud and tax-evasion charges. Internationally, it has been widely accepted that Khodorkovksy, although no saint, did not have a fair trial and was suffering the consequences of challenging the state. He had made financial contributions to those who lobbied in the State Duma for his interests and he led initiatives against corruption and was in favour of democracy. Yukos, with its claims of Western standards in corporate governance, was a competitor to Russian state-owned oil companies.

Generally, the Russian state has asserted its interest in nationalising the oil and gas sector and has not tolerated competitors, which has made it difficult for global oil giants Shell and BP as they have expanded into Russia with an eye to the vast profit potential there. It comes at a price. In December 2006, Gazprom, the state-owned gas conglomerate, bought a controlling stake in Sakhalin-2, the energy project in Russia's remote Far East, for $7.45 billion (£5 billion), which analysts said was below the market price. Royal Dutch Shell, the global oil company, sold 50 per cent plus one share in the project, cutting its holding from 55 to just under 27.5 per cent, and was to receive US$4.1 billion (£2.75 billion) for ceding control of the project. Earlier Russia's environmental agency had warned of environmental breaches and had threatened to withdraw Shell's licence. By this deal, Shell reduced its potential gains from the project, but gained the assurance of the Russian state's support.

BP, another multinational oil company, has experienced harassment while operating its business in Russia. In June 2007, the Russian–British joint venture TNK-BP, half owned by BP, sold its stake in the Kovykta gas field to Gazprom for US$700–900 million (£470–602 million). This price was a fraction of the stake's true value. Analysts saw this as another example of the Kremlin squeezing Western oil firms.

A former unit of TNK-BP became subject to a claimed Russian criminal investigation into alleged large-scale tax evasion. In March 2008, the group's Moscow offices were searched, and a TNK-BP employee was charged with industrial espionage. This came at a time when relations between Russia and Britain were strained after the mysterious 2006 poisoning in London of

Alexander Litvinenko, a former Russian agent who was critical of the Kremlin. Russia had refused to extradite the main suspect in the case to London.

Also in 2008, BP suspended foreign employees seconded to TNK-BP because of a lack of clarity on their visa status. BP and Russian law enforcement agencies said there was no connection between the visa dispute and the raid or tax-evasion allegations. In May of the same year, the FSB made a second search of BP's Moscow office.

There was speculation that the Kremlin was trying to force TNK-BP's Russian owners, a consortium of oligarchs, to sell their stakes to state-controlled Gazprom. A lock-in agreement that prevented them from selling had expired at the end of 2007.

In general, the Russian government does not tolerate criticism. William Browder, chief executive of Hermitage Capital, a foreign portfolio investor in Russia, was a frequent critic of Gazprom and how it conducted its business, including awarding contracts to parties on favourable terms. The company has rejected some of these criticisms as ill founded. In November 2005, the Russian authorities refused to renew Browder's visa, effectively barring him from the country. Hermitage Capital now claims it was a victim of attempted fraud in Russia. In June 2007, a lieutenant colonel in the Russian interior ministry seized documents of Hermitage Capital in a claimed tax investigation and used these to try to extort US$367 million (£246 million) from three subsidiaries of the Hermitage Fund. HSBC, the trustee of the Hermitage Fund, has filed criminal complaints in Russia.

Journalists have sometimes suffered, even losing their lives, if they expose corruption and wrongdoing in Russia; but crimes against them almost always go unresolved (see Chapter 20). Russian business interests and not just the Kremlin are likely to react to public criticism that can harm them.

Regulators who do their job properly run the same kind of risks as the journalists. In September 2006, Andrei Kozlov, first deputy chairman of the Central Bank, who was in charge of cleaning up the banking system and had closed down dozens of banks, was shot dead in a Moscow street. His killing was widely considered to be related to his work.

Russian business has had interests to protect but in the credit crisis of 2007–09 it has conceded a lot of power to the state, and oligarchs have queued for government bailouts. By late 2008, the dramatic oil price decline in recent months had hit exports, and Russia's trade surplus (the extent by which export revenue exceeds import revenue) had fallen dramatically. At one stage in October 2008, the interbank lending rate, at which banks can lend each other money, was 22 per cent, its highest level in 10 years.

The Kremlin blamed the United States for the global economic crisis, although some economists said that Russia's own policies had led to many of its problems. To protect itself against potential crisis, Russia had accumulated international currency reserves (gold, foreign currency, special drawing rights and IMF reserve positions), which were the third largest in the world. The Central Bank of the Russian Federation has, however, spent tens of billions of dollars from these in defending the rouble, although it has since become devalued. Some analysts criticised this strategy, which had avoided an immediate hit to the currency but had cost the country money. In late December 2008, Russia's reserves had dropped well below US$500 billion (£334 billion), depleted from nearly US$600 billion (£402 billion) when the oil price had been high.

Some analysts suggest that if the global financial crisis persists for another year or two, Russia's reserves could run out. The credit crisis of 2007–09 is not, however, a repeat of the 1998 Russian crisis, as prime minister Vladimir Putin said in a countrywide televised question-and-answer session in December 2008. He said that in 2008, the state-run banks, Sberbank, Vneshtorgbank, Gazprombank and Bank of Moscow, which control 60 per cent of banking assets in Russia, had strong balance sheets.

But that was not the whole story. Between May and October 2008, the Russian stock market's value had declined by 75 per cent in line with the credit crisis. In Russia, shares rather than mortgage-backed securities provide backing for credit. The decline in value meant that business owners had to cover their borrowings with extra cash, selling equities to raise it, which led in a vicious circle to further share price falls. The inflow of lending from foreign banks, on which Russia has long heavily depended, had declined.

In the real economy, factories and businesses were closing, while many staff wages and supplier bills were going unpaid. Banks were less ready to grant consumer loans, contributing to a decline in foreign car sales and stagnation of property prices. Even beer production had declined.

Owners of the country's wealth voted with their feet. In October 2008, capital flight from Russia was running at US$12–16 billion (£8–11 billion) a week.

The 2008 government bailout of Russia amounted to an estimated 13 per cent of GDP, higher than any other in the G8 group of countries. The government focused on rescuing banks, but also on construction and retail, which are linked with other industries in the supply chain.

Generally, there is a feeling in Russia, exacerbated by the credit crisis that started in June 2007, of a transfer of wealth from private hands to the state, which is the opposite to what happened in the Yeltsin era. In April 2008, a bill on foreign investment in strategic industries was signed into law. The legislation requires any foreign investor to have government approval before buying more than a 50 per cent stake in one of 42 strategic sectors, including oil and gas, the media, defence, mobile telecommunications and fisheries. At the same time, Russian business seeks foreign partners, outside Russia as well as in it, although the credit crisis starting in June 2007 put some expansion plans on hold.

Russia's invasion of South Ossetia in Georgia, in August 2008, reminded the world of the region's instability, and investors are now shying away from the Russian stock market. But as Mark Mobius, director at Templeton Emerging Markets Equity Group told *The Times* in October 2008, Russia is moving in the longer term towards a market-operated economy with a strong legal underpinning.

19

Pooled investments

Introduction

Pooled investments are where investors put money into a single fund, which a fund manager then invests on their behalf. In this chapter we will look at the various kinds available, including money market funds, exchange-traded funds and hedge funds.

Overview

In countries other than the United States and Canada, 'mutual funds' is a generic term for pooled investments, sometimes known as collective investments.

These vehicles pool money from investors and invest it in securities, including shares, bonds and short-term money market instruments, commodities and commercial property. The fund manager decides how to invest money allocated to the fund.

In the United States and Canada, 'mutual funds' has the specific meaning of open-ended funds, a type that can create or redeem as many more units as required to meet investor demand. The equivalent in Europe is open-ended investment companies. These funds have a net asset value (NAV) per share, which is the dollar value of a single share in the mutual fund, based on the value of the fund's underlying assets less its liabilities divided by the number of shares outstanding. The NAV is calculated at the end of each business day. The funds sell units at the NAV plus a sales charge, and buy back at the NAV.

Within the spectrum of pooled investments, there are closed-ended funds, known in Europe as investment companies, which have a fixed number of shares in issue and trade on the stock market, and whose price could be at a premium or discount to the NAV.

In relation to open-ended funds, the EU has benefited from cross-border selling of undertakings for collective investment in transferable securities (UCITS). Closed-ended funds do not fall under UCITS regulations but have a great deal of investment freedom in their own right, including gearing and investing in illiquid assets such as hedge funds.

In December 2001, the UCITS III Directive was adopted, providing a European passport for investment managers throughout the EU, and broadening the activities they may undertake. The EC noted in a statement on proposed revisions to the directive that European investment funds to which UCITS III applies are on average five times smaller than US funds and cost twice as much to manage.

In January 2009, UCITS IV was passed. The directive will be implemented by July 2011 and will allow UCITS managers to further develop their cross-border activities. It will create economies of scale, give a greater choice of investment funds to investors and increase investor protection by ensuring that retail investors receive clear, easily understandable and relevant information when investing in UCITS funds. According to the EC, about 40 per cent of UCITS originating in the EU are sold in third countries, mainly Asia, the Gulf region and Latin America.

Asset allocation

Funds have their own investment objectives, such as growth or income. Some fund managers operate on a top–down basis, which means that they start with the global macro-economic view; others take a bottom–up approach, focusing initially on the investments and only then on broader economic factors.

Asset allocation is about how the fund manager divides the investment income across stocks, bonds, cash and other assets such as commodities and real estate. Some funds invest in blue-chip companies and others in smaller growth companies. They may invest in the United States or Europe, in a specific emerging market, or elsewhere perhaps more widely.

Individuals investing in a mutual fund can select the mix of assets to suit their risk profile and age. The younger they are, the more risk they may feel inclined to take because they have longer to wait. Cash and cash equivalents are the safest investments, with equities much riskier and commodities riskier still. To invest across different assets is to diversify. This aims to limit losses and fluctuations. If one asset is doing badly, others may be doing well. Diversification can also reduce the profit potential from investing exclusively in a winning share or sector.

Our fund managers' most useful tool
No. 3: A good pair of shoes

**Over the past year, we personally interviewed the management
of over 4,000 companies worldwide.**

Aberdeen Investment Trusts ISA and Share Plan

There's nothing like being able to judge for yourself.
For us, we won't add a company to our portfolios without first
holding a personal interview with its management and even
when we do invest, we visit our investments thereafter at
least once a year.

We are dedicated to finding reasonably-priced companies,
supported by an excellent business, with a strong balance
sheet and talented management.

Our investment companies cover the UK, Asia and specialist
sectors, as well as international markets. You can invest in
these trusts from £100 per month or £1,000 lump sum.
We offer daily dealings for lump sum investments.

Do remember that the value of shares and the income
from them can go down as well as up. You may not get back
the amount invested. No recommendation is made, positive or
otherwise, regarding the ISA and Share Plan.

If you have doubts about the suitability of any investment for
your needs, please consult an independent financial adviser.

To find out more:
Request a brochure: **0500 00 40 00**
www.invtrusts.co.uk

2008/9 ISA deadline
Friday 27th March 2009

Aberdeen Asset Management PLC

We operate independently and only manage assets for third parties, allowing us to focus solely on their needs, without conflicts of interest. We now manage over £110 billion of third party assets from our offices around the world.

Our clients access our investment expertise across three asset classes: equities, fixed income and property.

We package our skills in the form of segregated and pooled products across borders. We invest worldwide and follow a predominantly long-only approach, based on fundamentally sound investments – we do not chase market fads.

Our investment teams are based in the markets or regions in which they invest. Clients understand our process and portfolios because they are transparent.

Asset allocation **Investment by mandate**

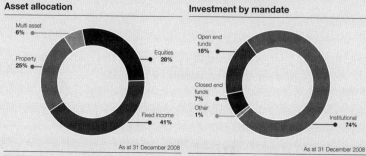

Asset allocation:
- Multi asset 6%
- Equities 28%
- Property 25%
- Fixed income 41%

As at 31 December 2008

Total Funds under management £110 billion

Investment by mandate:
- Open end funds 18%
- Closed end funds 7%
- Other 1%
- Institutional 74%

As at 31 December 2008

At Aberdeen we pride ourselves on original thinking and research. We also believe strongly in portfolio transparency. Implicit in our style is a rejection of commoditised products and closet indexing: our business therefore stands or falls on whether we can genuinely add value to clients' assets.

Our equity process dates from the early 1990s. The process is continuously evolving but its central tenets are an emphasis on original research, the identification of businesses that we can understand and the elimination of downside risks through price disciplines. While it originated in Asia, our approach works equally in developed markets, since fundamentals drive returns over the long term.

Our aim is to add value by identifying good quality securities, defined chiefly in terms of management and business models, which are attractively priced.

Stock selection is the key source of equity alpha. We downplay benchmarks in portfolio construction since these provide little clue to future performance, we always visit companies before investing, making thousands of visits annually to existing and prospective holdings. Every contact is documented in detail. If a security fails our screens, we will not own it, irrespective of its index weight.

Our mainstream strategies are simple: we buy-and-hold, add on the dips and take profits on price run-ups. This reduces transaction costs and keeps portfolios focussed. We rarely pursue short-term returns for mainstream strategies, albeit for specialist portfolios, activity may be more dynamic.

We employ around 90 equity investment professionals globally. Portfolio decisions are made collectively, and we avoid cultivating 'star' managers. Cross-coverage of securities also increases objectivity and lessens reliance on individuals.

We manage 13 investment companies that give you the opportunity to tap into some of the most dynamic investment markets around the world – with Aberdeen's team of professional fund managers to support you.

Our investment companies' expertise focuses on five areas: the UK, Asia, globally invested funds, specialist funds focused on a particular market sector and tracker funds. In this way, the range allows you to pinpoint investment markets very precisely, so you can meet particular needs within your portfolio.

Investing in our range of investment companies is easy and cost effective. We offer four ways to invest – and two of them are tax efficient. Just choose whether you want to invest in our Share Plan, Investment Plan for Children, tax-efficient ISA or make an ISA transfer. Other than 0.5% government stamp duty, our low cost investment plans mean that there is no additional cost to you on buying the shares. Our Share Plan and Investment Plan for Children have no initial charges, and our ISA transfer and ISA have a low annual charge of £24 (Plus VAT).

Whichever investment company interests you, please ensure that it is suitable for your tolerance for risk. Higher risk investments such as investment companies may compensate for their high volatility and uncertainty by offering potentially higher returns than lower investments. But this is not guaranteed.

The source for all figures: Aberdeen Asset Managers, as at 31 December 2008

Specialist types of fund

Money market

Money market funds are mutual funds investing in short-term debt instruments. In the United States, they can be treasury funds, which can invest in treasuries or in government agencies like Fannie Mae or Freddie Mac. Otherwise, they can be prime money market funds, which invest in commercial paper.

This type of fund started in the United States in the 1970s. The SEC published regulations governing them in 1983. The funds came to offshore Europe in the 1980s, where there were no SEC regulations. The funds relied on credit ratings from rating agencies to provide reassurance.

The funds have a main aim of preserving capital, but they also seek liquidity and competitive, sector-related returns. The main performance benchmarks include the LIBID and SONIA indices, as discussed in Chapter 6. Money market funds are not engaged in leverage and pay lower interest than other fixed-income investments such as bonds. The returns may not keep up with inflation.

In compensation for the modest returns, investors have looked to the money market funds to keep their money secure, but there is no government guarantee and, occasionally, the confidence may be misplaced. In September 2008, money market funds saw an outflow not far short of US$200 billion (£147 billion) in a week after a fund 'broke the buck' by offering a return lower than the cash invested. Reserve's Primary Fund, the oldest money market fund, would return only 97 cents on the dollar. This was an extremely rare event, triggered by unprecedented market conditions; according to the Institutional Money Market Funds Association, it was a result of exposure of the Reserve Fund to unsecured Lehman debt securities.

The SEC is to review money market funds as a priority for 2009. The influential Group of 30 (G30), an international body of leading central bank financiers and academics, published its recommendations on the topic in January 2009. From their international perspective, they take the view that money markets ought to be regulated like special purpose banks.

Commodity index funds

Commodity index funds give investors exposure to commodity prices and not to the share prices of the businesses associated with them. Pure commodity exposure of this kind at a low cost is a useful way to diversify an investment portfolio given that commodity returns do not move in synch with equities or bonds.

Commodity funds were popular with investors trying to beat the credit crisis of 2007–09 but, after July 2008, commodity prices collapsed. For more on commodities and related cycles, see Chapter 14.

Split-capital investment companies

The split-capital investment company is a type of closed-ended investment company that has more than one class of share capital. Usually, one type of share is for income and receives all the income generated by the trust, and the other is for capital gain. The trust has a fixed lifespan, perhaps seven years, compared with the unlimited life of other investment companies. At the end of its life, its remaining assets are distributed among shareholders.

In the bear market from March 2000, split-capital investment companies saw their share prices plunge. When one fund collapsed in value, others followed because a number were linked by cross-share holdings and the funds had high levels of debt. The FSA subsequently conducted its largest-ever investigation into the split-capital trust sector and, in December 2004, agreed a final £194 million negotiated settlement with 18 out of 22 firms under investigation, with no admission on their part. On subsequent consultation, the Treasury decided that investment companies should not be regulated as products by the FSA, taking the view that the listing rules were an appropriate mechanism for split caps, and noting that the FSA had already tightened these in response to the problems.

Venture capital trusts

Venture capital trusts (VCTs) are quoted companies that invest in small growth companies and aim to make capital gains for investors. They have been described as a form of investment company. VCTs were launched in the UK in 2005 to encourage residents to invest in UK higher-risk unlisted companies that need start-up, early-stage or expansion capital. There are significant tax breaks for private investors.

There is very little trading in the shares and market makers may offer a wide spread. The annual charges tend to be higher than for conventional investment companies, partly because the funds are small and lack economies of scale, but also because of the heavy research that some VCT managers carry out into sometimes small, not very transparent, companies. The VCT plans an exit from its investments through a stock market listing or a takeover.

Real-estate investment trust

The real-estate investment trust (REIT) was created in the United States in 1960. The product has since been popular in Australia, Japan, Hong Kong,

France and the Netherlands as a way for retail investors to invest in a diversified property portfolio through a tradable investment asset; it was launched in the United Kingdom in January 2007. The REIT is a quoted company that conducts a property rental business. It pays neither corporation tax on rental income nor capital gains tax, and must distribute most of its earnings to shareholders.

Exchange-traded funds

An exchange-traded fund (ETF) trades all day like a stock but has the diversification of a mutual fund. Each unit in the fund tracks the movement of an entire stock market index or sector, or alternatively perhaps commodities.

The ETF is open ended and can issue an unlimited number of units to meet demand. The product was already well established in the United States when it was launched in the United Kingdom.

Global inflows into exchange-traded funds reached US$200 billion (£147.2 billion) in 2008, according to Financial Research Corporation.

Hedge funds

Hedge funds are a form of pooled investment mainly for institutional investors. No one agrees on the exact definition of a hedge fund but, in broad terms, it is a specialist type of pooled investment that is free to invest in all financial instruments or markets, including high-risk instruments. It is a global operator and may employ a range of investment strategies, involving gearing (borrowings) and taking short positions (selling securities it does not own in order to profit from a falling market), as well as taking long positions.

Structurally, the hedge fund is often a limited partnership and has unregulated status, but its investments may not be promoted to the general public. Many hedge funds are registered in the Cayman Islands where there is lighter regulation, but some prefer registration in Luxembourg or Dublin for the European exposure that this secures. The fund may be managed elsewhere, in which case the manager, as opposed to the offshore fund that it manages, may be regulated. In Europe, funds are typically managed from London because of the commercial clout that derives from being regulated by the FSA. London is by far the largest hedge fund management centre in Europe, but most hedge fund management is from the United States, accounting for a market share of 65 per cent in 2008.

The hedge fund managers are often ex-investment bankers and other specialist financiers who give up highly lucrative jobs to set up a fund, and who know enough about markets to exploit a sophisticated tool book of modern investment vehicles. They normally invest their own money alongside that of

investors, and will reveal how much. They are attracting the capital of sophisticated investors, including, increasingly, pension managers who use hedge
funds to diversify their funds in a way uncorrelated to their equity positions.
There have been start-ups even in late 2008 and later, in the throes of the credit crisis.

The hedge fund will typically charge investors a management fee of
1.5–2.0 per cent, whether the fund rises or falls in value, and a performance fee
of 20 per cent, although some funds charge more. The hedge fund will profit
from any gain but will not partake in any losses. In the difficult year of 2008,
some hedge funds offered to cut fees if investors stayed with them, or they
penalised redemptions. Most firms did not get a performance fee that year and,
given a reduction in funds under management because of redemptions, saw a
decline in management fees. Some paid their managers bonuses, but smaller
ones than in better times.

Hedge fund strategies

The strategies and combinations of strategies used by hedge funds vary enormously, but have in common that they aim at absolute returns, as opposed to
those relative to the market. The funds are supposed to be agnostic to market
direction, although heavy losses in 2008 suggest that this is not the case.

Hedge funds may still hedge, which is to buy shares likely to rise, and take
an offsetting short position in those likely to sell. This was the theme of the
first hedge fund, set up in the late 1940s by Alfred Winslow Jones, a former
journalist. Selling short, usually with a long position as well for hedging, is in
itself a strategy. It was the most profitable one in 2008.

Arbitrage funds try to take advantage of temporary price differences
between securities. Arbitrage is risk free when buying the same security at different prices but riskier when attempting to capitalise on temporary deviations
in the prices of different securities.

Convertible arbitrage arises through mispricing on convertible bonds,
which are bonds with a right to switch into shares at a given price. Convertible
arbitrageurs have sought to make a gain through buying the bonds and selling
short the underlying shares. Once the bond has been re-priced against the
shares, the manager would make money.

Bans on short selling of financial stocks in September 2008 hit convertible
arbitrage funds hard because the funds could not short stocks in the financial
sector, which issued more than 50 per cent of convertibles. The regulatory concerns about short selling are related to market abuse, but regulators have not
been able to find evidence in certain high profile suspicious cases.

Statistical arbitrage is an extension of pairs trading, where two greatly correlated stocks that temporarily diverge are traded in pairs. In pairs trading,

when one stock outperforms the other in a divergence from the usual correlation, the trader takes a long position in the weaker performer in the expectation that it will rise, and a short position in the other, so hedging the position against whole market movements. Usually, the cost of taking one position is compensated by returns from the other. When the divergence is corrected, the trader makes a profit. This strategy does not have much risk, but it needs good timing to work well.

In statistical arbitrage, the trader takes the same approach but on a large portfolio of stocks. The trader takes a long position on underperforming stocks and a short position on outperforming stocks, seeking to profit from anomalies of usual correlation. Traders act fast and make often tiny profits. They may rely on models, as did LTCM, a high-profile hedge fund that used statistical arbitrage among other techniques and collapsed in 1998 (see Chapter 15).

Other techniques include trading on a global macro basis, or investing in underpriced securities issued by problem companies. Fund managers may seek to capitalise on temporary price extremes arising from takeover activity.

Multi-strategy funds move from one technique to another on clients' behalf. After hedge fund losses in 2008, and the collapse of many funds, there may be a tendency toward multiple strategies to avoid putting all the eggs in one basket. Gearing has declined. LTCM had borrowed more than 25 times the amount investors gave it, according to a US government working group. According to the Alternative Investment Management Association (AIMA), by early 2009, gearing in hedge funds was less than twice what investors provided, compared with 30-plus times leverage reported in the banks. In addition, the amount of leverage should not be considered alone. What matters is its relationship with volatility, which is how risky it is.

'The popular image of hedge funds as high risk and highly leveraged today is a misconception,' says AIMA. 'Most hedge fund investors want stable returns more than anything else and all the main hedge fund strategies exist really to provide that. Our research shows that hedge fund returns have been less volatile and higher over the last 10 years than other asset classes.'

Hedge funds are owned by institutional investors, high-net-worth individuals and funds of funds. Pension funds had 1.9 per cent of their assets in hedge funds in 2008, down from 1 per cent in 2006, according to the National Association of Pension Funds.

A typical hedge fund investor historically was a high-net-worth individual but is now a very sober institutional investor, according to AIMA. The interest is because the majority of these funds deliver stable returns in a risk-controlled manner. This has historically been delivered except in exceptionally volatile periods such as the final quarter of 2008.

It is just as well that this stability exists, because hedge funds are not fully liquid. In a start-up fund, a two-year or longer lock-up period may apply, giving managers freedom to use investors' money for that period. Even after that, investors cannot withdraw money at any time, and may be able to do so only quarterly or monthly, perhaps out of kilter with investing strategies. Hedge funds may split the fund, so that one part is in liquid assets with access to quick redemptions and the other has a longer lock-in period.

Hedge fund regulation

Hedge funds typically set up account facilities with the prime brokers owned by banks. The prime brokers are custodians of their assets, offer financing and lending services to hedge funds, enabling them to use leverage, as well as technological support. They may help with consulting and regulatory compliance services. They provide operational support and introductions to investors. They typically deal with many hedge funds and so can benefit from economies of scale.

One of the main lessons for hedge funds from the Lehman collapse is that they are not using enough prime brokers to diversify risk.

There is fear of a systemic risk from hedge funds destabilising the economy, perhaps by investing together in the same direction or becoming too heavily geared, and this has been the subject of major concern at international policy level. So far it has not happened, and there is no evidence that this risk even exists.

Hedge funds are reluctant to reveal their investment strategies because others may copy them, thereby influencing security prices and undermining profitability. This can conceal fraud. The scandal surrounding the secretive Madoff investment fund (see Chapter 11), although it is not technically a hedge fund, has drawn attention to this risk.

There is global momentum toward more regulation of the hedge fund industry which, despite some protests from the industry, seems unstoppable. Hedge funds may not have caused the global credit crisis of 2007–09, but they are paying a big price for it, and not just in their losses. In January 2009, the EC launched a consultation on hedge funds which was widely expected to result in international regulatory initiatives from the G20.

In the United States, but not in London, a loophole allows hedge fund managers with fewer than 15 clients, which could be funds, not to register with the SEC. In late January 2009, US senators Chuck Grassley and Carl Levin introduced US legislation to close the loophole.

There is a move toward global convergence of hedge fund regulation, with a focus on, among other things, transparency. This is fully supported by AIMA.

20

Forecasters, persuaders and commentators

Introduction

In this chapter we will look at the roles of stock market analysts, economists and strategists, public relations, investor relations and journalists. These professionals play a key role in the dissemination of information and, in some cases, the selling of it.

Analysts

Fundamental

The stock market analyst focuses on the dynamics of particular markets and makes trading and investment recommendations. The approach is usually fundamental analysis, which focuses on accounting figures and ratios, based on the financial statements, and on prospective figures.

In stockbrokers and banks, the analysts are on the sell side, providing support for salespeople as well as for investment bankers (see Chapter 7). Their research is distributed to the firm's clients.

The major institutional investors employ buy-side analysts, who tend to have a broader role than their sell-side counterparts, with less focus on individual stocks and sectors, and their research is disseminated internally.

The analyst produces valuation models on an individual company based largely on forecasts of its future plans and prospects. He or she comes up with figures that are often in line with those of other analysts.

The sell-side analyst may cover only six or seven companies in a sector and will continually issue new notes on each company to assess how corporate or market developments affect valuation. Analysts use informed guesswork to compensate for the lack of key company data available, and this accounts for variations in forecasts although, to avoid falling foul of regulations and the law, companies disseminate information to analysts simultaneously and equally.

The Spitzer settlement of April 2003 on Wall Street was about alleged conflicts of interest between analysts' research and investment banking. New York Attorney General Eliot Spitzer found that Henry Blodget, a Merrill Lynch internet company analyst, had in private e-mails disparaged an internet stock that he was recommending to clients. Spitzer found other instances of biased recommendations across the industry.

Ten global investment banks settled the matter with the SEC, the NYSE, the National Association of Securities Dealers and Spitzer. As part of the redress, the banks agreed to separate their research and investment banking departments to prevent the passing of information. There is some feeling that the Spitzer settlement was politically motivated. The settlement has, however, set an international agenda.

Analysts in today's markets still give specific recommendations to buy, sell or hold a given stock, or similar, although in at least one investment bank they have started moving away from this approach. Financial institutions in the United Kingdom, unlike in the United States, are not required to disclose what proportion of their research consists of sell recommendations, but it is small. The sell recommendations can offend the companies that provide these analysts with most of their information. The companies may also be, or potentially be, corporate clients of the firm's lucrative investment banking division.

To add to the pressure on analysts, there are constraints on anybody gaining access to or using price-sensitive information. Analysts' written research reflects such constraints, their oral liaison with favoured clients perhaps less so.

Technical

Technical analysts are in a minority and are relatively unaffected by the above complications. They are likely to work independently, but a few are employed by large financial institutions. The technical analyst focuses on charts of price movements, index changes and related movements such as moving averages and trading volume. One aim is to make forecasts based on perceived past trends. Day traders may use technical analysis to pinpoint entry and exit points for trades. Some combine technical analysis with fundamental analysis and others are 'pure' technicians.

Technical analysis is based around trend theory, expressed in such observations as 'The trend is your friend' or 'The trend is a trend until it's broken.' Trend theory has its foundations in Dow Theory, a building block of modern technical analysis. As the theory goes, the trend will eventually hit a high point where investors will not buy further, which is resistance, and sellers emerge. Conversely, the price may fall to the support level, which is where investors have stopped selling. The more a resistance or support line is tested, the more effective it is considered. Technical analysis claims not to identify the absolute top or bottom, but rather to show when a trend has clearly started and when it has clearly ended.

Patterns in share price charts, such as the bearish head and shoulders, depict a struggle between supply and demand, based on trend theory, including continuation of the trend and breakouts. As a back-up, the analyst uses indicators that focus on, among other things, whether the market is over-bought or oversold, its relative performance and its rate of change. The indicator charts, viewed against those of the share price, can signal, rightly or wrongly, where traders could open or close a position. Moving averages, perhaps the most popular indicator, are considered good at indicating direction but not the point at which you should enter a trade.

Technical analysis has more critics than supporters. Fund manager Ralph Wanger considers that it has a following because of the illogical appeal of patterns, and hedge fund trader Victor Niederhoffer goes so far as to say that trends do not exist, which undermines the concept at root. Wall Street trader Jim Rogers has said he has never seen a rich technician except those who sold their services. Academics have largely dismissed technical analysis as inconsistent with financial theory.

There are others who are more convinced about the value of technical analysis. They are more likely to be traders than investors, particularly in currencies and commodities, where fundamental analysis techniques, as used in stock picking, are not available. Many private investors have invested in software incorporating technical tools. Marty Schwartz, a renowned Wall Street trader, claims he had lost money in 10 years of trading based on fundamental analysis, and only when he switched to technical analysis did he become rich.

Today, specialist techniques of technical analysis such as Japanese candles or Elliott Wave Theory have dedicated followers, but also detractors. Technical analysis has some links with astrology, widely considered a pseudoscience. Chris Carolan's article 'Autumn Panics and Calendar Phenomenon', which won the United States-based Market Technicians Association's Charles H Dow Award for the best technical analysis paper in 1998, examines the case for a correlation between the lunar calendar and stock market panics. The late William D Gann, a trader using mathematics-based techniques, has become a cult figure whose methods are promoted by certain publishers. Not everybody knows that Gann did not make as much money from trading as some of his promoters suggest, let alone that he was a closet astrologer.

The value of technical analysis has been debated even at international level. Professional bodies help to give the profession cohesion. The International Federation of Technical Analysts is linked to member societies of technical analysts in the United Kingdom, the United States, Australia and many other countries. These bodies promote expensive professional courses with examinations. There are attempts, occasionally successful, to link these courses with bona fide university programmes. There are technical analysis conferences.

The educational and conference circuit is a key way for an industry with a precarious existence and credibility to survive. Technical analysts still struggle to make their voices heard. Some survive only because they combine their efforts with helping to design and promote investment software or with journalism, including chartist-type newsletter writing, as well as lecturing and course writing. Some quite distinguished technical analysts are unemployed.

Economists and strategists

The economist generates ideas on the functioning of the economy, and will seek to understand central bank behaviour. The strategist has a broad-based focus, making calls on various asset classes and markets.

The economist and strategist alike focus on statistics that throw light on, among other things, trends in inflation, interest rates and currency movements. Their forecasts are often wrong, which is understandable, given that there are so many unknowns. It is hard, for example, to assess how much the weak pound will stimulate exports, when it is uncertain how far companies will pass on the benefit to customers rather than absorb it into their profit margins. What counts for more than the forecasts is the quality of analysis underlying them.

Many of these experts did not foresee the credit crisis of 2007–09 but, for those who remain in work, it has given them a focus. On 15 September 2008, N Gregory Mankiw, a professor of economics at Harvard University, wrote in a blog ahead of teaching his regular introductory economics course: 'I would like to thank all my friends on Wall Street for doing so much to spark interest in economic issues. You have gone beyond the call of duty, and your timing could not have been better.'

Public relations

Financial public relations (PR) agencies create an image for companies. They promote this to analysts, shareholders, investors and the media. The business has come a long way from the 1960s when messengers delivered press releases by hand. In those days, companies did not communicate properly with investors, and stockbrokers did not publish much research. The development of modern PR owes a lot to takeover bids, which were big in the 1980s. Government privatisations in those years meant that PR had to communicate with private investors en masse.

The value of PR, however, was, and still is, hard to quantify. It is to justify their significant billing that PR agencies keep a careful track record of publicity they have generated.

External PR is now a main conduit through which major listed companies speak to the press, particularly on controversial issues. This way, companies can standardise and time their information flow to suit their corporate and regulatory requirements. The large companies also use their own corporate affairs departments. The skill of financial PR professionals is to control media flow invisibly.

Some do it better than others. At its best, PR is masterly. A striking example was PR about the three NatWest executives who, in October 2004, were extradited to the United States to face trial over Enron-related activities. The invisible hand of PR guided the national press away from its instinct to criticise the NatWest Three and towards portraying them as victims.

A PR campaign persuaded journalists to focus their wrath instead on whether the US government was morally, and should have been legally, justified in extraditing the NatWest Three using the Extradition Act of 2003, rushed through parliament to assist extradition of terrorism suspects. The press followed the PR line in objecting that the United States could act without evidence shown to a British court but the reverse was not true. If Britain wanted to extradite an individual from the United States, it would have to produce evidence to a US court.

The NatWest Three were forced to go to jail in the United States, and journalists treated them almost as folk heroes. They did not ascertain the full facts. As Robert Wardle, then head of the SFO, later said, most of the evidence against the three men was in the United States, and evidence produced would have been sufficient to secure extradition even under the old legislation.

It is because financial PR agencies can deal consistently and expertly with the media and the City in a crisis that many companies will hire one on a retainer as a fail-safe. For most of the year, the agency will tick away at maintenance level. If, however, a crisis arises, the agency will seek to protect the company's public image. The company will want minimum impact on the share price. Today, many of those who assess a company's value will focus on its reputation as much as on its financial statements.

The PR agencies also represent companies during a takeover period or IPO, and play a major role in distributing company results.

The relationship between PR executive and journalist in developed economies is symbiotic. The competent PR executive will package their story for journalists initially in a press release, complete with prepared quote from a senior company executive, and provide back-up discussion on the telephone, which may add value but inevitably provides the company's message. Sometimes PR agencies will besmirch their client's competitors with verifiable facts, but they will not leak privileged information, as once some did, due to the risk of being held responsible for market abuse.

The good PR executive knows much that is price sensitive. In December 2008, the SEC filed a civil suit charging a Lehman broker, Matthew Devlin, with running a US$4.8 million (£3.2 million) insider-dealing operation using information about takeovers to which his wife, who worked at public relations firm Brunswick, had access. His wife told the press she had no knowledge of what was going on.

Such lawsuits are rare. The PR agencies need a good reputation, and the industry's rapid growth is a testimony to its success. In 1986, British companies spent £37 million on PR; by 1996 that figure had risen to £250 million (data from *The Invisible Persuaders: How Britain's Spin Doctors Manipulate the Media*, by David Michie, published by Bantam Press, 1996).

In the United Kingdom, a few PR agencies have emerged as leaders who de facto control the national press's agenda. According to Hemscott Adviser Rankings in November 2007, the top-ranked financial PR advisers by total market capitalisation of stock market clients were Brunswick, Maitland Consulting, Finsbury, Financial Dynamics and Citigroup Dewe Rogerson.

Investor relations

Investor relations (IR) is about how a quoted company liaises with present and prospective investors. An IR function keeps the market informed of price-sensitive information without making selective disclosures. In this way, it tries to obtain a fair valuation for the company's shares. The IR team answers analysts' questions and provides them with up-to-date figures for their spreadsheets, as well as helping investors to understand the company better, and journalists who require a deeper understanding than most. The IR team provides capital market and strategic feedback to the company.

The team oversees press conferences on shareholder meetings, one-to-one meetings with shareholders, the IR section of company websites and company financial reports. The shift in communications is toward interactive data and electronic disclosures. Part of the job is to transmit information on intangible values such as the company's corporate governance policy. The IR team is aware of stock market patterns and works with the corporate secretary on legal and regulatory matters affecting shareholders.

The real value of IR is to limit the downside to reputation and share price in difficult times for the company, including during hostile takeover bids. Good IR can add most value when a company must disseminate bad news or capital markets have lost confidence. This happened to UK retailer Marks & Spencer in April 2008 when some investors objected to the board's decision to promote Sir Stuart Rose from chief executive to chairman. Another such crisis arose in the same month when the Royal Bank of Scotland announced a rights issue after it had said it would not need to, which angered some shareholders.

The credit crisis of 2007–09 has given IR officers (IROs) a chance to show their skill. According to the United Kingdom-based Investor Relations Society in its January 2009 'Informed' bulletin, IROs expressed concern that in 2008 any statement to investors was portrayed as negative, resulting in unrepresentative price falls. A spokesman for the society said: 'Feedback from IROs suggests that they are focusing on the long-term story of their company and its balance-sheet strength, and not on short-term growth, and are refuting rumours. The story they put across is the business, not the share price.'

Some companies still outsource IR, but the profession has developed in its own right over the last couple of decades. The Sarbanes–Oxley Act 2002 (see Chapter 12) requires of US-quoted companies, among other things, enhanced financial disclosure and accuracy, including for off-balance-sheet transactions, which has increased the importance of IR. The industry now attracts former professionals such as analysts, fund managers, accountants and investment bankers. This trend has increased industry salary levels and status.

It is a reflection of the industry's status that, according to an April 2008 US survey of IROs conducted by Korn/Ferry International and the National Investor Relations Institute, at least four out of five IROs now report to the chief financial officer or chief executive officer. Almost half of the respondents in Fortune 500 companies (based on an annual list of the 500 largest companies in the United States) have responsibilities other than IR, including financial media relations, corporate communications and financial analysis.

Increasingly, IR professionals face dilemmas arising from regulatory complexity. In January 2009, the FSA fined Wolfson Microelectronics £140,000 for failing to make timely disclosures to the market, which has raised new uncertainties about how much companies should disclose. There is a feeling that the UK regulator acted inappropriately, or at least disproportionately, in fining Wolfson for not disclosing price-sensitive information as soon as possible, given that the company expected that, based on other, more positive information, its 2008 forecast revenue would remain the same.

The FSA has taken the position that if bad news is likely to have an effect on the share price, companies should disclose it and cannot refrain from doing so if they feel that good news offsets the bad. The onus lies with the Board to decide on whether information is price sensitive.

The FSA's action against Wolfson has, however, left IROs with a dilemma in how to advise companies, according to Mark Hynes, managing director of Transparency Matters Ltd. The IR industry does not want to advise companies to put out too much information, which could confuse the market and be useful for competitors or, at the other extreme, advise them to make incomplete disclosure, which could amount to not informing the market properly.

Even if a company wants to disclose everything, there is an issue whether it is so structured to know everything and to be able to give this information to IR to disclose, Hynes says. There would be a risk of two companies in the same sector putting out different levels of information, with a further complication for multinational companies following different rules in various jurisdictions. There is also uncertainty about the timing of an announcement.

The FSA rules leave it all up to the company to decide whether or not to disclose. In the United States, it is different. In October 2000, the SEC ruled that all US publicly traded companies must disclose material information to all investors at the same time. Contrary to some initial expectations, this has not led to excessive market volatility.

Journalists

Financial journalists take the basic information in a news release and any information they can muster, often directly from PR people, to build their own news piece. Some use chunks of the news release verbatim. There is often little time or incentive to do substantial extra spadework. The news agencies often have the most superficial reporting, but they are usually the first to publish, as befits their role as wholesalers of news.

The other end of the spectrum is investigative journalism. The type of journalist who does this work is a rare breed, who probes rather than accepts, gathers documentary evidence, tapes phone calls, arranges meetings with shady informers in pubs, is not afraid of antagonising people, and can attract personal threats and libel actions. Such a journalist takes pride in uncovering scandals, however, and, if they have their facts right, is not afraid to make enemies. Such journalists tend to be loners and may work as freelancers. The late Lorana Sullivan, most recently attached to the *Observer*, was such a journalist. A foundation has been established in her name in New York and Britain, with an aim of improving the standards of investigative journalism.

Such journalists may work on stories for days, even weeks. They sometimes get closer to the truth, or at least one part of it, than other journalists due to their tenacity. Some argue this is what journalism should be about. The majority connected with the media, including some newspaper proprietors, see such an approach as a luxury in today's cost-conscious times.

Most journalists hover between the extremes of rewriting press releases and investigative journalism, trying to add at least some value. The industry ideal is to have two named sources for every story, but journalists, pressed for time, often make do with less.

Some journalists in the trade press see their job as simply to provide useful information for their target audience. Others have a strong sense of public duty. They may name and shame known fraudsters and criminals in their publications, and applaud heroes of law enforcement and regulation.

They can get it wrong. Most journalists had applauded Eliot Spitzer's crusades against financial services industry corruption between about 2002 and 2006, his second term as New York State attorney general. They turned on Spitzer, however, after he resigned from his subsequent post as New York governor in March 2007 following allegations that he had spent more than US$15,000 (£10,472) on personal encounters with prostitutes. The aggressive tactics and political gains that had hallmarked Spitzer's public career became, for the first time, widely reported.

Online media, with instant publication, is a fertile source of rumours and, it is feared, of market abuse. Back in 2005, two journalists working as tipsters in the *Daily Mirror* under the name of the City Slickers were found guilty of market abuse from ramping shares in their column and profiting from the resulting share price movement. Fast forward to the credit crisis, and it has been widely suggested that unscrupulous hedge funds manipulated journalists to publish reports that helped send down share prices, so enabling them to make money from short positions.

The reports were not confined to mainstream media. It is becoming harder to define the journalist. National newspaper reporters are unmistakably in the trade, but the status of bloggers and new media is less clear, particularly when they do not conform to the old standards. Such concerns have been addressed in a study, 'What is financial journalism for? Ethics and responsibility in a time of crisis and change', published in November 2008 by Polis, a media think tank in the London School of Economics and Political Science. The study notes an identity crisis for journalists, and queries whether journalistic privileges should apply to, for example, bloggers.

The SEC has formally set out measures it will take before it subpoenas journalists to force them to reveal their sources, but according to Polis, how far this would apply to a non-traditional journalist is not entirely tested. It says that financial journalism needs an overhaul to meet the demands of reporting modern markets and the financial system.

There is some feeling that hasty reporting exacerbated the credit crisis of 2007–09. Careless headlines or injudicious reporting are at risk of becoming serious, self-fulfilling prophecies, said Richard Lambert, director general of the Confederation of British Industry and a former editor of the *Financial Times*, in a December 2008 speech at the Reform Media Group.

In early 2009, the UK Treasury Committee was examining the role of the media in the banking crisis and whether journalists should operate under any sort of reporting restrictions over the period. Unsurprisingly, news media responded unanimously in opposition to such restrictions.

The media said, among other things, that more aggressive regulation would increase the authority of unregulated sites such as financial bulletins and chat rooms, which would be disastrous for the investing public. Some said that to impose restrictions on what mainstream media could cover would lead to public uncertainty and assumptions of a worst-case scenario. Another argument was that, in making information available to all the public simultaneously, the financial media act against the creation of false markets and contribute to the proper functioning of the financial markets.

The press freedom of the West has not yet properly spread to parts of the developing world. In Russia, for example, the state has seized control of independent media, and now controls most, but not all, media coverage within the country, although it cannot control foreign reporting so easily.

In November 2008, the Russian prosecutor general's office told news organisations not to spread panic when they reported on financial institutions; it warned that inspections might be carried out. There was sensitivity about using the words 'collapse' or 'crisis', and some journalists had already been questioned. Some of the few independent voices within Russian media argued that this was censorship.

Journalists in Russia who insist on an independent voice may be risking their lives. Paul Klebnikov, editor of the Russian edition of *Forbes*, was shot dead by gunmen in July 2004 as he left his Moscow offices. He had published the country's first rich list, outing the 100 wealthiest people in Russia, which analysts said was the most likely reason for his death. He was one in a list of more than 20 journalists killed in Russia during the Putin administration in Russia. Another victim was Anna Politkovskaya, a Russian journalist known as a critic of the Kremlin's aggressive actions in Chechnya. In October 2006, she was found shot dead in her Moscow apartment block.

In a February 2009 video interview with the *Economist*, Julia Latynina, a columnist on *Novaya Gazeta*, Russia's most independent newspaper, where Politkovskaya had worked, said that there had been three journalists killed on the newspaper, and that journalists had to be worried when they touched the 'vital points of the state, the things that interest the Kremlin'. She said these are: war in Georgia, war with the Ukraine, and trading oil and gas.

'If you touch these points, you may be punished severely by the state,' Latynina said. 'But if you touch any other point, you can be punished by anyone else.'

21

Personal finance

Introduction

In this chapter we will look at the broad spectrum of personal finance and how it has fared in the economic crisis. We will see how wholesale markets have impact on the retail.

Overview

Personal finance is linked with the fortunes of wholesale markets. We have already seen how the credit crisis of 2007–09 started with subprime mortgage sales in the United States, which affected house prices, then savings, and ultimately led to a global meltdown, which hit consumers and personal finance.

Business looks after its interests first. In October 2008, the UK government rescued RBS after it had run into severe financial problems and, as part of the arrangements, Sir Fred Goodwin was to stand down as chief executive. He left RBS on 1 January 2009 with a very substantial pension, giving him £703,000 a year, which attracted government and media protest.

Around the same time across the Atlantic, governments and consumers alike were calling for restrictions on executive pay. The governments were looking to the banks to play their part in restoring public confidence in return for having state aid. The banks were slow, however, to pass on the benefits to consumers. The recession that had evolved in the credit crisis led to job losses. In the real economy, consumers stopped spending and, by early 2009, Americans were losing jobs at the rate of 700,000 a month.

Grow your wealth confidence

Kleinwort Benson has been a trusted adviser to private clients for over 200 years, the majority of whom have been with us for over two decades. We have a strong tradition of client trust, achieved through transparency in all that we do. We are reassuringly small at the point of contact resulting in a highly bespoke and personalised service.

For an insight into how we can increase your wealth confidence please email: Derek.Wright@kbpb.co.uk or call: +44 (0) 203 207 7400.

www.kleinwortbenson.com

Kleinwort Benson

PERSONAL FINANCE & THE GLOBAL FINANCIAL MARKETS

2007 and 2008 has brought home to everyone that the financial markets are globally intertwined and that when well-known institutions lose money in these markets, then the knock-on effects can have a very serious effect on our lives and personal finances. The UK banks were amongst the most global of their peers, with HBOS and RBS both having very significant loans and investments in the US mortgage market, and both being brought down by these exposures. These banks are now being forced to re-trench; loans for mortgages and for small businesses are now far harder to obtain and are charged at much higher margins over base rates than before, and the fees and charges for such loans are also much higher.

Just as financial markets have become global, so too has the economic policy response. Although each nation's politicians and Central Banks announce policy for their own jurisdiction, in practice these responses need to be, and are, broadly similar and co-ordinated. Thus interest rates everywhere are converging upon zero and most governments have announced short term stimulus plans of tax cuts and increased spending, which will need to be offset in the longer term by tax increases and spending restraint. It is important to note that if the UK had attempted these policies unilaterally, then much of the benefits of these policies would have gone to other economies. Today's global economic problems require global policy responses.

What began as a problem in one small sector of the US mortgage market has now spread out and affected most people in the Western world, either directly via the effects on their ability to borrow or more indirectly via the change in prices in all sorts of financial markets that have impacted pensions, savings, life insurance and mortgage products.

Although it is Central Banks that apparently set the official interest rate for each economy, from which the interest rates on variable-rate mortgages are derived, over one half of UK mortgages are now fixed-rate deals of varying maturities. Here it is the cash futures markets' expectations of future interest rates that drives the price at which a bank can borrow (and hence lend on) at a fixed rate over say 3 or 5 years. If the markets do not believe that a Central Bank will be able to keep rates at a low level over that period then the expectations of higher interest rates will be reflected in the futures markets, and so push up the rate for a fixed-rate mortgage deal.

At the upper end of the mortgage market, private banks offer their clients the option of mortgages in other currencies. Historically, interest rates in the UK have been higher than in other currencies, and so by borrowing in euros there can be a benefit in the form of less interest paid together with the possibility of reducing the capital value of the mortgage through changes in the value of the pound in the foreign exchange markets. So for example, taking out a mortgage in US dollars can result in a lower capital amount to repay if the pound rises against the dollar (or a higher capital amount if the pound falls against the dollar). Such mortgages are not necessarily the speculation that they may seem – if a UK investor buys a property in Spain and rents it out, then the euro income stream is a very good match for the euro mortgage payment stream (and the euro debt a match for the euro asset value) and so actually would reduce the foreign exchange risk that the UK investor is facing.

Many people in the UK have one or more of pension plans, endowment policies, insurance bonds, unit trust savings or PEPS and ISAs. For the most part the value of these savings products is directly determined by the behaviour of the world's financial markets, and in particular the stock (or share) markets around the world.

The institutional stock market investors, who are responsible for managing the assets in these products offer their clients significant exposure to international markets. This is for two major reasons; firstly diversification, for most people their future income depends on the prospects for the UK economy, and so to have all of one's wealth invested in the UK market which is also heavily dependent on the UK economy is not wise. It makes sense to diversify some of that risk by investing in other countries. Secondly the UK economy is quite heavily biased towards certain industries such as finance and media and away from other industries such as heavy manufacturing and technology. By investing in other stock markets , a broader exposure to the full breadth of the global economy can be obtained for investors.

Different investment managers go about investing in international equity markets in different ways. Some go about it in a "top-down" manner, first selecting which countries they think will perform best and concentrating the portfolio in those areas, and then selecting the best companies in those markets. Others are "bottom-up" investors who just focus on investing in the best companies, wherever they happen to be in the world.

What often surprises investors is that their investment managers make very little attempt to make money from "market-timing" – i.e. selling down lots of their shares when they expect markets to fall, and buying lots of shares when they expect markets to rise. The major reason for this is that experience has taught these managers that "market-timing" is extremely hard to do successfully, even though they are seen to be the experts. Thus most investment mangers seek only to perform better than a particular stock market index, not to actually make money. They do however believe that they will make money for their investors over the long term, as over the long term the stock markets have delivered real returns reflecting the real growth of the world economy.

In the end, every aspect of personal finance is intertwined, whether it is interest on savings or mortgages, the value of pensions or the value of savings plans – all are reliant on the movements of the financial markets, and today the financial markets are globally interdependent.

Mortgages

By this stage on either side of the Atlantic, many had either suffered, or faced the possibility of, repossessions. In the United Kingdom in late 2008, RBS had pledged not to begin the repossession process until customers were six months or more in arrears, up from three months. Other lenders did not rush to follow suit.

The declining value of houses was another concern. In the United States, the S&P Case-Shiller National Home Price Index reported that prices in the last three months of 2008 had fallen 18.2 per cent from the same period in 2007. Many Americans were tied to their job because they lacked mobility. They could not sell their house, or at least not at the right price.

The state of the housing market helped to push down the price of bank shares, a factor dragging down the rest of the stock market. Mortgage securities proved toxic and corporate bonds were risky. The savings and investment schemes of consumers suffered. On the bright side, those in work were paying much lower interest rates on mortgages after governments had reduced bank rates to almost nothing.

Savings and investment

Consumers had not given enough attention to where they invested their money. Many UK investors had been lured by the prospect of better interest rates than at home through cross-border placing of deposits within the European Economic Area. The problem was not just exposure to local markets.

Some banks under the European Union's passporting system offer their home protection scheme to investors outside their country. In this case, if an institution should fail, the level of protection would vary country by country. The Netherlands compensation would provide up to €100,000 per investor, which is better than the UK scheme, the Icelandic compensation scheme offers less. Fortunately, when Icelandic banks ran into problems in 2008, the UK government intervened on behalf of UK investors. In Ireland, the government has guaranteed all savings in Irish banks until 2010, but the country itself is now perceived as a risk.

In the United Kingdom, Northern Rock became one of the strongest banks for protecting policyholders since February 2008, when it was taken into public ownership.

Pensions

Consumers can retrieve savings, but the money in their pensions is tied up for years and, even on retirement, only a proportion may be released as cash.

Most pension funds are invested heavily in equities, which had plunged in value during the credit crisis. In April 2009, the FTSE 100 index of the United Kingdom's largest companies was down 33 per cent on the same time the previous year, and, in the United States, the Dow Jones Industrial Average has fallen 40 per cent.

Even some cash funds, which are meant to be safe, had lost money. For those contributing to a pension for the long term, there may be time to recoup losses. For those who needed to buy an annuity for retirement in early to mid 2009, the timing was, to say the least, unfortunate.

The way that most annuities work is that they offer a guaranteed income, supported by the life insurance company's investments in fixed interest investments, typically long-term government bonds. If the bond yields go up or down, so do the annuity rates. In early 2009, under its quantitative easing programme, the Bank of England bought back UK government bonds in large quantities. As a result, the price of the bonds rose and the yield, a percentage of the price, fell. Annuity rates fell and, by March 2009, were down 10 per cent on the previous year.

If this was not enough of a hit to pensions, there were fears that US insurance broker Aon was setting a trend when, in early 2009, its British arm cut back contributions to employees under the company's defined contribution pension scheme. This is the most common type of company pension, where cash is invested in a retirement fund, and the size of the pension pot depends on the fund's performance.

If other companies follow Aon's lead, it will end up that employees must pay more from their own salaries to get the same levels of retirement income. Back in 1999, Aon was one of the first to close its final salary scheme to new members. This is the most favourable type of pension scheme for employees because it pays out a proportion of their salary on retirement. Final salary schemes have declined drastically, due in part to weaker stock market returns and rising longevity. Another factor was the July 1997 move by Gordon Brown, then Chancellor of the Exchequer, to abolish tax relief on dividends paid into pension schemes.

In 2012, the United Kingdom will see the launch of personal account systems to complement existing pension provision. Employers, employees and, through tax relief, the Government will together contribute at least eight per cent of income per year to a pension pot. This is considerably less than many contribute to pension schemes now, and there are fears that it could become a new lower standard.

Role of pension funds in global financial markets

Pension funds are believed to own about one-third of the stocks and bonds traded in the West. A change in fashion among their investment consultants can move markets. For companies and governments, pension promises can have significant influence on everything from the cost of borrowing and the price of shares to the volume of inward investment. Pension funds have a significant role to play in global financial markets.

From a financial markets perspective, pension funds can be categorised into:

Defined contribution funds

Members have their own investment accounts, usually with some choice how they are invested. The accumulated accounts are used to buy benefits at retirement. In the markets defined contribution funds are suppliers of capital (equity and debt).

The following three categories are all different types of "defined benefit" fund, which offer benefits according to a pre-agreed formula:

Unfunded state pension funds

States variously provide unfunded public sector pensions, minimum state pensions (social security) and state earnings-related plans for private sector employees. These unfunded plans can be viewed as another form of government debt, with added demographic exposure.

The consequences of default are, however, quite different to ordinary government debt. The Irish government has, at the time of writing, proposed to "claw back" part of its civil servants' pensions through targeted taxation.

The extent of any unfunded state pension promises is often unclear due to poor disclosure and woolly national accounting; indeed they are often kept off-balance sheet in national accounts.

Unfunded private sector funds

In some countries, such as Germany, these are the most common approach to providing pensions for private sector workers. They can be viewed as another form of corporate debt, but with additional exposure to demographic risks. Changes in accounting standards mean that these are not as opaque as they once were and some of their supporters complain of the unfairness of marking pension liabilities to market when debt is carried at par value.

Funded defined benefit plans

These can be private or public sector. In the private sector, funded plans are usually established in response to tax incentives.

Contributions are paid to meet the cost of new benefits promised, as well as any historic deficits. Regulations covering the process for setting contributions vary widely from one country to another. The EU recently adopted some minimum principles-based standards, however actual implementation differs by country. The US has a prescribed process for calculating minimum contributions.

One key advantage of funded plans is that they impose some discipline on costs. By requiring the sponsor to set aside capital which it cannot use for its own ends it is less likely that unrealistically high benefits will be promised. In the UK, declining real yields and unexpected improvements in life expectancy have rendered some benefit levels unrealistic. In funded private sector plans this has generally led to future benefit levels being scaled back and retirement ages increased; meanwhile unfunded state arrangements have been slow to adapt.

A funded plan can be compared to a hedge fund that has issued debt (the pension promises) and invested in "long" assets, which might include bonds, equities, cash, hedge funds, private equity or commodities. The two components can behave in quite different ways.

Over the last five years, greater transparency in accounting for pension costs, and increasing awareness of the risks, have encouraged sponsors and their advisers to look for ways to reduce the mismatch in behaviour of assets and liabilities:

- Investment strategy is becoming more closely linked to the liabilities with Trustees and plan sponsors seeking to avoid unnecessary, unrewarded risks.

- There is greater interest in "risk sharing" designs intended to pass some of the investment (and longevity) risks back to plan members. They can be compared to with-profits (or participating) insurance contracts and suffer the same lack of transparency as their main downside.

Typically, at the end of its life a funded defined benefit plan will be bought-out with an insurance company. This usually requires a cash injection or for benefits to be scaled back to bridge the gap between the plan's own funding target and the insurance company's cautious pricing basis. Most plans are run on the basis that this would occur a long time into the future when most of the liabilities have been run off.

How do financial markets price in pension exposure?
Pension plans affect market prices in two ways:

- Pension exposure is usually priced directly into transactions.

- A country's pension system affects the perceived general degree of risk of investing in that country.

The US, UK and International accounting standards now all price pensions, broadly speaking, using market-consistent assumptions with AA-rated bond yields used for discount rates. Until recently this was the benchmark for pricing pensions particularly in M&A transactions. However, greater awareness of the issues, and the widening yield gap between AA rated and 'risk free' assets has led some organisations and individuals to take a more cautious attitude to pension risk, and to price more conservatively.

In the UK, the Pensions Act 2005 greatly increased corporate exposure to pension risk, which led to a huge rise in demand for specialist transaction advice. Analysts have also identified so-called "pension zombies", companies with funding deficits sufficient to absorb profits for the foreseeable future. Their shareholders will only see a return if the pension plan's investment strategy pays off.

At a country level the pension promises made by the public and private sectors, and the robustness of the pensions systems, will affect patterns of economic growth, consumption and social cohesion. This exposes investors to potential risks which are difficult to assess. Countries with pension systems that are perceived as unsustainable are less likely to attract inward investment and their governments' costs of borrowing may be affected.

Conclusion: What are the current pension trends affecting capital markets?

- Much greater awareness of the risks of funded defined benefit plans. We expect closures of such plans to continue in countries where this is possible.

- Greater scrutiny of pension arrangements in transactions: in some cases preventing transactions from taking place.

- Higher levels of investment in swaps and bonds by pension funds looking to hedge part or all of their financial risks.

- Greater diversification of "return seeking" portfolios leading to more investment in absolute return funds, hedge funds and private equity.

- Slow development of the market for longevity risk transfer, other than buy-out.

- We expect the UK buy-out market to stabilise with lower, steadier rates of growth going forward.

- Some governments will struggle with ageing populations and over-generous state pensions. This will be a source of social instability and we expect such governments to look for politically-acceptable ways to "default" on these promises.

Simon Banks
Principal
Punter Southall Transaction Services

In emerging markets, the problems are more fundamental. The ex-Soviet countries have seen bank failures, leading to losses of life savings. At the Fifth International Risk Management Conference in Almaty in April 2009, industry professionals suggested that Kazakhstan's private pension funds, which are owned by the banks, could collapse. The culture in these countries still veers towards spending money and perhaps keeping a little under the mattress.

Insurance

By early 2009, many consumers across Europe and the United States were buying or keeping only essential insurance. In China, life insurance is considered unlucky in a culture where to talk about death is taboo, and such traditional thinking has become more prevalent in the recession, as Deidre Walsh, managing director at China Green, noted at the European Insurance Forum in Dublin in early 2009.

In the United Kingdom, the FSA had already focused on some insurance mis-selling issues, including in relation to Payment Protection Insurance (PPI). The product is designed to protect people who have taken a loan or credit card but cannot pay related debts due to illness or unemployment. The FSA found that many UK consumers had overpaid for PPI, or claim they were mis-sold it due to the many exclusions in their policy.

The UK Competition Commission said that, from February 2010, lenders would not be able to sell PPI at point of sale, or as single premium policies (where a lump sum covering the cost of insurance is added to the loan).

Consumer protection and confidence are at the core of the Retail Distribution Review in the United Kingdom, a key part of the FSA's retail strategy. The review comes into effect in 2012.

Globally, a debate rages whether product disclosure and consumer education can reverse the lack of public confidence in financial services. As consumer advocate Mike McAteer pointed out at the November 2008 annual conference of the Committee of Insurance & Occupational Pension Supervisors in Frankfurt, such measures do not prevent mis-selling.

The poorest users of financial services have not been hit the hardest by the credit crisis. Micro-finance, the provision of loans and other financial services to poor individuals in emerging countries, is affected, however, by aid reductions. The micro-loans are made against real assets like cows and chickens. They are for setting up small businesses or doing something else productive for the community, but sceptics say that some recipients may be using them to pay off credit cards.

The world's rich people have lost the most from the crisis, unsurprising given that they have large holdings in equities and property. In March 2009,

Forbes magazine reported that the world's billionaires had an average net worth of US$3 billion, down 23 per cent in 12 months. There were 743 billionaires in the world, down from 1,125 a year earlier. Steve Forbes, chairman and CEO of Forbes, said in a video report that the billionaires' losses meant not less money to play with, but rather less capital with which to nurture the global economy.

Globally governments, regulators and risk managers talk of a new era in banking, with an emphasis on consumer protection. The erstwhile star bankers tell another story. In a few years, they say, the credit crisis will be forgotten, new products reaching new heights of flexibility will be developed, and the cycle of the last few years will repeat itself.

A final word

The credit crisis of 2007–09 has brought some convergence to global markets but national interests still prevail.

The Group of 20 (G20) meeting in April 2009 ended amicably but had revealed differences in agenda. The United States had looked for a substantial spending stimulus, but Germany and France resisted this. France, unlike the United States, had sought tougher international regulation of financial institutions and markets.

In early 2009, the global credit crisis and recession was showing no real signs of abating and more global convergence was under discussion. It will not happen quickly, despite encouragement from Barack Obama, a US president who has wooed the world. Regulators are not fast at keeping up with industry developments. Credit rating agencies have made big mistakes. Major banks have almost collapsed. One constant is that markets remain heavily weighted against the consumer.

The old wisdom applies. The public must be properly cynical. Everybody in the City is trying to sell a product, service or idea. Investors, now more than ever, need to make informed choices. I hope this book has helped.

Members of the Financial Stability Forum

The Financial Stability Forum brings together senior representatives of national financial authorities such as central banks, supervisory authorities and treasury departments, international financial institutions, international supervisory groups, committees of central bank experts and the European Central Bank. What follows is a list of current members.

Australia

Australian Securities and Investments Commission	www.asic.gov.au
Australian Prudential Regulation Authority	www.apra.gov.au
The Treasury	www.treasury.gov.au
Reserve Bank of Australia	www.rba.gov.au

Canada

Bank of Canada	www.bank-banque-canada.ca
Canada Deposit Insurance Corporation	www.cdic.ca
Department of Finance	www.fin.gc.ca
Office of the Superintendent of Financial Institutions	www.osfi-bsif.gc.ca
Ontario Securities Commission	www.osc.gov.on.ca

France

Autorité des Marchés Financiers	www.amf-france.org
Banque de France	www.banque-france.fr

Ministère de l' Économie   www.minefi.gouv.fr

Germany

Bundesanstalt für Finanzdienstleistungsaufsicht   www.bafin.de
Bundesministerium der Finanzen   www.bundesfinanzministerium.de
Deutsche Bundesbank   www.bundesbank.de

Hong Kong SAR

Hong Kong Monetary Authority   www.hkma.gov.hk
Office of the Commissioner of Insurance   www.info.gov.hk/oci
Securities & Futures Commission   www.hksfc.org.hk
The Treasury   www.info.gov.hk/tsy

Italy

Banca d'Italia   www.bancaditalia.it
Commissione Nazionale per le Società e la Borsa   www.consob.it
Istituto per la Vigilanze sulle Assicurazioni Private
     e di Interesse Collettivo (ISVAP)   www.isvap.it
Ministero dell'Economia e delle Finanze   www.tesoro.it

Japan

Bank of Japan   www.boj.or.jp
Financial Services Agency   www.fsa.go.jp
Ministry of Finance   www.mof.go.jp

The Netherlands

Autoriteit Financiële Markten   www.afm.nl
De Nederlandsche Bank   www.dnb.nl
Ministerie van Financiën   www.minfin.nl

Singapore

Ministry of Finance   www.mof.gov.sg
Monetary Authority of Singapore   www.mas.gov.sg

Switzerland

Swiss National Bank   www.snb.ch

United Kingdom

Bank of England   www.bankofengland.co.uk
Financial Services Authority   www.fsa.gov.uk
H M Treasury   www.hm-treasury.gov.uk

United States of America

Board of Governors of the Federal Reserve System   www.federalreserve.gov
Federal Deposit Insurance Corporation (FDIC)   www.fdic.gov
Federal Reserve Bank of New York   www.newyorkfed.org
National Association of Insurance Commissioners (NAIC)   www.naic.org
Office of the Comptroller of the Currency (OCC)   www.occ.treas.gov
US Commodity Futures Trading Commission   www.cftc.gov
US Department of Treasury   www.treasury.gov
US Securities and Exchange Commission (SEC)   www.sec.gov

International organisations

Bank for International Settlements (BIS)   www.bis.org
European Central Bank (ECB)   www.ecb.int
International Monetary Fund (IMF)   www.imf.org
Organisation for Economic Co-operation and
    Development (OECD)   www.oecd.org
The World Bank   www.worldbank.org

International standard-setting bodies and other groupings

Basel Committee on Banking
    Supervision (BCBS)   www.bis.org/bcbs/index.htm
Committee on Payment and Settlement
    Systems (CPSS)   www.bis.org./cpss/index.htm
Committee on the Global Financial
    System (CGFS)   www.bis.org/cgfs/index.htm

International Accounting Standards Board (IASB)   www.iasb.org
International Association of Deposit Insurers   www.iadi.org
International Association of Insurance Supervisors (IAIS) www.iaisweb.org
International Organisation of Securities
   Commissions (IOSCO)   www.iosco.org

Economics, statistics and money markets

Euro – the Official Treasury Euro Service	www.euro.gov.uk
European Bank for Reconstruction and Development	www.ebrd.com
European Commission	www.europa.eu.int
Financial Reporting Council	www.frc.org.uk
Institute of Economic Affairs	www.iea.org.uk
International Energy Agency	www.iea.org
National Association for Business Economics	www.nabe.com
National Bureau of Economic Research	www.nber.org
National Statistics	www.statistics.gov.uk
Organisation for Economic Co-operation and Development	www.oecd.org
The Treasury	www.hm-treasury.gov.uk
The World Bank	www.worldbank.org
World Economic Forum	www.weforum.org
World Trade Organisation	www.wto.org

Appendix 3

Exchanges

American Stock Exchange	www.amex.com
Athens Stock Exchange	www.ase.gr
Australia Stock Exchange	www.asx.com.au
Bolsas y Mercados Españoles (Spanish Stock Exchange)	www.bolsasymercados.es
Borsa Italiana (Italian Stock Exchange)	www.borsaitalia.it
Bourse du Luxembourg	www.bourse.lu
Bratislava Stock Exchange	www.bsse.sk
Bucharest Stock Exchange	www.bvb.ro
Budapest Stock Exchange	www.bse.hu
Bulgarian Stock Exchange, Sofia	www.bse-sofia.bg
Chicago Board Options Exchange	www.cboe.com
Cyprus Stock Exchange	www.cse.com.cy
Deutsche Borse	www.exchange.de
Dubai International Financial Centre	www.dubaiifc.com
EUREX (European derivatives exchange and clearing house)	www.eurexchange.com
ICE Futures Europe	www.theice.com
IntercontinentalExchange	www.theice.com
Irish Stock Exchange	www.ise.ie
JSE Securities Exchange (South Africa)	www.jse.co.za
Ljubljana Stock Exchange	www.ljse.si
London Metal Exchange	www.lme.co.uk
London Stock Exchange	www.londonstockexchange.com
Malta Stock Exchange	www.borzamalta.com.mt
Moscow Stock Exchange	www.mse.ru
NASDAQ	www.Nasdaq.com

NASDAQ OMX and OMX Nordic Exchanges	www.nasdaqomx.com
	www.nasdaqomxnordicexchange.com
National Stock Exchange of India	www.nse-india.com
New York Mercantile Exchange	www.nymex.com
NYSE Euronext	www.euronext.com
	www.nyse.com
NZX (New Zealand Stock Exchange)	www.nzx.com
Oslo Stock Exchange	www.ose.no
Prague Stock Exchange	www.pse.cz
Singapore Exchange	www.ses.com.sg
SIX Swiss Exchange	www.six-swiss-exchange.com
SWX Europe (Swiss Exchange)	www.swx.europe.com
Tokyo Stock Exchange	www.tse.or.jp
Toronto Stock Exchange	www.tsx.com
Warsaw Stock Exchange	www.gpw.com.pl
Wiener Börse AG	http://en.wienerborse.at

Appendix 4

Miscellaneous

Chartered Insurance Institute	www.cii.co.uk
Competition Commission	www.mmc.gov.uk
Corporation of London	www.cityoflondon.gov.uk
Daily Speculations: fascinating website about, and including contributions from, US hedge fund trader and former academic Victor Niederhoffer	www.dailyspeculations.com
Department for Business Enterprise & Regulatory Reform	www.berr.gov.uk
Ethical Investment Association	www.ethicalinvestment.org.uk
Federation of European Securities Exchanges	www.fese.be
FTSE International (details of indices)	www.ftse.com
IMMFA: Institutional Money Markets Funds Assocation	www.immfa.org
Khodorkovsky & Lebedev Communications Center	www.khodorkovskycenter.com
Lloyd's of London	www.lloydsoflondon.co.uk
Neil Daswani: excellent insights on how cyber criminals operate	www.neildaswani.com
Office of Fair Trading	www.oft.gov.uk
Serious Fraud Office	www.sfo.gov.uk

Multilateral trading facilities (and similar), Europe

BATS	www.batstrading.co.uk
Chi-X	www.chi-x.com
Equiduct	www.equiduct-trading.com
Nasdaq OMX Europe	www.nasdaqomxeurope.com
Turquoise	www.tradeturquoise.com

News and analysis

BBC News Online (Business)	www.bbc.co.uk/business
Bloomberg News	www.bloomberg.co.uk
Breakingviews	www.breakingviews.com
Citywire	www.citywire.co.uk
Dow Jones Newswires	www.dowjones.com
Useful website of economics journalist David Smith	www.economicsuk.com
Exclusive Analysis: a strategic intelligence company that provides evidence-based forecasts for violent and political risks worldwide	www.exclusive-analysis.com
Financial Research Corporation: a consulting services provider in relation to mutual funds and other areas	www.frcnet.com
FT.com	www.ft.com
iMoneyNet: a provider of money market mutual fund information and analysis	www.imoneynet.com
International Financial Services London	www.ifsl.org.uk
Lipper: a global provider of mutual trust information	www.lipperweb.com
PA News	www.pressassociation.press.net
Red Herring magazine: US high-tech company developments	www.redherring.com
Reuters	www.reuters.co.uk

Post-trade organisations

The Depository Trust and Clearing Corporation	www.dtcc.com
Euroclear	www.euroclear.com
LCH.Clearnet Limited	www.lch.com

Trade associations and similar

Accounting Standards Board	www.asb.org.uk
Alternative Investment Management Association	www.aima.org
Association of British Insurers	www.abi.org.uk
Association of Financial Guaranty Insurers	www.afgi.com
Association of Investment Trust Companies	www.aitc.co.uk
British Bankers Association	www.bvca.co.uk
British Building Societies Association	www.bsa.org.uk
British Venture Capital Association	www.bvca.co.uk
Chartered Institute of Public Relations	http://ipr.org.uk
Committee of European Securities Regulators	www.cesr.eu.org
International Association of Insurance Supervisors	www.iais.org
International Federation of Technical analysts	www.ifta.org
International Swaps and Derivatives Association	www.isda.org
Investor Relations Society	www.ir-soc.org.uk
Investment Management Association	www.investmentuk.org
Investment Company Institute	www.ici.org
National Association of Pension Funds	www.napf.co.uk
Public Relations Society of America	www.prsa.org
Reinsurance Association of America	www.reinsurance.org
Securities Industry and Financial Markets Association	www.sifma.org
The Futures and Options Association	www.foa.co.uk
The International Underwriting Association of London	www.iua.co.uk

Glossary

Accelerated book build Where the bank takes a selling company's shares onto its books and offers them to investors. It will sell the shares within one or two days.

Alternative Investment Market A junior market established by the London Stock Exchange in 1995. This enables trading in smaller companies.

Alternative trading system A trading system that matches buy and sell orders but is not regulated as an exchange.

American depositary receipts Certificates issued by a US bank representing shares in a foreign stock traded on a US exchange.

Arbitrage To profit from a price difference in the same product trading on different markets.

Asset allocation How the fund manager divides investment income across stocks and other investments.

Asset-backed security A debt security backed by a pool of assets or collateral consisting of cash flows from such a pool.

Bad bank A bank used to hold non-performing assets.

Balance of payments A record of all money flows into and out of a country.

Balance sheet A statement of an organisation's total assets and liabilities on a specific date.

Baltic Exchange A membership organisation in the global maritime market place, and a provider of independent daily shipping market information.

Bank for International Settlements An international organisation that fosters international monetary and financial cooperation and serves as a bank for central banks.

Basel II An international regulatory capital requirement for banks and other financial services companies.

Basis differential The difference between the futures price and the underlying commodity.

Beauty parade Process by which banks compete for the job of book runner for a company's IPO.

Best execution Brokers' obligation to provide the most advantageous order execution for customers, including best price.

Bid rigging An illegal agreement between competing firms by which they coordinate their bids to artificially increase the price of goods or services offered to customers.

Big Bang Deregulation of the London stock market on 27 October 1986.

Bill of exchange An order by one person to another to pay a specified sum to a person on a given date.

Black–Scholes model A model used for valuing options, first articulated in 1973 by Fischer Black and Myron Scholes. The model's main insight is that the option is priced by implication if the stock is traded. The model uses factors that include intrinsic and time value, volatility, the underlying stock price and the risk-free rate of return. The model is widely used today as an approximation but it makes assumptions that may not apply, including a constant risk-free interest rate, continuous trading and no transaction costs.

Boiler room An operation that sells dubious investments to the public, and may pretend to be a stockbroker.

Bond A debt instrument issued for more than one year to raise capital by borrowing from investors.

Book runner The managing or lead underwriter in debt and equity issuances.

Bought deal Where a bank buys securities itself from an issuer and resells them in the market.

BRIC economies Brazil, Russia, India and China.

Broker (insurance) Intermediary who arranges insurance with underwriters for clients.

Broker-dealer A firm that buys securities for itself and for others.

Building society A member-owned financial institution that takes deposits and provides loans.

Buy side Describes the fund manager or institutional investor side of the investment business (as opposed to the broker-dealer or banking side).

Call option An option giving you the right to buy the underlying securities at the exercise price of the option.

Capital account The part of the balance of payments (see separate entry) that tracks the purchase or sale of assets.

Capital asset pricing model The CAPM, as it is called, is a model that finds the required rate of return on a stock by comparing its performance with the market.

Capital gains tax A tax on profits from selling assets such as shares.

Captive insurer An insurer owned by the company for which it provides cover.

Cash-box play A form of capital raising in which the deal is structured for a non-cash consideration.

Catastrophe bonds Also known as cat bonds. They are high-yield bonds, insurance-linked, and intended to raise money in case of a catastrophe. If the issuer, an insurance or reinsurance company, suffers a loss from a given catastrophe, its obligation to pay interest or repay the principal may be forgiven and used instead by the sponsor to pay its claims to policyholders.

Central bank A country's main monetary authority. It will, among other things, regulate the money supply, issue currency, hold the reserves of banks and oversee financial stability.

Central counterparty An entity that stands between counterparties to trades, acting as buyer to every seller and seller to every buyer.

Central counterparty clearing Where a neutral central counterparty comes between the buyer and seller to reduce risks, with transactions netted before they are settled.

Central Fund Part of Lloyd's security. Lloyd's levies a premium on policies written and the proceeds go into the Central Fund, which pays claims if members cannot meet their obligations.

Central securities depository An organisation that holds securities and conducts related administration; it may have clearing and settlement functions.

Certificate of deposit A deposit with a bank or other financial institution for a fixed period, usually paying a fixed interest rate.

Chapter 11 of the Bankruptcy Code A part of US federal bankruptcy law that gives a bankrupt company a chance to reorganise its business and become profitable. All significant business decisions must be approved by a bankruptcy court. Chapter 11 bankruptcy filings can be strategic.

Clearing The link between trading and settlement.

Closed-ended fund A fund that trades on the stock market with a fixed number of shares in issue. In Europe, these are called investment companies.

Collateral Security on a loan that is given up in case of default.

Collateralised debt obligation A security backed by pools of assets.

Collateralised loan obligation A collateralised debt obligation (see above) referencing leveraged loans.

Combined Code on Corporate Governance Sets out UK standards of good practice in, for example, board composition and development, remuneration, accountability and audit, and relations with shareholders.

Commercial paper Short-term unsecured debt issued by companies.

Commodity index fund Fund that gives investors pure commodities exposure, meaning to commodity prices and not the share prices of businesses associated with them.

Consumer Price Index An index measuring cost of consumer goods and services. A measure of inflation.

Contingent commissions Commissions paid by insurers to insurance brokers in exchange for steering business their way.

Convertible arbitrage A strategy of buying convertible bonds that seem mispriced and selling short the underlying shares with a view to making a profit. This is a hedge fund (see separate entry) strategy.

Convertible bonds A bond with a right to switch into shares at a given price.

Corporate bond A bond issued by a company, with a maturity date usually at least one year after issue.

Corporate governance How a company conducts its corporate affairs and responds to stakeholders, employees and society.

Covered bond A corporate bond (see separate entry) but covered by a pool of assets in case the originator should become insolvent.

Covered warrant An exchange-traded packaged derivative mainly for retail investors. It is a security and not a contract.

Credit crunch A serious shortage of money or credit. The term is commonly used to describe the 2007–09 credit crisis.

Credit default swap A form of credit derivative contract. The buyer makes regular small payments to the seller in return for a payout if the underlying asset defaults.

Credit rating agency A firm that issues credit ratings for companies. The higher its rating, the better the credit terms a borrower will receive. The rating is a paid-for service, which has called into question its independence.

Credit union A not-for-profit financial institution owned by its members.

CREST The central securities depository for UK markets and Irish stocks. Crest operates an electronic settlement system, and can physically hold stocks for customers.

Current account The part of the balance of payments that tracks the country's exports and imports.

Dark liquidity pool Volume of trades created from institutional orders and concealed from the public.

Deficit When more money is spent than taken in.

Defined contribution pension scheme Where cash is invested in a retirement fund on the pension holder's behalf, and the size of the pension depends on how well the retirement fund has performed.

Demutualisation The process by which a mutual society, owned by its members, becomes a public company, owned by shareholders.

Derivative A financial contract, the value of which is derived from a traditional security, asset or index.

Designated market maker A form of market maker on the NYSE, previously called specialist (see separate entry).

Direct market access A service offered by some stockbrokers enabling private investors to place buy and sell orders directly on the order books of the LSE.

Discounted cash flow The present value of future cash flow, calculated by multiplying projected income by the discount factor.

Discount rate The rate of interest by which US banks can borrow from the Federal Reserve. The term also means the interest rate used to find the present value of future cash flows.

Discount window A mechanism by which the Federal Reserve lends to commercial banks.

Discretionary broker Broker who can deal and make investment decisions for clients without their specific approval.

Dividend A payment made to shareholders, taken from the company's profits.

Dividend yield Dividend per share as a percentage of the share price.

Dow Jones industrial average An index of stock market prices based on 30 US blue-chip stocks.

Downgrade clause This is a clause in a reinsurance contract saying that if a reinsurer's rating with a credit rating agency falls below a trigger, the primary insurer may void the contract or require collateral.

Earnings per share Earnings of a company divided by its total shares outstanding.

Efficient market A market where prices on shares and other assets reflects all known information.

Electronic communication network A system that brings buyers and sellers together for electronic trade execution.

Equitas A Lloyd's reinsurer established in 1996 to reinsure liabilities in Lloyd's syndicates on policies written from the 1930s until the end of 1992. It is the world's largest solvent run-off reinsurer.

Eurex German–Swiss derivatives exchange.

Eurobond An international bond denominated in a currency not belonging to the country of issue.

Euronext.liffe London-based derivatives exchange owned by NYSE Euronext. It was formed in January 2002 from the takeover of the London International Financial Futures and Options Exchange (Liffe) by Euronext.

EURONIA Euro overnight index average, which is the benchmark weighted-average overnight interest rate for the euro. It is published in London.

European Economic Area An arrangement by which some non-member states of the European Union can participate in the European single market.

European Union A political and economic union of 27 member states.

Excess-of-loss reinsurance Where the insurer pays the initial layer of a valid claim and the reinsurer pays the balance up to a set figure.

Excess spread The net interest from assets, after payments to bondholders and expenses.

Exchange controls Regulations restricting convertibility of one currency into others.

Exchange Rate Mechanism System for aligning exchange rates of EU currencies. This was introduced by the European Community in March 1979.

Exchange-traded commodities Exchange-traded funds (see separate entry) that invest in commodities.

Exchange-traded fund An open-ended security that trades all day like a stock but has the diversification of a mutual fund. It will track the movement of an index, sector, foreign markets or commodities.

Execution only A service enabling customers to buy or sell shares without having advice.

Exercise price The price at which an option holder may buy or sell the underlying security.

Facultative reinsurance This provides a reinsurer with cover for specific risks not covered in its reinsurance treaties.

Fair value Amount at which assets are traded fairly, which is often identical to market price.

Federal Reserve Bank One of 12 regional banks servicing a reserve district in the US. These are operating arms of the Federal Reserve System.

Federal Reserve System The central banking system of the United States.

Final salary pension scheme Where the pension provision is a proportion of the pension holder's salary on retirement.

Financial Action Task Force on Money Laundering An international organisation that recommends anti-money laundering procedures and identifies countries where they are inadequate.

Financial futures Futures (see separate entry) based on a financial instrument such as shares. The agreement is to exchange a cash sum reflecting the difference between the initial price of the underlying asset and its price on settlement. Interest rate futures enable buyers to hedge against adverse interest rate movements.

Financial guarantors Another name for monoline insurers.

Financial Industry Regulatory Authority The largest non-governmental regulator for all securities firms doing business in the United States. FINRA is a self-regulatory organisation and the successor to the National Association of Securities Dealers.

Financial reinsurance A form of reinsurance arranged for financial or strategic reasons, with little or no risk transfer from the insurer to the reinsurer.

Financial Services Action Plan A 1999 initiative intended to harmonise financial services markets in the European Union.

Financial Services Authority The UK financial services regulator.

Flipping Buying or selling shares quickly. This can be a way to make money quickly from new issues.

Forward A contract to buy or sell an asset in the future at a price agreed today.

Forward rate agreement A contract by which a party pays a fixed interest rate and receives a floating interest.

Freight derivatives Financial instruments for trading in future levels of freight rates. They include forward freight agreements and options based on these.

Front-month contract The futures price on the earliest of the delivery months.

FTSE 100 A share index of the 100 biggest UK companies by market capitalisation.

Fund of hedge funds A fund that invests in a number of hedge funds.

Future A buyer's and seller's agreement to receive and deliver a specified amount of an asset at an agreed price on a future date.

Gaming Using knowledge of money flows into dark liquidity pools for financial gain. For example, traders may execute small orders to obtain information about volumes.

Gearing Use of borrowed money to try to increase returns. The US term is leverage.

Gilts UK government bonds.

Giovannini report The Giovannini reports, published in 2001 and 2003, focused on barriers to EU cross-border clearing and settlement, and how to overcome them. They were the work of an expert group, the Giovannini Group, created by the European Commission as part of its aim of integrating capital markets.

Glass–Steagall Act The US 1933 legislation that separated investment banking from commercial banking. It has now been repealed.

Great Depression An economic crisis that started with the 1929 stock market crash and continued into the 1930s.

Grey market A market in shares before they are issued, or off exchange.

Gross domestic product Measure of the value of goods and services an economy produces.

Haircut A percentage reduction in an asset's market value.

Hard commodities Products of extractive processes, including oil and metals. Cycles run on a longer time frame than in soft commodities.

Hard insurance market Where insurance costs are rising and in shorter supply. This is part of the insurance cycle.

Hawala An informal banking system, which works by allowing cheap and unrecorded money transfers.

Hedge fund A flexible and lightly regulated investment fund, sometimes using innovative trading techniques. This is a fund for institutional investors or wealthy individuals. A hedge fund typically charges up to 2 per cent management fee and 20 per cent performance fee. Hedge funds suffered in the 2007–09 credit crisis. There are global moves underway to regulate the industry.

Hedging Making an investment to reduce or eliminate the risk in another investment.

ICE Futures Europe's leading futures and options exchange for energy products. It is part of IntercontinentalExchange, a US company.

Identity fraud Pretending to be another to obtain goods or services.

Incurred-but-not-reported claims Estimates of future insurance claims.

Index option Option on stock market indices.

Inelastic Where price fluctuation makes little difference to demand, as for the price of soft commodities in the developed world.

Insurance broker Intermediary between insurance companies and their clients.

Interdealer broker An intermediary for those market participants who want to trade in large amounts without revealing who they are.

International Financial Reporting Standards Rules and guidelines established by the International Accounting Standards Board for companies to follow when preparing financial statements. More than 100 countries allow, or require, companies to comply with IFRS standards.

International Monetary Fund United Nations agency established partly to maintain order and foreign exchange stability.

International Organisation of Securities Commissions An international organisation for regulators of securities and futures markets from across the world. It aims to promote high standards of regulation, to unite in efforts to establish standards, and to exchange information and help.

In the money Where the asset price is more than the exercise price of the option. The difference represents the option's value.

Intrinsic value How far the underlying asset's value surpasses the exercise price of an option. An option only has intrinsic value when it is in the money (see separate entry).

Investment adviser A specific US term for a firm or person that advises clients on how to invest their money.

Investment banking The business of raising capital, trading and selling securities and advising on mergers and acquisitions.

Investor relations How a quoted company liaises with investors, keeping them informed of price-sensitive information and tries to obtain a fair valuation for the company's shares.

IPO A company's first offering of equity to the public.

Jobber This was a term for a dealer in shares who only traded with brokers. In 1986, jobbers were replaced with market makers.

Junk bond A high-yield bond rated below investment grade because of the issuer's perceived high default risk.

Latency The delay between when something starts and when it happens. It is measured in milliseconds and typically refers to the speed of electronic trading on exchanges and multilateral trading facilities.

Lender of last resort Provider of loans when nobody else can or will.

Leverage See gearing.

LIBID London interbank bid rate. This is the rate at which a bank will borrow from other banks.

LIBOR London interbank offered rate. This is the rate at which banks will lend money to each other.

Limit order Minimum selling price or maximum buying price, set by the client.

Liquidity Ease of buying or selling an asset for cash at a fair price.

Lloyd's A specialist insurance market that makes up around half of the London market. It has a large global licence network.

Lloyd's managing agent An agent that employs underwriting staff and manages one or more syndicates on behalf of Lloyd's members (companies or Names). There are about 47 managing agents, mostly owned by listed companies or backed by insurance-related capital.

LMX spiral London market excess-of-loss risk, passed, between insurers and syndicates in the 1980s and sometimes coming round full circle. Eventually there were huge insurance losses on the risk.

London Metal Exchange The world's leading non-ferrous metals market.

Long-tail insurance Insurance where the liability may be discovered and claims made many years after the loss, as in asbestos-related cover.

Long Term Capital Management LTCM was a high-profile hedge fund that used statistical arbitrage (see separate entry) among other techniques. The fund had more than 25 times gearing; it relied on a model that failed after Russia defaulted on its debts in 1998. LTCM eventually collapsed.

Maastricht Treaty 1991 treaty signed in Maastricht, the Netherlands, with the aim of establishing a single European currency and creating economic cooperation in Western Europe.

Madoff, Bernard A Wall Street adviser who turned out to be a major fraudster. In December 2008, it was revealed that he had defrauded investors out of US$50 billion.

Malware Abbreviation for malicious software. This is software designed to harm a computer system.

Margin Collateral that a client deposits with, for example, a derivatives dealer or spread betting firm.

Market capitalisation The share price of a company, multiplied by the number of shares in issue.

Market maker A firm quoting both a buy and sell price in a financial instrument, and which will trade at that price.

Market Reform Group A group that aims to identify inefficiencies in the London insurance market's processes and to develop technological solutions.

Mark to market This is to record the value of a financial instrument or portfolio daily, based on the market price for the instrument or a similar one. The process enables assessment of profits and losses and of whether margin requirements are satisfied.

Microfinance Covers loans and other financial services to poor individuals in emerging countries, particularly China and India.

Micro-insurance Insurance for low-income people. It has low premiums and provides low coverage.

Monetary policy A central bank's management of interest rates and money supply to influence the economy.

Monetary Policy Committee A Bank of England committee that meets monthly to decide the official interest rate.

Money laundering Concealing the origin, ownership and destination of illegally obtained money by converting it into assets that cannot easily be linked with these.

Money market funds Mutual funds that invest in short-term debt securities.

Money markets Wholesale markets for trading short-term securities such as commercial paper, treasury bills and certificates of deposit.

Monoline insurer A company that provides insurance protection to buyers of financial instruments.

Multilateral trading facility A system that links multiple parties, including investors or investment firms, and enables them to trade financial instruments.

Mutual funds In the US and Canada, open-ended funds (see separate entry). Outside these two countries, a generic term for pooled investments.

Names Individuals who underwrite insurance through syndicates at Lloyd's.

Nationalisation To turn a private entity into one owned by the state.

Net asset value per share The currency value of a single share in a mutual fund. This is based on the value of the fund's underlying assets less its liabilities, divided by the number of shares outstanding.

Netting When trading parties net off a positive value against a negative value, making it necessary to pay out only a net amount.

Nil paid rights The rights to which shareholders have not subscribed in a rights issue.

Nominal value The value of a security set by the issuing company, with no relation to market value. It is the same as par.

Non-performing loan Loan where the borrower has stopped making payments.

Non-proportional reinsurance Where the reinsurer pays only if the loss is beyond the insurer's retention.

Note A short-term bond.

Notional amount The nominal amount used to calculate payments on products used in risk management. This sum does not usually pass from one party to another.

Off balance sheet Where an asset or debt is not on the balance sheet.

Open-ended fund A fund that can create or redeem as many more units as are required to meet investor demand. In the United States, such funds are mutual funds; in Europe, they are open-ended investment companies fit this category.

Open-market operations Where the central bank buys and sells securities. It is a main method of monetary policy.

Open offer An offer of new shares to existing shareholders on a pre-emptive basis. Unlike in a rights issue, shareholders cannot sell their right to buy new shares in the open offer.

Option A derivative giving the right to buy or sell a security at a predetermined price, the exercise price, within a specified period.

Order-driven trading system Where buy and sell orders for securities are automatically matched on a central computer system.

Out of the money Where the underlying asset price is less than the exercise price of the option.

Over-collateralisation The extent to which the principal balance of a mortgage pool may exceed that of the tranche securities.

Overnight index swap An interest rate swap where the overnight rate is exchanged for a fixed interest rate.

Over the counter Not traded on an exchange.

Pairs trading Where two greatly correlated stocks that temporarily diverge are traded in pairs. When one of a pair of stocks outperforms the other in a divergence from the usual correlation, the pairs trader takes a long position in the weaker performer in the expectation that it will rise, and a short position in the other, so hedging the position against whole market movements. Usually, the cost of taking one position is compensated by returns from the other. When the divergence is corrected, the trader makes a profit.

Par See nominal value.

PATRIOT Act The USA PATRIOT Act of 2001 (Uniting and Strengthening America by Providing Appropriate Tools Required to Intercept and Obstruct Terrorism) expanded the definition of terrorism to include domestic terrorism; it gave law enforcement agencies more ability to search messages and records as well as to detain and deport immigrants suspected of terrorism. It gave the Secretary of the Treasury more authority to regulate financial transactions, particularly those involving foreigners. Critics say that the act has eroded civil liberty protections.

Payment protection insurance Insurance protecting people who take out a loan on credit card and cannot pay debt on these due to illness or unemployment.

Ponzi scheme Fraud where investors are lured into an investment scheme by promised high returns, but are paid only with the cash from earlier investors. The structure collapses when cash outflow exceeds inflow. The concept was named after Charles Ponzi, an Italian immigrant to the United States who, in 1919–20, took more than 15 million dollars from investors on this basis. The Madoff fraud (see separate entry), revealed in December 2008, is the biggest example so far of a Ponzi scheme.

Pooled investment Where investors put money into a single fund.

Preferred stock Gives a priority claim on profits over common stocks.

Premium A fee the insured pays the insurer for insurance cover. This is also the market price for an option.

Price–earnings ratio Share price divided by earnings per share. This is how the market rates a company.

Primary dealer A bank or broker-dealer that may trade directly with the US Federal Reserve.

Principles-based regulation This places greater reliance on principles and outcome-focused high-level rules for regulatory purposes than on prescriptive rules. The FSA has embraced the approach, which contrasts with the rules-based approach common in the United States. It puts more of an interpretation onus on firms and discourages lawyers from seeking loopholes in the rules.

Private equity Investment in unlisted companies.

Proportional reinsurance Where the reinsurer takes a percentage share of the policy.

Prospectus Directive This has introduced a 'single passport for issuers', making securities available to investors either through a public offer procedure or by admitting their shares to trading.

Protection and indemnity associations Mutual insurance cooperatives that operate in the London insurance market and mainly insure their members against marine risks not covered by Lloyd's or company policies.

Public relations Creating an image for a company and promoting this to analysts, shareholders, investors and media. It can be in-house or through PR agents. This is about controlling information flow, and helps companies particularly in crisis situations or during the results reporting season.

Public sector national debt Previously named national debt, this is the United Kingdom's national government debt.

Quantitative easing A central bank's creation of new money and its injection into the financial system.

Quote-driven trading system An electronic exchange system where, unlike in an order-driven market, prices are derived from quotations of market makers or dealers.

RAPIDS An Australian structure for pre-emptive offers, which sets an accelerated institutional offering and a longer retail offering on the same terms.

Real-estate investment trust A way for retail investors to invest in a diversified property portfolio through a tradable asset. This was created in the United States in 1960, has been popular since in Australia and elsewhere, and came to the United Kingdom in January 2007.

Reinsurance Where an insurance entity spreads its risk by buying protection from a reinsurer.

Reinsurance Directive An EU directive, implemented in December 2007 or, in some countries, later, that created a single regulated market for pure reinsurance business.

Reinsurance to close A procedure at Lloyd's where a closing syndicate year passes its portfolio of policies and reserves, covering claims forward, to future years. This way, each annual venture is brought to an end.

Repo A sale and repurchase agreement. This is a short-term money market instrument. The borrower sells a security to a lender and agrees to buy it back at a fixed price at a later date.

Repo rate The rate at which banks can borrow money from a central bank.

Reserve ratio The ratio of a bank's reserves to deposits.

Residential mortgage-backed security A type of security whose cash flows come from residential debt such as mortgages, home-equity loans and sub-prime mortgages.

Retail service provider An interface between retail brokers and the wider equity markets. The providers are required to match best buying and selling prices on the order book.

Retrocession Where a reinsurer reinsures its business with another reinsurer, a retrocessionaire.

Return on capital employed Profits before interest and tax, expressed as a percentage of year-end capital employed. This is a measure of management efficiency.

Rights issue Where a company invites existing shareholders to purchase additional shares in the company.

Rolling spread bet Where the basis for pricing a spread bet (see separate entry) is the cash price.

Sarbanes–Oxley Act of 2002 The emergency legislation introduced in the United States after the Enron fraud. The act introduced tighter auditing controls and greater disclosure and reporting requirements, requiring the chief executive and chief financial officers to sign off financial reports, with criminal liability if this report turns out to be incorrect. The act has been widely criticised as being too severe and has caused US financial markets to lose business to London.

Savings and loan association A financial institution that takes in savings deposits and makes mortgage loans. Also known as a thrift. Similar to a building society.

Scrip issue Free shares that reduce the share price, but not the value of the total investment.

Securities and Exchange Commission The US securities regulator.

Securitisation Conversion of credit into tradable securities.

Sell side The broker-dealer/banking side of the investment business. The sell side sells securities to investors such as fund managers.

SETS The London Stock Exchange's electronic trading service. It combines electronic order-driven trading with market making.

Settlement The process of exchanging cash for securities and vice versa.

Shadow banking Off-balance-sheet activity by financial institutions, including trading high-risk derivatives through structured vehicles.

Side car A reinsurance company reinsuring one insurance company. The premium from the reinsured and the equity capital from investors are paid into a trust account that collateralises policies written by the side car.

Smurfing Where a large financial transaction is broken up into many small ones to avoid scrutiny under, for instance, money laundering regulations.

Soft commodity Commodities such as cocoa, sugar and coffee, affected by climate changes, and with inelastic (see separate entry) pricing in the developed world.

Soft insurance market Market where cost of insurance is low. This will be due to heavy competition and slacker policy writing. It is part of the insurance cycle.

Solvency II An EU Directive that sets risk-based standards of capital adequacy for insurers. It comes into force in 2012.

SONIA The sterling overnight index average. This is the rate for borrowing sterling overnight in London.

Special drawing rights International reserve assets created by the International Monetary Fund as an artificial currency consisting of a basket of national currencies. They supplement other reserve assets and were created amid concerns that gold and dollars alone were a limited means of settling international accounts.

Specialist A type of market maker, operating as a dealer representing a NYSE specialist firm, and aiming to facilitate trade on the exchange. Now renamed 'designated market maker'.

Spitzer, Eliot A former New York attorney general famous for investigating financial scandals. In April 2003, the Spitzer settlement with investment banks followed his investigation into alleged conflicts of interests between analysts' research and investment banking. A year later, Spitzer settled with insurance brokers following an investigation into contingent commissions and bid rigging (see separate entries). He became New York governor but resigned in March 2007 after revelation that he'd had liaisons with a call girl.

Split-strike conversion strategy This is a trading strategy with options (see separate entry), also known as a collar. It was used by self-confessed US$50 billion US fraudster Bernard Madoff (see separate entry).

Spot price Present delivery price on a commodity.

Spot transaction Where two currencies are exchanged at once, using an exchange rate agreed on the day.

Spread bet A way to trade on the movement of financial instruments by placing a bet.

Stamp duty A UK tax on buying shares or property.

Statistical arbitrage A trading strategy of hedge funds, which extends pairs trading (see separate entry) to a portfolio of stocks.

Stock exchange An organised exchange where brokers and dealers buy and sell securities.

Stock split The split of shares into a larger number with a proportionally lower unit value.

Straight-through processing Where the trade process for capital markets and payment transactions is conducted electronically without re-keying or manual intervention. This is used for foreign exchange.

Stress testing Assessing risk under a range of possible scenarios.

Structured investment vehicle A fund borrowing money by issuing short-term securities and then lending money by buying long-term securities at a higher rate.

Subpoena An official order requiring a person to testify or provide documents.

Sub-prime mortgage Mortgage given to a borrower with a poor credit history.

Sukuk An Islamic bond.

Swap A derivative by which two parties exchange assets or cash flows over an agreed time.

Syndicate A series of annual syndicates by a collection of individuals and companies that underwrite insurance risks at Lloyd's.

Systemic risk Risk that has impact on a financial market or an economy and not just on individual firms.

Takaful insurance An Islamic form of mutual insurance.

Technical analysis Study of past share price and other financial market movements on charts in the hope of identifying trading patterns. The aim is to predict future market performance or, for traders, to help choose investment entry and exit points.

Thrift See savings and loan association.

Tick Smallest unit price change.

Ticker tape A continuously transmitted paper ribbon on which security price quotes are written. In the days before modern technology they were used to record stock prices.

Tier 1 ratio The part of a bank's capital consisting of shareholders' equity plus irredeemable and non-cumulative preference shares.

Tier-one clients The biggest and most important clients of an investment bank.

Tranche A slice of a securities or structured finance deal.

Treasury bill Short-term government debt security.

Treaty reinsurance An agreement covering insurance risks in a given class or classes of business without evaluation of individual exposures.

Tripartite authorities H M Treasury, the FSA and the Bank of England in the United Kingdom. They have responsibility for cooperation in the area of financial stability.

UCITS III The UCITS (undertakings for the collective investment of transferable securities) III Directive, launched in December 2001, provided a European passport for investment managers throughout the European Union and broadened the activities they may undertake. The UCITS IV Directive will be implemented by July 2011. It will allow UCITS members to further develop their cross-border activities, creating economies of scale and increasing investor protection. Investment companies are excluded from UCITS.

Underwrite In investment banking, this is to guarantee a given price for a given number of securities to the issuer in exchange for a fee. In insurance, underwriters decide whether to accept a risk for the client, and on what terms.

Venture capital trust A quoted company that invests in small growth companies, aiming to make capital gains for investors.

Virus A software program that can reproduce itself and damage programs on the same computer.

Warrant The conventional warrant is a product that may be used to buy a specified number of new shares in a company at a specified exercise price at a given time, or within a given period. Warrants, unlike call options, are issued by the company and last for years, not months. See also covered warrant.

Wash trade A transaction that gives the impression that a purchase and sale have been made, although there has been no change in ownership.

Worm A type of virus (see separate entry) that spreads across computers on a network without user intervention. It may exploit a software design fault.

Writer (of option) Seller (of option).

XBRL Xtensible business reporting language. This is a computer language enabling additional data to be attached to financial information. When the data is transferred between systems, it will be recognised.

Yield The return on an investment. For a stock, the current yield is the dividend divided by the share price.

Zero coupon bond A bond sold at a deep discount from face value and which pays no coupon. On maturing, the bond is redeemed at face value.

Further reading

Books quickly become out of date. You can often gain more from checking the websites of trade associations, banks, central banks and regulators.

At the same time, the right book can be a revelation, and can be helpful, for instance, in explaining the background to the credit crisis that started in June 2007.

Notably, in December 2008, when events had deteriorated, there were 35 financial and economic books in the top 500 best-selling books on amazon.com, the online bookseller.

I favour those written by experts and with the author's genuine voice, but this combination is a rarity. The books below are my choice.

Accounting

Parker, R H (2007) *Understanding Company Financial Statements*, 3rd edn, Penguin Business. A concise overview.

City of London

Davidson, A (2008) *How the City Really Works*, 2nd edn, Kogan Page. This is my gossipy but accurate take on London's financial markets.

Stoakes, C (2007) *All You Need to Know about the City: Who Does What and Why in London's Financial Markets*, Longtail Publishing. A clear overview, if lacking some detail.

Valdez, S (2007) *An Introduction to Global Financial Markets*, Palgrave. A superb primer. Not quite a beginner's book but not too technical either.

Clearing and settlement

Norman, P (2007) *Plumbers and Visionaries*, John Wiley & Sons. A ground-breaking account of the history and future of the securities settlement industry in Europe.

Commodities

Rogers, J (2007) *Hot Commodities: How Anyone Can Invest Profitably in the World's Best Market*, John Wiley & Sons. An enthusiastic and well argued book about the commodities boom. Rogers, a former partner of hedge fund guru George Soros, is a highly successful investor, although not a trader. He does not mince his words about his enthusiasm for commodities and China. He criticises the monetary policy of ex-Soviet countries, the United States and, more recently, the United Kingdom. It is worth supplementing a read of this book with watching his broadcasts on Bloomberg TV and elsewhere, available on YouTube.

Derivatives

Kolman, J (2007) *Naked Option*, Harriman House. Entertaining and eerily topical fiction.

Economics and world affairs

Cooper, G (2008) *The Origin of Financial Crises: Central banks, credit bubbles and the efficient market fallacy*, Harriman House. A compelling analysis of forces behind the credit crisis of 2007–09. The book presents a case that financial markets are inherently unstable.

Ferguson, N (2008) *The Ascent of Money: A Financial History of the World*, Allen Lane. A historian's sweeping account of the history of money, the book takes the reader from tribal life with no concept of money through to the Enron scandal and the securitisation of home mortgages. His underlying theme is the evolution of money through natural selection.

Galbraith, J K (1992) *The Great Crash, 1929*, Penguin Business. A readable account of the 1929 US stock market crash.

Gladwell, M (2002) *The Tipping Point*, Abacus. A superficial but compulsively readable book about how social epidemics start. The author's broad themes are applicable to financial markets.

Greenspan, A (2008) *The Age of Turbulence*, Penguin (published with new epilogue). A fascinating autobiography by the former chairman of the US Federal Reserve, who, many believe, bears some responsibility for getting the United States into the credit crisis of 2007–09.

Krugman, P (2008) *The Return of Depression Economics and the Crisis of 2008*, Allen Lane. An excellent and accessible overview.

Peston, R (2008) *Who Runs Britain?... and who's to blame for the economic mess we're in?*, Hodder Paperbacks. A big-name journalist's penetrating look at the British economy.

Taleb, N N (2004) *Fooled by Randomness*, Penguin. Entertaining and iconoclastic book about how models do not work.

Equities

Blodget, H (2008) *The Wall Street Self-Defense Manual*, Random House Business Books. Surprisingly cautious (and sound) advice from the analyst whose e-mails helped to trigger the US Spitzer investigation of conflicts between research and investment banking.

Burns, R (2005) *The Naked Trader*, Harriman House. An entertaining and useful book for the home trader of equities.

Davidson, A (2007) *The Complete Guide to Online Stock Market Investing: the Definitive 20-Day Guide*, Kogan Page. Practical online stock market investing clearly explained.

Graham, B (2005) *The Intelligent Investor*, HarperBusiness. The classic on value investing.

Hobson, R (2007) *Shares Made Simple*, Harriman House. An overview of how the stock market works from a seasoned journalist's perspective.

Shipman, M (2006) *The Next Big Investment Boom: Learning the Secrets of Investing from a Master and How to Profit from Commodities*, Kogan Page. A useful book on investing from an author who practises what he preaches.

Thompson, S (2009) *Trading Secrets, 20 Hard and Fast Rules to Help You Beat the Stock Market*, FT Prentice Hall. A book focused on market timing rather than individual stock picking. The author, drawing on research from *Investors Chronicle*, where he is companies editor, dissects historical, technical and economic data to find lessons for investing.

Boiler Room. A film, but too good to exclude from this list; starring Ben Affleck, it reveals the sales techniques of the boiler rooms. Authentic and not yet dated.

Fun stuff

Anderson, G (2008) *City Boy*, Headline. A fun exposé, with insight into the results-focused culture of the City of London.

Reingold, D (2007) *Confessions of a Wall Street Analyst*, Collins. A great exposé.

Hedge funds

Coggan, P (2008) *Guide to Hedge Funds*, The Economist. A journalistic trot through the basics of hedge funds. Clear and useful, although an updated edition is needed.

Media

Davidson, A (2008) *The Times: How to understand the financial pages*, 2nd edn, Kogan Page. A clear guide to the business pages of any newspaper.

Davies, N (2008) *Flat Earth News*, Chatto & Windus. A brilliant exposé about how overworked journalists repackage news.

Money laundering

Lilley, P (2006) *Money Laundering: The Untold Truth about Global Money Laundering, International Crime and Terrorism*, 3rd edn, Kogan Page. An overview in an easy-to-read style.

Regulation and compliance

Mills, A (2008) *Essential Strategies for Financial Services Compliance*, John Wiley & Sons. A lively guide to issues and solutions in regulation and compliance, written from a compliance officer's perspective.

Russia

Lucas, E (2008) *The New Cold War*, Bloomsbury Publishing. The best of the books on Russia's business environment.

Risk management

Shirreff, D (2004) *Dealing with Financial Risk: A Guide to Financial Risk Management*, Economist Books. An excellent overview, relevant in the credit crunch. Needs updating, however.

Technical analysis

Marber, B (2007) *Marber on Markets*, Harriman House. Entertaining, honest and illuminating about technical analysis. The author has worked for decades in the field.

Index

Index of advertisers

Contact details for advertisers

Aberdeen Asset Management plc	www.invtrusts.co.uk
ABIT – ABI Trust Ltd	www.abifinancial.com
Charles Stanley & Co	www.charles-stanley.co.uk
Corporation of London	www.cityoflondon.gov.uk
Deutsche Bank	www.fbfx/TT
ESCAP – EAP School Management	www.escp-eap.eu
Eurex Frankfurt	www.eurexclearning.com
Global Bank of Commerce Ltd	www.globalbank.org
IBFX / Interbank FX	www.ibfx.com
J P Morgan Asset Management	www.jpmorganinvestmenttrusts.co.uk
Kleinwort Benson Private Bank	www.kleinworthbenson.com
London Stock Exchange	www.londonstockexchange.com
Punter Southall & Co	www.pstransactions.co.uk
The Wine Investment Fund	www.wineinvestmentfund.com
World Gold Council	www.gold.org

ALSO AVAILABLE FROM KOGAN PAGE

ISBN: 978 0 7494 5084 7　　Paperback　2008

Order online now at www.koganpage.com

Sign up for regular e-mail updates on new
Kogan Page books in your interest area

ALSO AVAILABLE FROM KOGAN PAGE

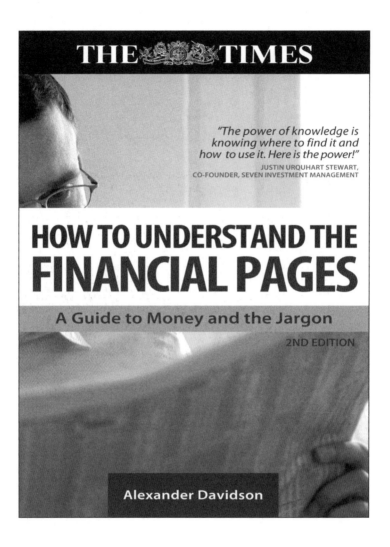

THE TIMES

"The power of knowledge is knowing where to find it and how to use it. Here is the power!"

JUSTIN URQUHART STEWART,
CO-FOUNDER, SEVEN INVESTMENT MANAGEMENT

HOW TO UNDERSTAND THE FINANCIAL PAGES

A Guide to Money and the Jargon

2ND EDITION

Alexander Davidson

ISBN: 978 0 7494 5144 8   Paperback   2008

Order online now at www.koganpage.com

Sign up for regular e-mail updates on new
Kogan Page books in your interest area